PLAYS TWO

J B Priestley

PLAYS TWO
THEY CAME TO A CITY
SUMMER DAY'S DREAM
THE GLASS CAGE

Introduction by Tom Priestley

OBERON BOOKS

LONDON

They Came to a City first published by Samuel French in 1944, *Summer Day's Dream* first published by Samuel French in 1950, *The Glass Cage* first published by Samuel French in 1958.

First published in this collection in 2004 by Oberon Books Ltd (incorporating Absolute Classics)
521 Caledonian Road, London N7 9RH
Tel: 020 7607 3637 / Fax: 020 7607 3629
e-mail: oberon.books@btinternet.com
www.oberonbooks.com

ISBN: 1 84002 293 0

Cover design: Andrzej Klimowski

Printed in Great Britain by Antony Rowe Ltd, Chippenham.

Contents

Introduction

Tom Priestley

This is the second volume of Oberon's collected plays of J B Priestley; the first contained comedies, but these plays here are all 'straight' or serious plays. But serious does not mean overly solemn. If the main thrust is the interplay of character and the presentation of ideas comes second, they both provide the audience with entertainment and emotional involvement interspersed with humour and insight into human behaviour.

The underlying themes of my father's work are the nature of Englishness and the relationship between the sexes, the latter exploring the essential differences, instinctive and intellectual, between men and women. Beside this the subject of the first two plays here is the Utopian ideal.

The First World War, despite all its horrors, produced the forlorn hope of radical social change; but while Russia was transformed by the Communist Revolution, the Western world returned more or less to the *status quo ante*, with social stagnation, economic decline, the slump, mass unemployment and the rise of Fascism. The Second World War, with its total involvement of whole populations, revived that hope; politicians and intellectuals began to consider the shape a new society could take, and the changes in planning and attitudes required to effect it.

While JBP described himself as a socialist, he never joined any political party, and when, to everyone's surprise, he stood for parliament himself in the 1945 election, he stood as an independent. His socialism was rooted in his background in Bradford, home of the Independent Labour Party, which owed much to the non-conformist chapel traditions of community. It was a socialism balancing the rights of the individual with the needs of society, avoiding the extremes of dogmatism and rigid control which emerged in the communist countries.

They Came to a City starts with a relatively standard premise: a random group of people representing a variety of social backgrounds find themselves in a totally unexpected situation, and the drama grows from their reaction to that situation and their interaction as characters. There is a suggestion of my father's favourite theme – Time – in the way all these characters find themselves mysteriously gathered outside the gate of an unknown city – they meet, introduce themselves, form various alliances and when the gate suddenly swings open, make their way into the unseen city. We never see inside the city itself. Act Two is set in the same place, outside the gate, but now at the end of the same day as the characters straggle out bit by bit to exchange opinions about their experiences in the city – some have found it invigorating and exhilarating; others have found it strange and distressing because the inhabitants of this unseen utopia share none of their prejudices, indeed positively reject them. Now the characters have to decide which of them will try to return to the life they originally came from and which will opt for a new life in this city. Some of the choices are unexpected, especially that of the two main characters, giving the play its inspirational ending.

The drama comes from the relationships formed and the choices between change or stagnation. While much of the discussion is political, it is not primarily a political play as much as a social and human drama. The centre of the piece is not about how such a city could be created, but about reactions to it once it exists.

In the event JBP was disappointed that postwar Britain seemed so drab and joyless despite the founding of the Welfare State; the austerity of the late 1940s failed to match the excitement expressed by some of the characters in *They Came to a City*.

He welcomed the 1951 Festival of Britain and celebrated it in one of his merriest comic novels *Festival at Farbridge*; for once austerity was laid aside for communal celebration.

They Came to a City opened at the Globe Theatre on 21 April 1943 and played for 278 performances. The identical cast appeared in a film version directed by Basil Dearden for Ealing which was released in August 1944 with a script by Dearden and Sidney Cole. Interesting to note that the sets for the stage play were designed by Michael Relph, who was to form a partnership with Basil Dearden to collaborate on a series of notable British films.

J B Priestley felt strongly that the development and possession of the atomic bomb was a grave setback for civilisation, and argued forcibly for the United Kingdom to take the moral lead in ridding itself of these weapons of mass destruction, and so became one of the founders of CND – the Campaign for Nuclear Disarmament.

Nevertheless the setting for *Summer Day's Dream* is an England reduced to basics by a nuclear war, rid at last of its position as a leading industrial nation and so driven back to a simple life of small scale agriculture, barter and homemade entertainment.

I remember him saying in conversation that if he could choose a period from history when he would rather live it would be the eighteenth century. As he wrote in *English Journey* he felt much of the industrialisation which marked the Victorian Age had ruined many fine areas of the country and enslaved people in factories.

At least the country people, though poor, lived a more natural life. His was an instinctive reaction, but as often he was trying to redress the balance from the assumption that the Industrial Revolution was an undeniable benefit for all.

So the Utopia of *Summer Day's Dream* is an England out of the rat race, reduced to third world status, but environmentally friendly. This ecological paradise is challenged by the arrival of representatives of the new world order, from America, Russia and, interestingly, India – members of an investigating commission come to assess the quality of some minerals which could be exploited. Again a human drama unfolds when the inhabitants of this utopia firstly discover the purpose of the commission, and then try to influence its outcome by reference to human values and a rejection of endless industrial development and globalisation for its own sake.

After the 1939–45 war my parents were advised to put their investments into land, and bought two adjoining farms on the Isle of Wight where we were living at the time. I wonder if this introduction to agriculture lay behind the choice of setting for this play: unusually for JBP, the countryside – indeed the country is a key character over which the drama unfolds.

Although the title comes from Shakespeare's, *Midsummer Night's Dream*, the play feels closer to *The Tempest*, set on an island invaded by outsiders, with the central character, Stephen Dawlish, a kind of Prospero, a wise old man commenting on life from his own rich experience; although my father was only fifty-five when the play was produced – it opened at the St Martin's Theatre on 8 Sept 1949 – he seems to speak personally through Stephen Dawlish, and indeed became more like him as he grew older.

The part was played with distinction by Sir John Gielgud on BBC television to celebrate my father's centenary in 1994.

Though set in the summer of its title, I can still remember the warm autumnal feel of the original production. I went up to Bradford, my father's hometown, for the first time to attend an opening with my parents; we travelled on to Newcastle with the actors. Perhaps this as why I have a great affection for this play, finding it imbued with warmth, humanity and love.

Working as he did in the naturalistic tradition of play-writing, JBP regretted the flatness of conventional middle class spoken English and envied the comparative richness of North American and Irish speech. Did this influence his decision to write a play set in Canada? Certainly, the background to *The Glass Cage* is fascinating.

He was visiting Canada and was struck by the talent and appearance of three actors he saw in Toronto in the middle 1950s: Barbara Chilcott and her brothers Murray and Donald Davis. So struck was he that he promised to write a play for them, and the result was *The Glass Cage*. It was produced by the Crest Theatre in Toronto and opened in London at the Piccadilly Theatre on 26 April 1957. Because it was a late play it has not appear in any previous published collection, and was largely forgotten until the West Yorkshire Playhouse presented a reading during their festival celebrating the work of J B Priestley in September 2001. The play was a revelation, even to the few of us who had seen it when it was first produced. Would one immediately recognise it as a Priestley play? It is certainly well crafted, and perhaps elements of the young Elspie have echoes of other young women in Priestley plays – Dinah in *The Linden Tree* or Carol in *Time and the Conways* – but see if you find a different tone in the language generally. As we have seen, J B Priestley was firmly against dogma of any kind, being a man of independent mind, and was as suspicious of religious as of political dogma. If the central theme of *The Glass Cage* is hypocrisy, there is a moving and unexpected resolution. Once again a group of outsiders, two brothers and a sister, threaten the complacency in this case of a household; but much is hidden and must be revealed.

If the household members are hypocrites, the outsiders are equally self-righteous, and both must be made to face the truth before they can advance. They have to escape from their cage.

In this play JBP comes closest to depicting evil in any of his dramatic works. But this evil gives way to redemption, and therein lies the richness and the fascination of the piece.

In all three of these plays his interest was in the group as much as the individuals; the dynamics of society, and one of his greatest skills was in writing effectively and dramatically for a selection of characters, retaining our interest in them all equally, so that the whole becomes bigger than the parts, and the balance is nicely struck: the individuals engage our attention and sympathy, but survive within the assembly; their personal change is reflected in the realignment of the whole.

London, 2003

THEY CAME TO A CITY

Author's Preface

They Came To A City: Thousands of performances of this play have been given, but nobody has seen it who did not see the original production, directed very adroitly by Irene Henschel, and played superbly by Googie Withers, Renee Gadd, Ada Reeve, Frances Rowe, Mabel Terry-Lewis, John Clements, Raymond Huntley, A E Matthews, Norman Shelley – one of the best casts I have ever had. It opened in 1943 and after a very successful tour it had a long run at the Globe Theatre. Since then it has been produced in many theatres abroad, and has been a great favourite with repertory and amateur companies here at home. It has also been filmed, with the original cast. I have read and heard many wildly different accounts of what this play is about, and I have been told, among other things, that it is really a study of the Integration of the Personality (see Jung), a drama of life after death, a slab of Left Wing propaganda, a plea for town-planning. My best reply perhaps is to describe how I came to write it. During the War I was impressed by the very different attitudes of mind that people had to any post-War changes, which were then being widely discussed. It seemed to me there was a play in this, so long as I could keep away from the mere play of debate, which I dislike, and discover an appropriate 'symbolic action'. I use the quotation marks because this is my own term and not generally known. Actually this play offers a good though perhaps rather crude example of the 'symbolic action' on which so many of my plays and novels are built. The unknown city gave me exactly what I wanted but it should be remembered that what is important in the play is not the city but the respective attitudes of the characters toward it. If there are still some prospective directors of this play among my readers here, I should like to warn them against turning it into a melodramatic production with much too heavy a bias against the older characters, a mistake that I think we contrived to avoid in the original production. It is not one of my own favourites, but I consider that much of the First Act is ingeniously contrived.

They Came To A City is a play I had more or less in my head from the early days of the war, but I did not write it until the Summer of 1942. It was not produced until early 1943 because we were waiting for John Clements to finish his film commitments (and his Joe Dinmore was well worth waiting for.) It first appeared in Bradford – my native town, and chosen for this opening at my special request.

After a very successful provincial tour, the best any play of mine has ever had, it opened at the Globe Theatre, London, in April 1943, I was fortunate in this play in finding a dramatic formula that enabled me to express, in dramatic form, the hopes and fears and sharp differences of opinion about the post-war world of various sections of the British people. This made it a topical play that nevertheless was not a war play. The eager response of audiences both in London and the provinces proved that people did not regard the Theatre simply as an easy escape from a difficult world, although of course a certain element – and, to my mind, a very necessary element – of escape must be present in this as in other arts. Even though I was exceptionally lucky in my cast and its producer, for the production itself was a brilliant example of team work, I owed much to my good fortune in hitting on this particular manner of treating the theme.

I must point out that the mounting drama of the Second Act would be impossible without the deceptively easy movement of the First Act: it was the First Act that was hard to write, not the Second. Again, the criticism that the City appears to offer nothing but hearty communal activities is really rather stupid, because obviously it is the communal activities that casual visitors, there for a few hours, would notice, and furthermore, my characters naturally single out what attracts *them.*

Finally, I feel I must explain that in my original stage directions all the characters arrive on the stage from the direction of the audience and return in that direction, the whole of the first part of the play, before day has dawned and shown my people the walls, taking place on darkened steps and gangways leading from the auditorium to the stage. I still believe that this is how the play should be done, but there were various good reasons why it was not found possible to carry out my original directions. *They Came To A City* could actually be produced in a ball without any proscenium or curtain, so long as the lighting, which would always have to be fairly intricate, could be adequately organised. And here again, I must confess that the average dramatic critic appeared to be far less responsive and receptive, far more hidebound in his ideas, than the average member of the audience.

J B Priestley
Brook, Isle of Wight
December, 1949

Characters

JOE DINMORE

MALCOLM STRITTON

CUDWORTH

SIR GEORGE GEDNEY

ALICE FOSTER

PHILIPPA LOXFIELD

LADY LOXFIELD

DOROTHY STRITTON

MRS BATLEY

They Came To A City was first produced at the Globe Theatre, London, in April 1943, with the following cast:

JOE DINMORE, John Clements
MALCOLM STRITTON, Raymond Huntley
CUDWORTH, Norman Shelley
SIR GEORGE GEDNEY, A. E. Matthews
ALICE FOSTER, Googie Withers
PHILIPPA LOXFIELD, Frances Rowe
LADY LOXFIELD, Mabel Terry Lewis
DOROTHY STRITTON, Renee Gadd
MRS BATLEY, Ada Reeve

Producer, Irene Hentschel

The action takes place during one day outside a strange city.

Note on the set:

This can be more or less elaborate according to the resources of the theatre, but the following features are essential. On the (actors') right a tower that is part of the city wall, and set in the face of this tower is a large practicable door, as strongly made as possible, that opens inward, with the hinges up stage. Then running across the stage from this tower is a wall that must have broad steps in front of it, with, if possible, a look-out alcove and then a walk that goes off left. There is also a downstage exit left in front of the steps. There should be a small seat down stage left and if possible a place to stand on the level of the top step, above this seat. Behind the wall, to represent the sky, should be a cyclorama, as big and as far back as possible. The tower, the steps, the wall, any seats or parapets, should appear to be made of the same material – stone, concrete, rough-cast, adobe, etc. The door suggests heavy plastic with a bronze tinge.

The lighting, which moves from early dawn to full daylight and then through sunset to dusk, should be as varied as possible. The sky should be grey, intense blue, and finally purple. Bright sunlight streams through the doorway, once the door is opened. In the last scene of the play, there is only a glimmer of daylight remaining, and Joe and Alice play in a spotlight.

ACT ONE

The curtain rises in complete darkness. Then LADY LOXFIELD enters at right proscenium opening, and is seen right centre, in a spotlight. She is a handsome, dignified woman in her late fifties, not without a certain graciousness, though we hardly ever see her at her best. She must have the voice of her class.

LADY LOXFIELD: (*Turning to call.*) Philippa! Philippa!
    (*She waits for a reply. Then with sudden urgency.*) Philippa!
PHILIPPA: (*Unseen yet.*) Yes, Mother. I'm coming.
LADY LOXFIELD: (*Impatiently.*) Well, where *are* you?
    (*Enter PHILIPPA at right proscenium opening, out of spot.*)
    Really, Philippa, how can you leave me alone – at a
    moment like this – when *anything* might happen – I can't
    imagine.
    (*PHILIPPA has now come into the spot, and they stand together.
    She is in her late twenties, a girl of no particular charm and
    appeal, but with more sense and character than would first
    appear. Both women are in ordinary walking dress.*)
PHILIPPA: (*With weary patience.*) But I wasn't leaving you
    alone, Mother. I was only just behind you. I stopped
    because I thought I heard somebody moving about.
LADY LOXFIELD: All the more reason why you shouldn't
    leave me. We must stick together.
PHILIPPA: (*Same tone.*) Yes, Mother.
LADY LOXFIELD: Can you still hear somebody?
PHILIPPA: No, not now.
LADY LOXFIELD: Where are we?
PHILIPPA: I haven't the foggiest.
LADY LOXFIELD: You haven't *any* idea?
PHILIPPA: No. All I know is that we're no longer in that
    beastly hotel in Bournequay – thank the Lord! (*After a
    pause.*) Perhaps we're dead.
LADY LOXFIELD: Philippa, don't be ridiculous.
PHILIPPA: Well, Mother, think it over. The last thing
    I remember was that horrible geyser going off with the
    most frightful bang –

LADY LOXFIELD: I thought it was a bomb.

PHILIPPA: No, it was the geyser.

LADY LOXFIELD: I shall make a serious complaint to the manageress.

PHILIPPA: You'll have to find her first, won't you?

LADY LOXFIELD: Philippa, I won't have you talking to me like that. Now let's be sensible. (*She moves a pace or two, then stops.*) Could we have been blown into the grounds?

PHILIPPA: No, this isn't Bournequay.

LADY LOXFIELD: (*Impatiently.*) Well, where is it, then?

PHILIPPA: I don't know, but I do know it isn't Bournequay. Doesn't smell like it. Doesn't taste like it. I know it isn't. (*She stops, listening.*) Listen! I can hear somebody again.

LADY LOXFIELD: (*In alarm.*) Philippa! Now –
(*Enter CUDWORTH at left proscenium opening.*)

PHILIPPA: Sh! (*She whispers.*) Yes, there's somebody over there.
(*CUDWORTH is spotted. They stare across to where CUDWORTH is now seen. He is a short, perky, inquisitive, rather aggressive middle-aged man, with a self-assured, staccato, rather Cockney voice. He is wearing the clothes a prosperous business man would wear in his office – no hat, etc. They look at each other a moment.*)

CUDWORTH: (*Confidently.*) Oh, good evening! I suppose it is evening, isn't it?

PHILIPPA: I suppose so, though we're a bit mixed up.

CUDWORTH: So am I. Better introduce ourselves, eh? Cudworth's my name.

PHILIPPA: I'm Philippa Loxfield. And this is my mother, Lady Loxfield.

CUDWORTH: How do you do?

LADY LOXFIELD: How d'you do, Mr Cudworth? Er – can you tell me if this is Bournequay?

CUDWORTH: (*Surprised.*) Bournequay? Don't suppose so. I never go to Bournequay. Don't like the place.

PHILIPPA: Neither do I. But where are we, then?

CUDWORTH: Now you've got me. Just going to ask you
that.

LADY LOXFIELD: Indeed! But – if you don't mind my
asking – how did you get here?

CUDWORTH: I don't know. Not like me not to know a
thing like that. But there it is.

PHILIPPA: You're just like us. Only I think the geyser
blew up.

CUDWORTH: Matter of fact, I thought I was dreaming.
Don't often dream. No point in it. But I was working late
at my office – going over some figures – and had just
finished. Then I must have dropped off.

PHILIPPA: (*Amused.*) He thinks he's dreaming us, Mother.

CUDWORTH: No, no. Some other explanation, of course.
But you're the first people I've seen. Let's move on a bit,
shall we? (*He moves forward cautiously, the light following
him, to centre, second step.*)

PHILIPPA: Go on, Mother.

LADY LOXFIELD: (*Vaguely.*) Well – I must say – but
I suppose we might as well – (*She moves forward cautiously
to centre, second step, with PHILIPPA close behind her, during
his following speech.*)

CUDWORTH: (*Staring about him.*) Place of some sort here.
First I've seen. Looks like a wall.
(*They now move into his light, which opens a little to include
them.*)

PHILIPPA: (*Staring about her.*) Yes, it is a wall. (*At centre,
one foot on the first step.*)

CUDWORTH: That's right. And better a wall than nothing,
if you ask me.

PHILIPPA: Certainly. Well, Mother, we're *somewhere* now.

LADY LOXFIELD: What's the use of saying we're
somewhere, if we don't know *where!* Really, Philippa!

CUDWORTH: Did you say your name was Loxfield? Not
in tin, are you?

PHILIPPA: (*Amused.*) I've never been in tin.

LADY LOXFIELD: (*With dignity.*) No. My husband was in
the Colonial Service, and when he died had just retired

23

from the governor-generalship of the Tago-Tago islands. He was Sir Francis Loxfield.

CUDWORTH: Never heard of him, but I'm a commercial man myself. Now then, what shall we do?

PHILIPPA: (*Pointing left.*) We'd better try that way.

CUDWORTH: All right. (*Moving to the top of the steps.*) There are two or three important wires I'd like to send as soon as we can find a post office that's open.

(*PHILIPPA begins to giggle.*)

What's the joke, young lady?

PHILIPPA: (*Moving up to the top of the steps.*) I believe you've got it all wrong. I'll bet anything there aren't any post offices round here.

LADY LOXFIELD: You don't know anything about it, Philippa. And I expect that Mr Cudworth will soon find a post office or something.

(*She goes to the top of the steps; PHILIPPA helps her.*)

Which reminds me I ought to have written to your Aunt Edith telling her not to think of coming to stay until the end of next week.

PHILIPPA: (*As they begin moving left.*) Perhaps it *is* the end of next week now.

CUDWORTH: (*Moving.*) That doesn't make sense, young lady.

PHILIPPA: Well, being here at all doesn't make sense to me.

LADY LOXFIELD: You're not tired, are you, dear?

PHILIPPA: (*Impatiently.*) No, I'm not, Mother. In fact, I'm enjoying it. (*Crossing top along the wall.*) Now, what happens there? (She hurriedly exits left.)

(*The other two follow her but hesitate a moment. Enter MRS BATLEY right proscenium opening, not spotted.*)

MRS BATLEY: (*Unseen.*) Excuse me!

LADY LOXFIELD: (*Calling.*) Philippa, not so fast, darling.

MRS BATLEY: Excuse me!

CUDWORTH: (*Stopping.*) I thought I heard somebody then.

LADY LOXFIELD: No. I don't think so. (*Calling.*) Now, Philippa, *do* be careful. Not so fast, Philippa!

PHILIPPA: (*Off.*) All right, Mother!

(*Exit LADY LOXFIELD and CUDWORTH up left. MRS BATLEY is now spotted. She is a short, compact, middle-aged working-class woman, poorly dressed, carrying a shopping bag or basket. Behind a certain outward diffidence, belonging to her class, she is oddly confident and serene. She moves centre to the steps.*)

MRS BATLEY: (*To herself, coolly.*) Couldn't 'ear me, though I could 'ear them. (*She sits on the second step.*) Talking English – that's one good thing. None o' that jabber, jabber, jabber, like them four foreigners in the train that day.

SIR GEORGE: (*Off stage left.*) Oh – I say!

MRS BATLEY. What's that?

SIR GEORGE: (*Nearer.*) I say!

MRS BATLEY: Well, what is it? Where are yer?

(*SIR GEORGE enters at left proscenium opening and is now spotted. He is a big, self-indulgent type of man about sixty, dressed in tweeds. He is carrying a golf club. He has the assured manner, the superficial good nature, and easy drawl of the landed upper class.*)

SIR GEORGE: Oh – look here – can you tell me how far I am from the club house?

MRS BATLEY: What club 'ouse?

SIR GEORGE: (*Surprised.*) Why, the West Windlesham Golf Club, of course.

MRS BATLEY: I'm sorry, but I never 'eard of it. I live out Walthamstow way meself.

SIR GEORGE: (*Horrified.*) Walthamstow! Good God – this isn't Walthamstow, is it?

MRS BATLEY: No, it isn't. Nothing like it. So maybe it's what you said – West What's-it –

SIR GEORGE: West Windlesham? Ought to be, because I was playing on the course there. But it doesn't look like it to me. D'you play golf? – no, I don't suppose you do –

MRS BATLEY: (*Much amused.*) Me – play golf! (*She laughs.*) Well, nobody never asked me that before. I 'ad to come 'ere to be asked that.

SIR GEORGE: Yes, very amusin'. Well, I was playing on the course there at West Windlesham – and I think one

of those two young idiots behind – I told 'em they were
too close – must have knocked me out with a long drive
or something. Then I must have been somewhere deep in
the rough – or rolled into a bunker – unconscious and so
on, y'know – and then started wanderin' about. That's all
I can think.

MRS BATLEY: I dare say that was it. I was doin' a bit o'
shoppin' meself –

SIR GEORGE: (*Ignoring her remark.*) Look here, if anybody
should ask for me, I'm Sir George Gedney. Sir George
Gedney.

MRS BATLEY: (*Without irony.*) Fancy!

SIR GEORGE: I suppose you haven't seen anybody about,
have you?

MRS BATLEY: Yes. There's two ladies and a gentleman just
went round that way. (*Pointing left.*) You'll catch 'em up if
you 'urry. I'm a bit tired meself or I'd 'ave caught up to
'em.

SIR GEORGE: (*Beginning to move up the steps.*) That way,
eh? I expect they know where we are. Live around here,
probably. Sure to, eh? (*He exits top left. He moves quickly
out left. We hear him calling, 'Oh, I say – anybody there?'*)
(*MRS BATLEY turns her head to watch him go, and listens
to him. Then she faces the audience again.*)

MRS BATLEY: (*Amused.*) 'D'you play golf?' 'e says. 'No
I don't suppose you do,' 'e says. 'Me play golf,' I says.
'Well, nobody asked me that before,' I says…
(*She stops now because MRS STRITTON can be heard calling
unseen from off right.*)

MRS STRITTON: (*Anxiously calling.*) Malcolm! Malcolm!
(*She enters through right proscenium opening.*) Malcolm!
(*Each of these has brought her nearer and at last we see her
spotted at right centre. She now sees MRS BATLEY. She is a
neatly dressed, fairly attractive, but anxious and inhibited
suburban woman in her thirties.*)

MRS BATLEY: It's not Sir George Gedney yer want, is it?

MRS STRITTON: No, I was calling for my husband. I'm
Mrs Stritton.

MRS BATLEY: (*Politely.*) Pleased to meet yer, I'm sure. I'm Mrs Batley. There was a short an' sharp sort o' gentleman – oldish, 'e was – that went with two ladies round that way. Could 'e be yer 'usband, Mrs Stritton?

MRS STRITTON: No, it doesn't sound like him at all.

MRS BATLEY: Was yer 'usband with yer?

MRS STRITTON: (*Rather distressed.*) Yes, we were together until about ten minutes ago. We're always together. We always have been.

MRS BATLEY: (*Philosophically.*) Well, that's 'ow some likes it. An' some don't.

MRS STRITTON: And then he said, 'Let's go along here.' And I said, 'No, Malcolm, let's try this way.' But I don't think he heard me. And now I don't know *what's* happened to him.

MRS BATLEY: Well, 'e'll be turning up, I expect. I 'eard them first three sayin' there's some sort o' wall round 'ere, so that ought to stop 'im wanderin'. I should sit down, dear, an' just give up worryin'. The minute you give up worryin' about 'usbands they always turn up.

MRS STRITTON: (*Rather tartly.*) Yes, but it was an accident. He wasn't *trying* to get away from me. He simply didn't hear me.

MRS BATLEY: I dare say. But 'e'll turn up. Excuse me askin', Mrs Stritton, but do yer live round 'ere?

MRS STRITTON: No, we live at Leamington. Mr Stritton is the cashier of a bank there.

MRS BATLEY: Fancy that!

MRS STRITTON: But we were going to stay with my uncle who has a large farm near Tewkesbury. And we were in the train, you see –

MRS BATLEY: (*After a pause.*) Yes?

MRS STRITTON: (*Hesitating.*) Well, I don't quite know what happened then.

MRS BATLEY: Same with me: I was shoppin' at the time meself –

MRS STRITTON: We were going through a tunnel. And then I remember Malcolm – my husband – saying, 'Are you all right, Dorothy?' And I said, 'Yes, dear, I'm all right. But what's happened?' And he said, 'I don't know. I wonder if we're dead.' And I said, 'Don't be silly, dear. Of course we aren't dead.'

MRS BATLEY: That's right. We'd feel different if we was dead.

MRS STRITTON: Just what I told him.

MRS BATLEY: Either we'd feel nothin' or we'd feel different. An' I feel just the same as I did. Feet achin' an' rheumatic pains in me legs, just the same. Besides, I've got me shoppin' basket, an' I wouldn't 'ave that if I was dead – that 'ud be silly. As I said – I was doin' a bit o' shoppin' at the time –

MRS STRITTON: (*Cutting in.*) I'm going back to look for him. (*She turns to the right exit.*)

MRS BATLEY: I wouldn't.

MRS STRITTON: But goodness knows where he may get to. (*Calling as her light fades.*) Malcolm! Malcolm! (*She exits right.*)

MRS BATLEY: (*To herself, calmly.*) One o' the worryin' kind. An' a fat lot o' good it does 'em.

(*Voices can now be heard left. They belong to ALICE FOSTER and MALCOLM STRITTON. ALICE is about thirty, cheaply dressed, looking at first sight too bold and handsome but vastly improving on acquaintance. MALCOLM STRITTON is about forty, neat, commonplace, the masculine equivalent of his wife. Note that none of the characters wear hats, except MRS BATLEY and MRS STRITTON.*)

MALCOLM: (*Off stage left.*) And what happened then? (*ALICE enters at left proscenium opening, followed by MALCOLM. They are not yet spotted.*)

ALICE: (*As she moves forward.*) So I go straight to the manageress and say to her, 'All right, Duchess, you can't want me to go any faster than I want to go, see? (*They are spotted at left centre.*)

I don't mind work but I like to eat when I'm working. And there's your uniform – such as it is – and there's your wonderful list of rules and regulations – an' you know what to do with it – and just give me my card, thanks.' So she does.

MALCOLM: Yes, but I don't see how that brought you here.

ALICE: Wait a minute, I haven't finished yet. So I go down into the bar, just to show my independence, and I have three gin-and-limes on an empty stomach. I walk out, still telling her in my mind what I think of her and her restaurant – and then – *bingo!*

MALCOLM: What does *bingo* stand for?

ALICE: It stands for *biff – wollop* – and black-out. I don't know whether I hit something or something hit me. But there's a black-out and the next minute, it seems, I'm wandering round here and asking you the way.

MRS BATLEY: I was doin' a bit o' shoppin' meself at the time.

ALICE: (*Turning to MRS BATLEY.*) Hello, didn't notice you.

MRS BATLEY: Excuse me, but is that gentleman with yer, Mr Stritton?

MALCOLM: Yes. I'm Mr Stritton.

MRS BATLEY: Well, yer wife's lookin' for yer.

MALCOLM: Yes, of course. I've been looking for her.

ALICE: (*Maliciously, turning back to him.*) Since when?

MALCOLM: No, really, I have. (*To MRS BATLEY.*) Where is she?

MRS BATLEY: (*Pointing right.*) Along there somewhere.

MALCOLM: (*Calling, but not loud.*) Oh – er – Dorothy!

ALICE: Say it as if you meant it. (*Shouting.*) *Dor-othy!*

MRS STRITTON: (*Off right.*) Malcolm! (*Nearer.*) Malcolm!

MALCOLM: (*Calling.*) Yes, dear, here I am.

ALICE: (*Shouting.*) Here he is.

(*MRS STRITTON enters at right proscenium opening.*)

MRS STRITTON: (*Now spotted.*) Oh – there you are, Malcolm. I've been looking everywhere for you.

MALCOLM: I've been looking for you, too, dear.

MRS STRITTON: You can't have been looking very hard.

ALICE: (*Cheerfully.*) Oh, he was.

MRS STRITTON: (*Ignoring this.*) Come along, dear, and don't let's waste any more time. We ought to find out exactly where we are. Unless, of course – your friend's already told you.

ALICE: (*Cheerfully.*) If you mean me, I haven't told him because I don't know. But he did ask me. After he'd asked me if I'd seen you.

MRS STRITTON: (*Coldly.*) Really! (*With impatience.*) Oh – come *along*, Malcolm.

MALCOLM: (*Hastily.*) Yes, of course. (*To ALICE.*) Excuse me. (*He goes to right centre and joins MRS STRITTON. They move up the steps centre, and then out up left. We hear her as they go.*)

MRS STRITTON: (*Indignantly.*) ...Looking everywhere for you...dreadfully worried...and there you are with that awful woman...who is she?...where did you meet her?...

MALCOLM: Dorothy! Really!

(*They exit top left.*)

ALICE: (*Cheerfully.*) Well, we know who wears the trousers there, don't we?

MRS BATLEY: I knew it before I saw 'im.

ALICE: (*Taking out some cigarettes.*) I guessed it before I met her. Have a cigarette?

MRS BATLEY: (*Pleased to be asked.*) No, thank yer, dear. Never took to it. What I'd like is to 'ave a proper sit down. Yer know what it is when yer've been shoppin'. An' I'd been on my feet all day before that. If yer'll excuse me (*Rises.*), I'll see if there's anything a bit more comfortable farther back 'ere. (*She crosses right and sits on the steps left of the door.*)

(*The light fades off her. Meanwhile ALICE is lighting her cigarette.*)

ALICE: Well, I feel better now. I don't know where I am or what's going to happen. But I feel better. And anyhow, I didn't know what was going to happen before this happened. So what's the odds? Here, are you still there? (*She turns to MRS BATLEY.*)

MRS BATLEY: (*Now sitting in the dark.*) Yes, I'm 'ere. 'Avin' a nice rest too, dear. Don't stop talking. I like to listen.

ALICE: That's all right, then, 'cos I like to talk. Not always, y'know. But when I'm in the mood I do. Ever been a waitress?

MRS BATLEY: No. But my cousin's youngest is a waitress. Looks nice in her uniform too, she do. My cousin showed me 'er photo.

ALICE: That's a life. I'm telling you. Talk about your feet! I've felt sometimes mine must be as big as footballs. And it's a mean life too. My God – it's *mean*. You wouldn't believe! Most of the time the management's trying to cheat the customers, and half the time the customers are trying to cheat the management. Proper monkey-house. The men aren't so bad – except, of course, half of 'em's got their pig's eyes sticking out of their head trying to imagine what you've got under your uniform. And some of 'em pinch you, too.

MRS BATLEY: That's right. One of 'em pinched me once. Upper Clapton Road it was, outside a greengrocer's.

ALICE: But the *women!* Not all of 'em, y'know. We used to get a lot of little tired ones that creep in and out like mice and can't thank you enough just for waitin' on 'em at all. I'll bet you're that kind. But half of the rest thought they were buying you along with their pot of tea and beans on toast. There's one sort with sticking-out eyes and a parrot nose – you know the sort I mean – my God, I could have killed 'em! What's the matter with people, anyway?

MRS BATLEY: They're all strung up inside dear, because they're not getting their bits of 'appiness. That's all.

ALICE: And then they want to take it out of somebody else?

MRS BATLEY: (*Coolly.*) That's right.

ALICE: Well, I don't see anything right about it. (*She rises, crossing left.*) Here, I say, where *are* we?

MRS BATLEY: Well, I 'aven't been able to work it out yet. Yer see, I was doin' my bit o' shoppin' –

ALICE: (*Cutting in.*) Mind you, empty stomach or no empty stomach, I ought to be able to stand three gin-and-limes, even pourin' 'em down ever so fast. But of course I was upset. I pretended not to be – y'know how you do? – but I was upset all right. Even so, what's three gin-and-limes?

MRS BATLEY: Price of a 'ard day's work, dear.

ALICE: No, I mean to say, what are they to anybody who's worked behind a bar the same as I have. I'd three years working in bars. Six months in London – out at Hammersmith. Then eighteen months in Newcastle, where they call you 'hinny'. Then six months in Birmingham. I didn't like Birmingham. Anybody can have Birmingham for me. Then – hello, what's this? (*She breaks off because JOE DINMORE enters at right proscenium opening, and is spotted. He is a fairly hefty, shabbily dressed, jaunty man about thirty-five or so, who assumes a rather rough, tough manner, which shows American influence. He stops and looks admiringly at ALICE.*)

JOE: (*In easy masterful style.*) Hello, Beautiful!

ALICE: (*Noting him but talking to MRS BATLEY.*) I might have known there'd have to be one of these conquering heroes and gorgeous beasts. I did think I might be going to have a rest from 'em, but what a hope!

JOE: (*Grinning.*) Talking to yourself, Beautiful?

ALICE: Don't call me beautiful –

JOE: Why? Aren't you? (*Moving to right centre of the steps centre.*)

ALICE: No, I'm not, though I've seen worse.

JOE: So have I. Lots.

ALICE: (*Sharply.*) But I don't like that tone of voice, so give it a rest. (*She crosses to him centre.*) And if you want to know, I was talking to my friend, who's sitting over there in the dark.

JOE: Why is she? (*Looking round at MRS BATLEY.*)

ALICE: Because she wants to sit down and have a rest and be quiet. And so would you if you were a woman.

JOE: If I'd been a woman I'd have packed up years ago.

ALICE: Women don't pack up. If they packed up, everything would pack up.

JOE: Well, it can, for me.

MRS BATLEY: (*Calmly.*) Perhaps it 'as.

(*ALICE laughs and crosses down left.*)

JOE: (*Turning to include her.*) Now, honest to God, that's just what I've been wondering. Yes, straight. Here, tell me this. Where are we?

MRS BATLEY: We ought to be somewhere Walthamstow way.

ALICE: (*Incredulously.*) Go on!

MRS BATLEY: We ought, I say, but we ain't.

JOE: Now you're talking sense, Ma. (*He rolls a cigarette, sitting right centre on the second step.*) You see, I was nursing a ship's engine. I'd been doing it right across the South Atlantic. It was an old engine. At least as old as I am. In fact, I'd say – older. Yes – older.

ALICE: (*With irony.*) Now are you sure? (*Crossing to him.*) I feel we ought to get this settled.

JOE: Now, Beautiful!

ALICE: (*Angrily.*) Oh – drop it.

JOE: (*Seriously.*) Here, you're not bad-tempered, are you?

ALICE: No, not as a rule.

JOE: Well then – take it easy. Nobody's trying to insult you.

ALICE: Now listen. I've been a waitress. I've been a barmaid. For ten years now I've had jobs where fellows like you come out with your *Beautifuls* and we have to pretend to think you're very witty.

JOE: The customer is always right, eh?

ALICE: Yes, and I could tell you plenty about that. But the point is, I want a rest from this *Beautiful* line just now, see?

JOE: Certainly. What's your name?

ALICE: Alice Foster. What's yours?

JOE: Joe Dinmore, Miss Foster. Or is it Mrs Foster?

ALICE: No, it isn't. What d'you do?

JOE: Well, I told you. I was at sea – down in the engine room. But I've done everything – except make money. I was in Australia one time – driving tractors. I was in South America one time, foreman on a railway gang.

ALICE: Didn't you ever try England?

JOE: Now and then, between times. But I was saving England up until I'd made my packet. It's a rich man's country. I've done a bit of docking. I was on a coaster one time. I –

ALICE: All right, Mr Dinmore. I get the idea. You've just tried this and that. And now you're trying this.

JOE: Well, I don't know about trying this. Last time
I remember anything I was down in the engine room,
Miss Foster. What about you?

ALICE: I walked out of my job. It was terrible anyhow.
I had three quick drinks, started worrying about myself,
rushed into the street – it was dark – and then – *bingo!*
I'm here.

JOE: Bingo – we're both here. I've been laying myself five
to one I'd waken up in the jug somewhere, with a head
on me like an old boiler. But if so, I don't see where you
come in, Miss Foster.

ALICE: I don't either. And this Miss Foster's getting me
down a bit.

JOE: I thought you wanted some politeness.

ALICE: All right, but don't overdo it. (*She turns up stage
and points to the sky, where it is now getting rapidly lighter.*)
What's happening over there?

JOE: It's getting a bit lighter, that's all. (*He lights his cigarette.*)

ALICE: (*Moving centre.*) What sort of place is this? (*She goes
up the steps a bit.*)

JOE: Reminds me of a place I saw in Peru one time.
(*As she goes forward and the dawn light comes up, they see
that MRS BATLEY is asleep comfortably, basket by her side.*)

ALICE: (*Pointing, whispering.*) She's asleep.

JOE: Good old Ma! Let her sleep.
(*During the next speeches they move quietly away from her,
and climb the steps – to look over the wall. The light is still
very dim and hazy.*)

ALICE: (*Not whispering now.*) It wouldn't be a kind of castle,
would it?

JOE: (*Rising.*) It might be, and then again it might be a
town. (*He follows ALICE up the steps.*) Lots of these old
towns have walls all round 'em. Seen 'em all over the
place.

ALICE: I've seen 'em on the pictures.

JOE: (*Looking down over the wall right.*) Can't see a thing yet.
(*ALICE joins him on his right.*)
Looks a hell of a drop, though. No getting in this way.

ALICE: (*After a pause, turning from the wall.*) I say, Joe –
I can call you Joe, can't I?

JOE: Certainly you can, Alice. (*Turning to her.*)

ALICE: (*Slowly, softly.*) What if there was something
absolutely *wonderful* down there? (*To the top of the steps.*)

JOE: How d'you mean, *wonderful?* (*He is standing on the third
step, elbow on the wall.*)

ALICE: (*Slowly, hesitantly.*) I don't know – quite. I'd know it
if I saw it, though. Something different. Not a bit like
London – or Newcastle – or Birmingham –

JOE: (*Grimly.*) No, nor Liverpool, Glasgow. Port Said, Aden,
Colombo, Bombay, Singapore, Sydney, New York, Los
Angeles, Chicago.

ALICE: (*Slowly.*) Ever since I could remember I've wanted
to come suddenly on something *wonderful,* all different.
To look over a wall and see it. To open a door and walk
into it. Don't laugh.

JOE: (*Seriously.*) I'm not laughing.

ALICE: You were smiling.

JOE: That's different, Alice. That's friendly.

ALICE: Yes, that's different. Just as this place would be
different.

JOE: Smiling, not laughing. Friendly, eh?

ALICE: Yes, all friendly. (*She stamps out her cigarette.*)

JOE: Like old Walt Whitman. I used to carry a little book
of his around with me – could spout it by the yard.
D'you know what he said? 'I dreamt in a dream... I saw
a city...' – what was it? – 'invincible to the attacks of the
whole of the rest of the earth. I dreamt that was the new
city of friends.'

ALICE: Yes, that's it, Joe.

JOE: Sounds fine, doesn't it? But I'm glad he said he only
dreamt it. What a hope!

ALICE: Well, I'm a fool, I suppose, but that's what I've
always wanted. And it's what – in a way – because I'm a
fool – I've always *expected.* I think that's why I've never
settled down – you know.

JOE: I'm just the chap who does know, Alice.

ALICE: I've thought that if I moved on and tried another job, somewhere else, it might somehow be *there*.

JOE: And it never was – was it?

ALICE: No, it never was, Joe.

(*They come down now. The light still grows. ALICE comes down the steps to left centre. JOE follows to the third step centre.*)

JOE: Ever called yourself a mug?

ALICE: Yes, but don't you try calling me one.

JOE: Okay. I've been calling myself one for – oh – fifteen years. No, longer.

ALICE: Steady. You're not that old.

JOE: I'm thirty-five.

ALICE: Well, what's that?

JOE: Nothing – yet.

ALICE: Guess how old I am.

JOE: (*Promptly.*) Twenty-two.

ALICE: Go on! I'm twenty-eight.

JOE: I don't believe it.

ALICE: (*Confidentially.*) And I look it. You wait. Mind, I'm a bit tired, y'know, and the old face is feeling it, what with one thing and another.

(*They look at each other a moment. JOE smiles.*)

JOE: You're all right, Alice.

ALICE: Thanks, Joe. (*To change the subject, indicating the door right.*) Here, what about the door?

JOE: Let's see. (*They have a look at everything on the right.*) Kind of watch tower. They have 'em in these old walled towns. I've seen 'em before.

ALICE: I dare say. (*She crosses right to the door.*) But does this strike you as being old?

JOE: No, it doesn't. (*He follows over to her.*)

ALICE: It doesn't me, either. Though of course they might have just done it up.

(*They are now looking at the door curiously. The scene is still growing lighter, though not full daylight yet.*)

JOE: Nobody's going to break down this door in a hurry.

ALICE: (*Who has been examining it.*) What's it made of?

JOE: Don't know. Looks like a kind of plastic to me. New stuff.

ALICE: There's nothing to open it with – no handle or anything.

JOE: No, it's not that kind of door. This door's either tight shut, as it is now, or it's wide open. (*He runs his hand over the door.*) That's the sort of door it is.

ALICE: I must say, men amuse me. (*She crosses back to right centre.*) You're suddenly talking about this door – all so proud and grand – just as if you'd helped to make it. I've noticed that before about men.

JOE: (*Looking hard at her.*) Here, what *d'you* know about men?

ALICE: (*Returning his look.*) I know plenty.

JOE: I'm sorry to hear it.

ALICE: (*Steadily.*) I left home when I was seventeen – wasn't anything for it – and went in the chorus with a touring revue. Had two years of that, though I was never any good. Been on my own, knocking around, ever since. Working, but trying to enjoy myself too. So you can just work it out for yourself. About men or anything else.

JOE: I see. But what are you telling me all this for?

ALICE: Oh. (*A slight pause.*) I see. (*She moves away to left centre.*)

JOE: I don't think you do, but we'll let it pass.
(*Suddenly he bangs loudly on the door. He wakens MRS BATLEY who is rather startled.*)

MRS BATLEY: My word, you made me jump.

JOE: Sorry, Ma.

MRS BATLEY: What are you doing?

JOE: I'm letting 'em know we're here.

MRS BATLEY: (*Calmly.*) That door'll open when it wants to open, and not before.

JOE: Now how d'you know that, Ma?

MRS BATLEY: I've got that feeling about it, that's all. Nobody ever takes much notice of me, but I 'ave these feelings about things.

ALICE: (*Crossing towards MRS BATLEY.*) So have I.

JOE: I'm landed here with a couple o' witches, am I?

ALICE: No, just a couple of women.

MRS BATLEY: Oh no, dear, there's more than the two of us. There's that gentleman and 'is wife – y'know, the one that was a bit jealous. Then there's a golfing gentleman – Sir George Gedney. Then there's two ladies – mother and daughter – with a little sharp gentleman.

JOE: Here, we're quite a party, aren't we?

MRS BATLEY: (*Looking left, coolly.*) This is the little sharp gentleman coming now.

(*They look left. Enter CUDWORTH at the top left entrance, looking rather hot and fussed.*)

CUDWORTH: Do you happen to know where I can find a post office? (*He stands left centre, immediately above the stone seat.*)

(*ALICE looks at him and then suddenly screams with laughter, sitting on the second step right centre. Then MRS BATLEY laughs because ALICE laughs. JOE grins. CUDWORTH stares at them in astonishment.*)

What's the joke? Go on. Tell me. Nobody can say I can't enjoy a joke. (*He moves a little towards right.*)

ALICE: (*Trying to recover.*) I'm sorry, Mr – er…

CUDWORTH: Cudworth's the name.

ALICE: (*Sits up and looks at him.*) Oh. Well, I'm sorry, Mr Cudworth, but honestly, I don't know why I laughed, but it suddenly come over me – seeing you standing there, all fussed, wanting a post office.

CUDWORTH: Can't see anything funny about it.

JOE: Well, why d'you want a post office?

CUDWORTH: Because I must send a couple of telegrams.

JOE: Urgent?

CUDWORTH: Very urgent. Business, y'know.

JOE: Oh – business. Making money.

CUDWORTH: That's it.

JOE: But d'you need some money very badly?

CUDWORTH: No. I've plenty. But that's not the point.

JOE: Well, what is the point, then?

CUDWORTH: One of these argumentative chaps, are you? (*Coming briskly down the steps centre.*) All right. You can't catch me. (*He pauses on the second step left centre.*) The point is – I'm engaged in some business operations. I can either succeed in 'em or fail in 'em. If I fail in 'em I look a fool and people begin to think I'm losing my touch. I don't want that to happen. And that's why I want to send a couple of telegrams.

MRS BATLEY: (*Dreamily.*) I said he was a sharp little gentleman.

CUDWORTH: So I am. And thanks for mentioning it. (*He crosses to below the door right.*) Now what about this door? Why are we all standing here arguing about nothing, when here's a door? (*He goes up to it and noses round it. Then he raps on it.*)

JOE: (*Crossing to left centre up the steps.*) We've tried that, only much louder. But go on.

(*CUDWORTH raps again, harder. He steps back and looks at the whole tower. JOE sits at the corner of the wall.*)

CUDWORTH: There's another tower arrangement farther along there (*Indicates to left.*) I've just been on there with a fool of a woman and her daughter. The woman's a snob. But she's happy now because Sir George Somebody's turned up. (*Irritably.*) Who are we, anyhow? What are we doing here?

MRS BATLEY: Well, I'm 'avin' a nice rest.

CUDWORTH: What do you do when you're not having a nice rest?

MRS BATLEY: Look after a 'ouse full o' people an' go out cleanin' three times a week.

ALICE: (*To CUDWORTH.*) Aren't you sharp and nosey?

CUDWORTH: Yes. And I'll bet you've never kept any job more than a year. Have you?

ALICE: You mind your own business. (*She lights a cigarette.*)

CUDWORTH: (*Chuckles.*) All right. But a lot of things are my business.

JOE: (*Who has been looking him over.*) Now I'd say you're one o' these chaps who started as a black-coated worker – clerk or what not – and then by never missing a trick and by giving all your mind to it pushed yourself pretty high up into the boss and capitalist class.

39

CUDWORTH: (*Who takes this as a compliment.*) And you wouldn't be far wrong either. What are you? Mechanic or something, eh?

JOE: Right. Mechanic or something.

CUDWORTH: Jack of all trades, eh?

JOE: Right.

CUDWORTH: Here today and gone tomorrow, eh?

JOE: Right every time.

CUDWORTH: Yes, and where's it got you?

JOE: Well, it's got me here. Where has your line got you?

CUDWORTH: If I told you what I was worth, you'd be surprised.

JOE: Surprised? I wouldn't even be interested.

ALICE: (*Reproachfully.*) Now, Joe, don't be rude. You don't look like a Joe. (*To MRS BATLEY.*) Does he?

MRS BATLEY: No, he don't.

JOE: Here, what *is* this? Are you women ganging up on me already? Know much about women, Mr What's it – Cudworth?

CUDWORTH: Yes. I keep away from 'em.

ALICE: I'll bet you do too.

(*CUDWORTH crosses slowly left centre.*)

Take your mind off your business, don't they?

CUDWORTH: (*Coolly.*) That's right. And always interfering. (*He turns at left centre to ALICE.*) Messy too.

ALICE: (*Indignantly.*) Messy! (*She sits up.*) What d'you mean, *messy?*

JOE: I know what he means.

(*ALICE looks indignantly at JOE.*)

Mind you, he's wrong. (*He raises both hands defensively.*) But, I know what he means. (*He crosses to the wall right centre, third and fourth steps, and leans on the wall.*)

CUDWORTH: Thought you would. (*He moves to the top of the steps centre.*) How many times have they got you into trouble – you know – spent your money, taken your mind off your work, landed you into quarrels, cost you your job – eh?

JOE: (*Grinning.*) I can't remember.

CUDWORTH: You see.

ALICE: (*Half humorous.*) I might have known when you started off with your *Hello, Beautiful*. In fact, I did know. I said so. (*To MRS BATLEY.*) Didn't I say so right at the start?

MRS BATLEY: Yes, dear. I 'eard you. But 'e's all right. No 'arm in 'im at all.

JOE: Thank you, Ma.

(*Enter PHILIPPA, excitedly, along the top, from left.*)

PHILIPPA: I say, Mr Cudworth, do you know what there is down there?

CUDWORTH: No, couldn't see a thing last time I looked down.

PHILIPPA: Well, you can now. There's a city. (*She looks over the back wall left centre.*)

ALICE: (*Rises.*) A city! (*She runs up the steps to right of PHILIPPA.*) Let's have a look.

(*She is followed by JOE and CUDWORTH, in looking down over the wall. CUDWORTH is left of PHILIPPA and JOE is at the right corner of the wall. It is now much lighter though not quite full daylight.*)

PHILIPPA: You see, it *is* a city, isn't it? Look – you can see the avenues and squares. I saw them distinctly a minute ago.

ALICE: (*Excitedly.*) I can see them. (*Joining JOE.*) It's all misty yet, but I can just see them. Look Joe!

JOE: I am looking, Alice, but I can't see any avenues or squares or anything but a lot o' ground mist.

PHILIPPA: (*Impatiently.*) You aren't looking *properly*.

CUDWORTH: (*Staring away.*) Well, *I'm* looking properly – staring my eyes out – and I can't see anything but mist. Shapes in it, of course, but they might be anything.

PHILIPPA: (*Impatiently.*) They aren't *anything*. I tell you, they're big buildings and houses and streets and squares and boulevards. It's a city. And a marvellous city. I distinctly saw it.

ALICE: I hope you're right. I believe you are too.

(*Enter MALCOLM preceded by MRS STRITTON left, on stage level, rather cross and argumentative.*)

MALCOLM: I'm *not* arguing, Dorothy. There's no point in having an argument when we don't know what's happened to us or where we've got to –

MRS STRITTON: But that's what I've been saying to you all along –

MALCOLM: Just let me finish, please, dear. I say – I'm *not* arguing, but I do insist that never for one single moment did I suggest we should go to Tewkesbury. It was your idea from the first.

(*MRS STRITTON turns and sees the door.*)

I'm not blaming you – why should I? – but I do say –

MRS STRITTON: (*Examining the door.*) No bell or knocker or anything.

MALCOLM: Even if there was, I don't see what right we have to start ringing or banging away. We don't know who lives there –

MRS STRITTON: (*Not loudly but in sudden rage.*) We can ask them where we are, can't we?

MALCOLM: Yes, I suppose so. But, y'know, it's still very early –

MRS STRITTON: (*Fiercely, moving to right centre.*) Malcolm, if you won't bang on that door, then I *will.*

MALCOLM: (*Moving slowly towards the door.*) Oh – well – of course – I'll do it –

JOE: (*Calling across.*) Don't bother, pal. We've all tried it – and they don't reply.

MALCOLM: Oh – thanks. (*He moves back left centre.*) You heard what he said, dear –

MRS STRITTON: Of course I heard what he said. (*And as if to show what she thought of it, she goes to the door and begins knocking on it loudly.*)

MALCOLM: (*When clearly nothing is happening.*) You see, dear –

MRS STRITTON: (*Exasperated.*) Oh, Malcolm, you are maddening. (*She sits down on the second step right centre.*)

ALICE: (*Cheerfully.*) We think there's a city down there.

(*MRS STRITTON ignores this and looks straight ahead. MALCOLM notices this and feels he ought to answer for her.*)

MALCOLM: (*With nervous cheerfulness at the foot of the steps left centre.*) Oh, really? A city?

ALICE: (*Cheerfully and casually.*) Yes. Come and see if you can see it.

(*MALCOLM exchanges a glance with his wife. She looks furious.*)

MRS STRITTON: (*Angrily.*) Well, go on, see if you can see it.

MALCOLM: Well, wouldn't you like to see if you can see it?

MRS STRITTON: (*Sharply.*) No, I don't believe anybody can see anything yet.

PHILIPPA: (*Calling across.*) I saw it quite clearly.

MRS STRITTON: (*Contemptuously.*) Oh, did you really?

PHILIPPA: Yes, I did. And I wish you wouldn't be so beastly bad-tempered.

MRS STRITTON: (*Angrily.*) What do you mean?

CUDWORTH: (*Coolly.*) She means bad-tempered, Mrs – er – (*To MALCOLM.*) What's your name? Mine's Cudworth.

MALCOLM: Stritton.

CUDWORTH: London?

MALCOLM: No, Mr Cudworth, Leamington. I'm in the West Midland Bank there.

CUDWORTH: Can't say I know it. Heard of it, of course, but can't really say I know it. I bank at Barclays. Have done for years.

JOE: (*Grinning.*) Where do you bank, Miss Foster?

ALICE: (*Promptly.*) Post Office Savings, Mr Dinmore. (*Moving to the top of the steps.*) What about you? (*She crosses to the right wall above JOE.*)

JOE. The London and Wide World Rolling Stone No Moss Limited.

(*CUDWORTH sits on the left end of the wall left.*)

MRS STRITTON: (*To MRS BATLEY.*) I think it's going to be warmer, don't you?

MRS BATLEY: (*Politely.*) I wouldn't be at all surprised, Mrs Stritton.

PHILIPPA: I'm beginning to wonder if we're not all crackers. (*Moving a little towards the top of the steps.*)

CUDWORTH: (*Puzzled.*) Crackers?

JOE: She means cracked, daft, bug-house, barmy.

CUDWORTH: Certainly not, Miss Loxfield. Silly idea!
Don't feel at all cracked myself. Just rather out of touch
with things, that's all.

PHILIPPA: Oh – well, for that matter, I feel all right.
Rather better than usual, though that's not saying an
awful lot. But I feel that something might *happen*.

ALICE: (*Heartily, taking a step towards PHILIPPA.*) Yes. So
do I.

(*They look at each other with a kind of quick understanding.*)

PHILIPPA: Yes – but – well, you look as if quite a lot had
happened to you already –

ALICE: (*Half humorous, half serious.*) Here, steady.

JOE: (*Butting in.*) I know what she means.

ALICE: (*Quickly.*) No, you don't, and you keep out of this.

PHILIPPA: But, you see, hardly anything happens to me.
Honestly.

JOE: Don't you do any work?

PHILIPPA: No.

JOE: (*Not roughly.*) Well, if you went and did some work,
perhaps something might start happening –

PHILIPPA: I know, but Mother'd have a fit.

JOE: Well, let her have a fit.

PHILIPPA: Oh – it's all right talking –

CUDWORTH: If you ask me, there's a lot to be said for
that old idea about women's place being in the home.

JOE: How many girls have you got in your office?

CUDWORTH: Six.

JOE: And how many women have you got in your home?

CUDWORTH: I haven't got any.

JOE: Well then, what's the use of telling us you think a
woman's place is in the home? You don't believe a word
of it. If you did, you'd pop those six girls from the office
in your home – and make a start that way.

CUDWORTH: Talk sense!

ALICE: (*To CUDWORTH.*) Don't mind him, Mr Cudworth,
he's only showing off.

PHILIPPA: I don't know. It sounds sensible to me.

ALICE: (*With humorous warning.*) Hoy!

PHILIPPA: No – I mean, people are always saying they believe this and that, but then you see that they don't behave as if they believed it. There's such a lot of *pretence* about.

CUDWORTH: (*Moving towards PHILIPPA.*) Quite right too. Has to be.

PHILIPPA: Why?

CUDWORTH: Got to keep up appearances, young woman. You'd be among the first to grumble if we started dropping our pretences. Sort of manners really. (*To the other two men.*) Aren't they?

MALCOLM: Yes.

JOE: No.

(*CUDWORTH sits on the lower wall, centre.*)

MRS STRITTON: (*Rising and turning to JOE, with sudden sharp effect.*) I believe you enjoy contradicting people, don't you?

JOE: Up to a point – yes.

ALICE: (*Unfriendly.*) I suppose you agree with everybody – eh?

MRS STRITTON: We're not talking about me.

(*She looks at MALCOLM, drops her head and crosses left centre, sitting on the stone seat. ALICE sits on the fourth step right centre. PHILIPPA is in the apex of the wall, above JOE.*)

MALCOLM: (*Nervously filling the gap.*) This – er – place rather reminds me of a town in France that we once saw. D'you remember, Dorothy? The Châteaux Country. Near the River Loire, y'know. Very beautiful old places they are too. Though of course this doesn't look particularly old. Quite new, in fact. But somehow there's a resemblance. Don't you think so, Dorothy?

MRS STRITTON: (*Hesitates – then.*) Yes, Malcolm, there is.

(*MALCOLM moves to MRS STRITTON, and sits on her right.*

Enter LADY LOXFIELD and SIR GEORGE.)

LADY LOXFIELD: But surely *she* was a Carmichael.

SIR GEORGE: Yes, rather. Her cousin married a cousin o' mine – you many have run into him – Tommy Basingworth. Nice little fella, Tommy, so long as you didn't have too much of him. His brother Archie – also my cousin, of course – married one of the Logan girls.

LADY LOXFIELD: Oh, good gracious – yes. Those Logan girls! Which one was it – Kitty?

SIR GEORGE: No, Dolly. Kitty came rather a nasty cropper, you remember. I used to go duck-shootin' with their brother – Piggy Logan.

CUDWORTH: (*Crisply cutting in.*) Used to be a Logan running the Thames and Medway Trust. Very sharp he was, too. Couldn't put anything past that Logan.

SIR GEORGE: Not the same family. Not very brainy, these Logans. (*Sitting right of CUDWORTH.*) Excuse me. You in the City?

CUDWORTH: Yes. Are you?

SIR GEORGE: Oh – good lord – no. Often wish I was. Got two or three potty little directorships that take me up to town now and then. That's all.

LADY LOXFIELD: Philippa! (*She takes PHILIPPA by the arm and they move to the corner of the wall, left.*)

PHILIPPA: (*Not eagerly.*) Yes, Mother?

LADY LOXFIELD: You remember that Mrs – er – well, I'd better not mention names – but the woman we met last week at Rhoda's – the one who mixed the cocktails – you *remember?* Well, Sir George has been telling me all about her, and I was perfectly right. She *was* – and not once but *twice!*

PHILIPPA: (*Who isn't interested.*) Was *what?*

LADY LOXFIELD: Di-vorced, darling. Just as I thought. And not once – but twice.

MRS STRITTON: (*Boldly.*) Well, you don't know whose fault it was.

LADY LOXFIELD: (*Coldly.*) I beg your pardon. (*Looking down at the STRITTONS below.*)

MRS STRITTON: I said – you don't know whose fault it was.

MALCOLM: (*Muttering caution.*) Dorothy!

(*LADY LOXFIELD gives them a stare and then turns away as she exits with PHILIPPA, top left.*)

SIR GEORGE: (*To CUDWORTH.*) Some of the fellas at the club seem to be makin' a very nice thing out of West Coast Manganese.

CUDWORTH: Don't touch 'em.

SIR GEORGE: Didn't think of doin', actually.

JOE: I was out on the Coast one time. It was hell.

SIR GEORGE: I wasn't addressin' you, y'know.

JOE: Well, (*Grinning.*) I wasn't addressing you.

SIR GEORGE: (*Ignoring this, to CUDWORTH.*) What d'you fellas recommend these days?

CUDWORTH: (*As if about to give a hot tip.*) Do you want some easy money?

SIR GEORGE: (*Eagerly.*) Yes.

CUDWORTH: So do I.

SIR GEORGE: Well?

CUDWORTH: That's all for the present. But I think I know where to find some easy money.

MRS BATLEY: (*Calmly.*) Except that yer can't find a post office.

CUDWORTH: (*Irritably.*) I know, I know.

MRS BATLEY: (*With no outward signs of mirth.*) That gives me a bit of a laugh, that does. If yer'll excuse me sayin' so, Mr Cudworth.

CUDWORTH: Here, don't you be vindictive.

JOE: I'm surprised at you, Ma.

MRS BATLEY: Oh, I don't know. After cleanin' an' doin' a lot of offices for sharp gentlemen like 'im, I think I'm entitled to a bit of a laugh now. An' I'll bet yer don't know 'oo cleans your office, Mr Cudworth.

CUDWORTH: (*Briskly.*) Well, that's where you're wrong. I do know. It's a Mrs Sutton, who lives at E. Fifty-six, Booker's Buildings, E.C.2.

(*ALICE moves to the top of the steps and stamps out her cigarette, as LADY LOXFIELD and PHILIPPA re-enter at top left, to left centre.*)

Matter of fact, she's a widow of a fellow who was once a clerk with me. Years ago. Years and years ago. He died long since. Edgar Sutton. I dreamt about him the other night.

47

SIR GEORGE: (*Rising – slowly, reflectively.*) My uncle Everard – who was years in the Straits Settlements and then came home to be Joint Master of the North Barsetshire – used to dream regularly, once a month, that he was being chased by a leopard. And his man, who'd been a long-service non-com in the Dragoons, absolutely reliable sort of feller, swore that on three separate mornings he'd seen a leopard coming out of my Uncle Everard's room – in North Barset, mind you. Which just shows you – that – well, things are pretty queer really – dreams and all that... Care for another stroll, Lady Loxfield?

LADY LOXFIELD: Yes, I'd like it. Philippa!

PHILIPPA: No, Mother, I'd much rather not.

LADY LOXFIELD: (*Firmly.*) And *I'd* much rather you came with us.

PHILIPPA: (*Emphatically.*) Mother, I want to stay here. (*They stare at each other, challengingly, a moment. There is a pause. The light is now much stronger, and now there comes a golden gleam from below, as if the city there were reflecting the dawn glow. ALICE, who has been staring down, now jumps up, pointing.*)

ALICE: (*Excitedly.*) Oh – Christians awake! – *look there!* (*JOE turns and PHILIPPA moves to right of ALICE. A distant, but clear, high fanfare is heard. LADY LOXFIELD and SIR GEORGE move to the back wall. The STRITTONS go up the steps to the right of the apex of the wall, between PHILIPPA and LADY LOXFIELD. CUDWORTH has moved to the left corner of the back wall. They all stare down, and take it in slowly.*)

SIR GEORGE: (*Casually.*) Rum sort of show.

ALICE: (*Indignantly.*) It's *beautiful.*

SIR GEORGE: Reminds me of that – what's it – Empire Exhibition at Wembley –

LADY LOXFIELD: I found that frightfully tiring – didn't you?

SIR GEORGE: Yes.

PHILIPPA: I'll bet this isn't a bit like it.

(*CUDWORTH moves back and sits at the left corner of the lower wall.*)

ALICE: (*Eagerly.*) Well, what do *you* think of it, Joe?

JOE: (*Slowly.*) I don't know.

ALICE: (*Disgusted.*) How d'you mean – you don't know?

JOE: I've seen places before that looked as good as this. You'd see 'em a long way off, after weeks at sea, and think you were sailing into Heaven. But when you get inside 'em – God, they *stank*.

ALICE: We're not talking about smells now.

JOE: I'm not either. I mean that when you got inside 'em, the carry on there was so terrible – poor devils sitting about in rags with their ribs showing through – kids crawling about the gutters with their faces all running sores –

PHILIPPA: (*Shuddering.*) Oh – shut up. (*She moves a little away.*) Don't spoil it.

JOE: (*Grimly.*) All right. I won't. But that's why I said I didn't know.

PHILIPPA: Anyhow, it's not like that down there. (*To ALICE.*) Is it? (*She returns to the wall.*)

ALICE: No, I'm sure it isn't.

CUDWORTH: (*After a pause.*) Looks very fancy to me. Too fancy. Don't care for anything fancy.

SIR GEORGE: Quite right.

MALCOLM: (*To his wife.*) What do *you* think of it, dear?

MRS STRITTON: (*Uncertainly.*) It's peculiar, isn't it? (*She comes down to the second step.*)

MALCOLM: Yes – it seems – a long way from home, doesn't it?

MRS BATLEY: (*Who has never moved.*) It don't to me.

MRS STRITTON: Doesn't it?

MRS BATLEY: No.

JOE: (*Coming down to the third step, surprised.*) But you didn't – (*He breaks off and stares at her.*) What are you trying to tell us, Ma?

MRS BATLEY: I'm not tryin' to tell you anything. But I 'ave my little ideas same as the rest of yer –

49

JOE: Quite right, Ma.

(*MRS STRITTON sits at the left of the stone seat left.*)

ALICE: Go on, Mrs Batley.

MRS BATLEY: No, dear, that's all.

(*The others stare at her, puzzled, then look down again.*)

LADY LOXFIELD: (*Dreamily, moving away from the wall.*) When I was a girl I went to Venice, I went for ten days... quite by myself... It wasn't easy to do that then...but I did it. Spring...nineteen hundred and nine... Venice in Spring...and before these terrible wars began and everything changed... I was only a girl, of course... young...and foolish...but I was very happy...very happy... (*She has moved towards the top exit left.*)

PHILIPPA: (*Who has been staring at her.*) But, Mother, you never told me! (*She moves towards LADY LOXFIELD.*)

LADY LOXFIELD: No, Philippa. I never told anybody. (*She shakes her head and exits left.*)

PHILIPPA: But you ought to have told *me*. (*She exits top left.*)

ALICE: Can't see any people about down there. And it's the people I want to see now.

CUDWORTH: Too early. Nobody up yet. (*He rises.*) Later on, they'll probably open that door.

SIR GEORGE: You going in, then?

CUDWORTH: Certainly. Place that size – well worth looking at.

SIR GEORGE: (*Joining him.*) Agree with you. Ought to be able to get a bath and some sort of breakfast. What d'you make of the place?

CUDWORTH: (*Confidentially.*) Can't say for certain yet, of course. But plenty of money there. No doubt about that. Can't put up buildings that size for nothing.

SIR GEORGE: Dunno about that. Some of these people seem to. Enormous buildings – cathedrals, palaces, all that sort of thing – and nobody in the place with tuppence to bless himself with. Seen that often. Spain, Italy, out East. You'd be surprised. Care for a stroll?

CUDWORTH: (*Beginning to move left with SIR GEORGE.*) All right. Might see a bit more farther along. Some of these people have the assets but don't know how to use 'em. (*As they exit top left.*) Take South America, for example...

(*JOE looks after them, then turns to ALICE, who is still staring down.*)

JOE: Did you hear those two?

ALICE: No, I wasn't taking any notice. Why?

JOE: Typical specimens o' the boss class. Grab, grab, grab – that's all they care about.

ALICE: And what d'you care about?

JOE: That's not the point.

ALICE: (*To his right.*) What is the point, then?

JOE: (*Emphatically.*) The point is – here's two typical specimens –

ALICE: (*Angrily.*) Oh – shut up about your typical specimens.

JOE: What's the matter with you?

ALICE: It isn't what's the matter with me, it's what's the matter with *you:* Here we are – and down there is a wonderful place, like nothing we've ever seen before. And all you can do is to shake your fat head and say you don't know what it's like, and then pay no more attention to it because you're bothering about your typical specimens of the boss class.

JOE: And so what?

ALICE: So I say you're as bad as they are – if not worse.

JOE: Like hell I am!

ALICE: (*Stormily.*) Oh, I might have known, I might have known.

JOE: Now listen –

ALICE: Oh – shut it! (*She pushes JOE aside and exits top left, running.*)

JOE: (*Stares after ALICE, then looks at MALCOLM.*) Did you hear that? What's the matter with her?

MALCOLM: I don't know, I'm sure.

MRS STRITTON: (*Unpleasantly.*) I'm surprised at you. You talked to her long enough.

MALCOLM: Now, Dorothy, you know very well I was looking for you –

MRS STRITTON: Yes, you told me that before.

MALCOLM: (*Wearily.*) All right. All right.

MRS STRITTON: (*Marching out left.*) It isn't all right.

MALCOLM: (*He looks for a moment as if he were about to follow her, but then restrains himself. Apologetically.*) My wife's rather upset...she isn't too strong...and this queer business, well, you can imagine. You see, by this time we ought to have been staying with her uncle. He has a large farm – two farms really – near Tewkesbury. And now of course we don't know where we are, and he doesn't either. So she's naturally upset. (*Hesitating.*) Perhaps I ought to go after her.

JOE: I wouldn't.

MRS BATLEY: (*Quietly.*) Neither would I. Leave 'er alone.

JOE: She's bad-tempered, that's what's the matter with her. And so is that other Judy – Alice. (*Coming down, he sits on the fourth step right.*) Here, Ma, how do you women get that way – all sugar and honey one minute, and the next minute tearing and spitting like wild cats? What causes it?

MRS BATLEY: Diff'rent things – same as you.

JOE: Oh no, not the same as us. I can't have that. (*To MALCOLM.*) Can you?

MALCOLM: No, I can't, I must say. (*He comes slowly to the bottom of the steps left.*) They seem to lose their temper so suddenly, and without any real reason. (*He lights a cigarette.*)

MRS BATLEY: No, Mr Stritton, there's allus a reason. Now Mrs Stritton, she went off in a 'uff, as yer might say, like that, 'cos, as you said, she's upset an' worried. An' I expect she's one of them who when they starts worryin' soon begin to worry about *everything*. So just 'cos she catches yer talkin' to that young woman, Alice, she feels more uncertain still – an' then she loses 'er temper with you just 'cos yer've made 'er feel like that just when she needed a bit o' comfort.

JOE: Ma, I can see you know it all. Now what about the other one – Alice? What made her fly off the handle?

MRS BATLEY: Well. I don't know that I ought to let on about 'er.

JOE: Go on, Ma. I'll keep it to myself. And so will Mr Stritton.

MALCOLM: (*Sitting on the second step.*) Oh – of course. Most certainly.

MRS BATLEY: That Alice is one that's had a lot of disappointments. Well, she meets you 'ere an' fancies you –

MALCOLM: (*Startled.*) Me?

MRS BATLEY: No, no – 'im. (*Indicating JOE.*) Then she's disappointed in yer, and that makes 'er mad at 'erself for expectin' anything, an' being disappointed again, and then she gets mad at you 'cos yer've made 'er mad at 'erself.

JOE: (*Gloomily.*) Ma, you've depressed me.

MRS BATLEY: Now, now! Just 'cos she was disappointed in you!

JOE: No, no, no. You've got it all wrong there, Ma. That's too simple altogether.

MRS BATLEY: It's better if it's simple.

JOE: Not with me it isn't. And I'll tell you why. I'm not a simple character. I'm complicated, I am. (*To MALCOLM.*) Are you?

MALCOLM: Well – no – I wouldn't say I was. But not simple, either. Somewhere between the two, I'd say.

JOE: (*Gloomily.*) My trouble is – I don't believe in the Revolution. I'm a revolutionary who can't believe in the Revolution. You can see where that lands a fellow. Nowhere. Or here.

MRS BATLEY: What you want's a nice little 'ome.

JOE: (*Shouting.*) I don't want a nice little home. I've spent my life running away from nice little homes.

MRS BATLEY: Yes, and where's it got you?

JOE: (*Ordinary tone again.*) I just said that. I'm nowhere. But that's because I can't believe in the Revolution.

MALCOLM: What Revolution?

JOE: The one that's on its way. Oh, you're for it all right. And wait till you see what it does to Leamington and the West Midland Bank. And I'll bet you're very, very fond of Leamington and the West Midland Bank. Aren't you?

MALCOLM: (*Decidedly.*) No, I'm not.

JOE: You surprise me.

MALCOLM: Leamington doesn't suit me. Never has done
And as for the West Midland Bank – well, to be frank –
(*He drops his voice cautiously.*) – I consider it to be
completely out of date and – and –

JOE: (*With a mock whisper.*) Go on. (*Sliding down a step.*) Tell
me the worst.

MALCOLM: (*In a whisper.*) An obstacle to true economic
progress.

JOE: Well, well, well!

MALCOLM: (*Very confidentially.*) And another thing.
I consider the chairman of the Bank, Sir Herbert
Groosby-Perkins, a mean and contemptible old toad.

JOE: That's fine. But what's the use of just whispering it to
me? Tell everybody. Shout it at the top of your voice.
I'll bet you daren't. Do you good, y'know. Time you let
off steam, after pussy-footing it in that Leamington bank
for years. Go on. Tell them. Let it rip. I'll dare you to.

MALCOLM: All right. (*He goes up the steps to the wall right,
and shouts down, very loud.*) I consider the chairman of the
Bank, Sir Herbert Groosby-Perkins, a mean and
contemptible old toad.

JOE: (*As MALCOLM turns.*) Good! How d'you feel?

MALCOLM: (*Smiling.*) I feel better.

(*MRS STRITTON dashes in, top left.*)

MRS STRITTON: (*Urgently.*) Malcolm, what on earth are
you doing – shouting like that? I thought you'd gone
mad.

MALCOLM: (*Smiling.*) No.

JOE: What's the use of saying No? Tell her you *have* gone
mad.

MRS STRITTON: (*Urgently, clutching him.*) Malcolm – Are
you – all right?

(*He nods, still smiling. Then he calmly but efficiently kisses
her, which both surprises her, and impresses her, so that she
stares at him. He gives another smiling nod and releases her,
coming down and sitting on the second step left. MRS
STRITTON sits on the wall up left centre.*)

MALCOLM: Why can't you believe in the Revolution, Mr
– er – ?

JOE: Call me Joe. I can't believe in the Revolution because
I've gone sour. I don't see people making anything good
together. They always seem to make something bad.
When they make anything good, they don't do it all
together but by themselves. But if the Revolution is to be
any use, they've got to be able to make something good
together. See what I mean?

MALCOLM: Not quite, Joe. Give me an example.

JOE: You know a house – or a pub – or one of those foreign
cafés – and it's good. No doubt about that, it's good. But
that's because one man's done it. But when you get a
town, a city, a country, what are they like, the whole
dam' lot of 'em? They're terrible. See?

MALCOLM: Yes, I see.

JOE: Pals of mine say, 'Ah, yes, but look at the conditions,
look at the system – all wrong.' I agree. The conditions
are stinking. The system's hell. All right. But that don't
convince me that people can make anything good
together. It doesn't seem to happen that way. I've gone
sour.

MRS STRITTON: (*After a pause.*) You talk a lot, don't you?

JOE: Yes, I talk and talk.

MRS STRITTON: What for?

MALCOLM: Here – steady, Dorothy!

MRS STRITTON: (*Rising.*) Why should I mind what I say
to him? He doesn't mind what he says. Telling you to
tell me you've gone mad!

JOE: I thought you might like him better mad. You've had
him sane long enough. And didn't seem to think much
of it.

(*MRS STRITTON turns away to the right wall.*)

There ought to be something somewhere in a man that a
woman can't control, one bit of him just out of her reach.

MRS BATLEY: Same with women.

JOE: Right, Ma. (*To MRS STRITTON.*) I talk and talk
because I like it, because I'm not sure of myself, because

55

I'm always finding things out. Why are you so
disappointed? What is it you want?

MRS STRITTON: I want three children and a large garden.

JOE: What have you got?

MRS STRITTON. No children and a small garden.

MALCOLM: You see, things have been difficult –

JOE: Don't make a personal issue of it. And no apologies.
She's heard 'em already, and we don't want to hear 'em.
Do we, Ma?

MRS BATLEY: Yes, I do.

JOE: Well, get together with her afterwards, and thrash it
out. (*To MRS STRITTON.*) Must they be your own
children and your own garden?

MRS STRITTON: (*Turning, takes a step forward.*) Yes, of
course. What do you think I want? To work in a day
nursery in a public park? (*With sudden passion.*) I want
my own children and my own place. (*She turns back to the
wall.*)

(*MALCOLM rises quickly.*)

JOE: (*After a pause, to MALCOLM.*) That's how it is, you see.
Nearly everybody wants *their own*.

MALCOLM: It's understandable, isn't it?

JOE: Yes, but then you say things have been difficult, and
my pals say the conditions are terrible, and I say the
system's all wrong. So let's change 'em, and up the
Revolution. But nearly everybody still wants their own
this and that. They still can't make anything good
together. So what chance have we with the Revolution?
And what chance have we without it? See what I mean?

MALCOLM: Up to a point. (*Sitting on the stone seat.*) But
I've never thought on those lines.

JOE: What lines have you thought on?

MALCOLM: Banking and credit. The private control of
public credit. That won't do, y'know, Joe.
(*MRS STRITTON moves to the top of the steps.*)
It simply won't do. We oughtn't to have it. I wouldn't say
this to everybody, of course –

JOE: Why not? Say it to everybody. Have it out with your
chairman, Sir Herbert Boogy-Woogy –

MALCOLM: (*Smiling.*) If I had it out with Sir Herbert Groosby-Perkins, he'd jolly soon have me out.

JOE: Well, you'll probably be out soon anyhow. Perhaps you're out now. After all, what are you doing here? What are we all doing here?

MRS STRITTON: Now you're beginning to talk sense. That's what I want to know. (*Moving down slowly to the second step.*) That's what's worrying me. Sitting here, chattering and arguing about nothing, and all the time we don't know where we are, how we've got here, why we're here, how we'll ever get back –

JOE: (*Rising, excited, pointing to the door.*) Hy – look!
(*The fanfare is repeated and MALCOLM rises as the door in the tower now slowly begins to open, until it is wide open. In the entrance thus revealed, there is light suggesting sunlight coming from an open space beyond but not seen. They stare at it in silence.*)

MRS BATLEY: (*Rising, calmly.*) Well, I'm goin' to 'ave a nice look round.
(*She exits right, through the doorway, not taking her shopping basket. The others, surprised, watch her disappear.*)

JOE: If you ask me, there's more in Ma than meets the eye. She's a dark horse, Ma is. Off she goes, first in, without turning a hair.

MRS STRITTON: Perhaps because she doesn't talk so much.

JOE: I wouldn't be surprised.
(*MALCOLM crosses to the door. He examines the entrance in a tentative kind of way.*)

MRS STRITTON: (*Rather alarmed.*) Malcolm. Be careful
(*Following him.*)

MALCOLM: Yes, dear. I just went to see what happens.
(*After a moment he reappears.*) It's all right. There are some steps the other side that go down to a roadway that leads you straight down into the city.

MRS STRITTON: Do you think – we could go in?

MALCOLM: (*With a shade of uncertainty.*) I don't see why not. After all, they opened the door – as if they expected people to come in this way. And it all – seems – a civilized sort of place –

MRS STRITTON: (*Hesitating, then making up her mind.*) All right, come on, then.

(*She exits right, followed by MALCOLM.*

JOE, humming or whistling casually, wanders in after them. He reappears a moment later, and stands in the doorway, looking towards the city.)

PHILIPPA: (*Off.*) Come along, Mother. (*She enters top left, and looks over the back wall at right centre.*)

(*As LADY LOXFIELD enters at top left.*) You can see lots of people down there now. They look awfully nice, too.

LADY LOXFIELD: Philippa darling, you don't know *what* they're like. How could you tell from that distance? They may be *awful.*

PHILIPPA: Well, they didn't look awful. (*Noticing the door, gasping.*) Hello! – the door's open. (*She comes down left centre to the third step.*)

JOE: Wide open. (*Crossing and sitting on the stone seat left.*) You go through there, down some steps, and in five minutes you're in the city. Ma led the way, and Stritton and his wife have just gone.

(*LADY LOXFIELD to the fourth step right centre.*)

PHILIPPA: Come on, Mother. Let's go.

LADY LOXFIELD: Now, Philippa, don't be childish. We don't know what this place is – or who these people are –

PHILIPPA: It's better than Bournequay, whatever it is – and the people can't be much worse.

LADY LOXFIELD: But we don't know what these people are like. They might kill us –

PHILIPPA: Why should they? And anyhow, the people in Bournequay were killing me.

LADY LOXFIELD: I think we ought at least to wait for Sir George and Mr Cudworth.

PHILIPPA: (*Gravely and decisively.*) Mother – I'm going straight through there *now*. If you'll come with me, I'll be glad. But whether you do or not, I'm *going*. (*She passes LADY LOXFIELD to the door.*)

LADY LOXFIELD: (*Putting a hand on her arm.*) Just a minute, Philippa. (*At the bottom of the steps.*) You're grown up and I can't prevent you from talking like that or behaving sometimes as if I were only a stupid encumbrance. But I can at least ask you not to be so cruel, not to try to hurt me.

PHILIPPA: (*Half impatient, half penitent, moving a step to LADY LOXFIELD.*) Mother, I'm *not*.

LADY LOXFIELD: (*With dignity, moving to the door.*) Come along then. (*Turning to JOE, just before leaving.*) If you're staying here a little longer, would you mind telling Sir George Gedney and Mr Cudworth that my daughter and I have gone down into the city?

JOE: I'll tell 'em.

(*LADY LOXFIELD exits through the doorway.*)

PHILIPPA: (*To JOE.*) I thought you'd have been the first in. Aren't you coming?

JOE: I dunno yet. Might. Might not.

(*PHILIPPA exits through the doorway. After a moment or two SIR GEORGE and CUDWORTH enter slowly, deep in talk, at top left.*)

CUDWORTH: (*Preceding SIR GEORGE to the top of the steps.*) So I said, 'You think that's smart, eh?' And he said, 'Well, it's good business, isn't it?' So I said, 'I don't know about that. Where's your option?' And he said, 'Don't worry about that, Mr Cudworth. I can have that option by tomorrow.' And I said, 'No, you can't, because it's here in my pocket.' You ought to have seen his face.

SIR GEORGE: Serve the fella right. Hello, where is everybody?

JOE: Gone through that doorway. Lady Loxfield and daughter went only a minute since, and told me to tell you.

SIR GEORGE: Door open, eh? Ought to see this place, don't you think, Cudworth? Might be something in your way, eh?

CUDWORTH: (*Coming down the steps followed by SIR GEORGE.*) Nothing like having a look round. Used to spend my holidays that way. Keeping my eyes and ears open. Picked up a controlling interest that way once in the Tormouth Trams. Sold out afterwards, of course. Trams no good to me.

SIR GEORGE: Quite. Don't blame you. Trams no good to anybody.

JOE: What is any good to you?

CUDWORTH: Trying to be smart?

JOE: Not specially.

CUDWORTH: Never pays with me.

JOE: I dare say. But what *is* any good to you?

CUDWORTH: Money is.

JOE: Why, what d'you do with it?

CUDWORTH: Make more money.

JOE: So what?

CUDWORTH: Now listen, and don't think you know it all. Have you been kicked about?

JOE: Yes. Plenty.

CUDWORTH: And that young woman along there – I'll bet she's been kicked about too.

JOE: I'll bet she has.

CUDWORTH: Yes, well, I haven't. Why? Too much money. Now – who's laughing?

JOE: Well, I'm not crying.

SIR GEORGE: (*Going over to him.*) But he had you there, though. Must have money. Don't I know it. Going to put this golf club down here. (*Putting his golf club right of the seat.*) Look a fool wand'ring round a strange town carryin' that thing, eh? Keep an eye on it, will you?

JOE: I don't promise. Are you what they call an aristocrat?

SIR GEORGE: (*After a slight pause.*) Dunno about that. I'm the seventh baronet, if that's anything. Got an old place in Wiltshire. Landed gentry, I suppose. Why?

JOE: I wasn't sure. But where you people made the mistake was in ganging up with these money boys. You ought to have ganged up with us – the crowd, the mob, the people without any money. I once read a piece by Disraeli where he said that. But you didn't. And it's too late now.

SIR GEORGE: I haven't the foggiest notion what you're talkin' about. Sorry! (*To CUDWORTH.*) You know what he's talkin' about, Cudworth?

CUDWORTH: Yes – and he's wrong. I must find a post office, then have a look round.

SIR GEORGE: Right you are! Lead on. (*To JOE.*) Excuse me! (*They go briskly through the doorway talking. JOE sits left end of the seat, looking rather morose. ALICE enters slowly, at top left, looking rather miserable too.*)

ALICE: Hello, Joe.

JOE: Hello, Alice.

ALICE: (*Hesitating.*) I'm sorry I told you to *shut it,* Joe.

JOE: That's all right. I talk too much.

ALICE: No, I went an' lost my temper. (*Sitting on the wall above the right end of the seat.*) I wouldn't have done it if I hadn't thought I was going to like you.

JOE: I know. That's what Ma said.

ALICE: Ma? Oh – her. Here, been talking me over?

JOE: No, she just happened to mention it. (*Pausing.*) Said I disappointed you.

ALICE: Well, you did, Joe. I'll admit it.

JOE: (*Looking up and hard at her.*) I'm no treat, y'know.

ALICE: If it comes to that, neither am I.

JOE: (*Still looking.*) Oh – yes, you are. I said that to myself the minute I set eyes on you and as soon as I heard you talking. 'Joe,' I said, 'this one's a treat.'

ALICE: (*Secretly delighted.*) I'll bet you didn't.

JOE: That's what I said to myself, and I've been thinking it ever since. (*He pauses.*) Look – (*Pointing.*) – the door's open.

ALICE: (*Seeing it, excited.*) Oh – Joe! (*She runs to the top of the steps.*) Is that where the others have gone?

JOE: Yes.

ALICE: And were you waiting for me?

JOE: I was hoping to see you again.

ALICE: Well, here I am. Come on, Joe. (*She runs down the steps to the door and turns.*) What are we waiting for?

JOE: I told you before – I've seen a lot of places.

ALICE: So have I, for that matter.

JOE: Not the way I have. Sailing in at dawn –

ALICE: (*Impatiently.*) And they looked wonderful – and then when you walked round 'em and had a few beers, they looked terrible. All ribs and running sores. I heard you.

JOE: All right, then – you heard me.

ALICE: But it's not going to be like that here –

JOE: How d'*you* know?

ALICE: Because I feel it isn't. (*Looking through the doorway.*) Besides, I've been staring at it for the last half-hour and it doesn't look that sort of place. (*She turns to JOE.*) And even if it might be – we're here, aren't we? We might as well move about a bit and make the best of it and see what there is to see. (*With a change of tone, after a pause.*) What's the matter with you, Joe?

JOE: I'm like you. I've had a lot o' disappointments, and I don't want any more.

ALICE: Come here, you big silly.

(*She stands expectantly, and slowly he comes towards her. When he is close, she kisses him, quickly. He tries to take her in his arms, but she slips back, eluding him.*)

Oh – no, you don't.

JOE: What – never?

ALICE: Never just here at this time of day.

JOE: Ah – that's different.

ALICE: And never anywhere at any time just by grabbing.

JOE: (*Slowly, staring at her.*) Okay. I'll remember.

ALICE: But you're coming with me to look at the city?

JOE: Yes, I'm coming with you.

ALICE: (*Happy.*) Joe! (*She flashes him a smile, then goes through the doorway.*)

(*JOE follows her. Curtain.*)

End of Act One.

ACT TWO

The set is exactly as we left it, with the door still wide open. But the lighting is different, suggesting the end of day, just as the previous lighting suggested early morning. The lighting is full at first, but a shade less brilliant and more mellow than that at the end of Act One. MRS BATLEY's shopping basket and SIR GEORGE's golf club are just where they were before.

After a moment, SIR GEORGE himself enters through the doorway, looks about for his golf club, finds it with pleasure, then sits down, lights his pipe, and smokes. Then MRS STRITTON, looking rather hot and bothered, arrives through the doorway, right.

MRS STRITTON: (*At right centre.*) Oh – Sir George!

SIR GEORGE: (*Noticing her, rising.*) What? Oh – yes – Mrs Stritton.

MRS STRITTON: Have you seen my husband – Mr Stritton – up here?

SIR GEORGE: Can't say I have. But I've only just arrived myself.

MRS STRITTON: He said if we missed each other, we'd meet up here.

SIR GEORGE: Quite. Well, there's plenty of time, y'know. I'd sit down and take it easy. (*As they do sit down, SIR GEORGE on seat, MRS STRITTON on the second step left centre.*) Exhaustin' sort of day we've had, really. Cigarette?

MRS STRITTON: No, thank you, Sir George. I don't smoke. I've tried several times, just to keep Malcolm – my husband – company, but I've never really enjoyed it. (*A pause.*)
Did you like this city?

SIR GEORGE: No, couldn't stand the place.

MRS STRITTON: No, I didn't like it either.

SIR GEORGE: Very sensible of you.

MRS STRITTON: But I know Malcolm likes it.

SIR GEORGE: Good God! You surprise me. Didn't think he was that sort of chap.

MRS STRITTON: What sort of chap?

SIR GEORGE: Well – the sort of chap who'd like this sort of place. In a bank, isn't he?

MRS STRITTON: Yes, the West Midland at Leamington.

SIR GEORGE: And a decent, steady sort of chap I'd have thought –

MRS STRITTON: (*Eagerly.*) Oh, he is.

SIR GEORGE: That other fella now – stoker or mechanic or whatever he is – fella who talks so much – well, it 'ud never surprise me if *he* liked this sort of place. Just his style, probably. Saw him once or twice, and he seemed to be enjoyin' himself I must say'.

MRS STRITTON: He and that waitress girl were pretending to do some work in that funny-looking factory when we had a look at it this morning. Then the next time I saw them they were dancing in those gardens –

SIR GEORGE: What gardens?

MRS STRITTON: Didn't you see those gardens where they were all dancing?

SIR GEORGE: No. I think I must have dropped off after lunch. Don't care about dancing in gardens, though, at any time. And shouldn't have thought your husband was the sort of chap who'd want to go dancing in gardens.

MRS STRITTON: No, Malcolm wasn't dancing in the gardens. It was Joe Dinmore and that girl Alice. But I must say Malcolm seemed to be enjoying himself, and absolutely wore me out dragging me round.

SIR GEORGE: Quite! A little of this sight-seein' goes a long way with me. Always did. Some good-lookin' gals, though, down there.

MRS STRITTON: (*Without enthusiasm.*) Oh, did you think so? I didn't.

SIR GEORGE: No, don't suppose you would. Like to see a few good-lookin' gals about. But too many people there for my taste. Fact is, I don't like people. Always enjoyed myself best where there haven't been people. A few decent fellas – old pals – and one or two reliable servants, that sort of thing – but not mobs of people. Have to get away from 'em. Ever try duck shootin'?

MRS STRITTON: Good gracious – no!

SIR GEORGE: No – silly question really. Wasn't thinking. But that's the sort of life. Even when I'm in Town, I like to sit quietly in the club. Sensible old-fashioned club, y'know. Nobody talks, and you can still get a decent glass of wine. But mobs of people – like you get in this place – all bouncing round looking so pleased with themselves – dreadful, dreadful! Hullo, here's Cudworth. (*CUDWORTH enters through the doorway, looking bad-tempered.*)

Well Cudworth, you look as if you'd had quite enough.

CUDWORTH: I have too.

MRS STRITTON: And I must say I don't blame you, Mr Cudworth.

CUDWORTH: How did you get on, Sir George?

SIR GEORGE: I didn't.

CUDWORTH: Same here.

SIR GEORGE: Wouldn't be paid to spend another day in the place. Though I must say, there weren't any offers. Rather the reverse, in fact. Fella in that bureau sort of place said to me, 'Well, what can *you* do?' So I said to him, 'Well, I used to do a good deal of huntin', and I still do some shootin' and fishin' – ' And the fella laughed, and said, 'Are you a savage?'

MRS STRITTON: (*Primly.*) I'm not surprised. (*She rises, and moves right centre.*) I must say, some of the things I heard and saw quite shocked me. I mean – no proper privacy – and – and niceness – or anything. Didn't you notice that, Mr Cudworth?

CUDWORTH: Up to a point. (*MRS STRITTON crosses to the door and looks out.*) Don't know about niceness. Not sure what niceness is, and don't care much anyhow. I said at first the place was too fancy, and I was right. But what got me down were the people. (*He moves to the bottom of the steps left.*)

SIR GEORGE: Bit peculiar, eh?

CUDWORTH: Peculiar? Barmy. (*Sitting on the second step.*) I said to one chap this morning – chap with a red beard

who laughed a lot – I said, 'Wouldn't suit me this at all.
Never got any proper work done.' So he said, 'What is
your work?' I told him. And d'you know what *he* said?

SIR GEORGE: No idea. But I'll bet it was something
damned insultin'.

(*MRS STRITTON has turned to listen.*)

CUDWORTH: He said, 'We don't call that work here.' So I
said, 'Well, what do you call it, then?' He said, 'We call it
crime.'

MRS STRITTON: (*Impressed.*) He didn't!

CUDWORTH: He did. And then he said if they caught me
at it, I'd be sentenced to a year's road-making.

SIR GEORGE: They're not civilized

CUDWORTH: Wait a minute. I've hardly started yet.
I thought this red-bearded chap must be mad – he
looked a bit mad – so I tried someone else, an old fellow
who looked serious enough. He asked me if he could do
anything for me, and so I said I'd like to meet a few of
their prominent business men in the same line as myself.
He didn't seem to understand that, so I explained – just
the rudiments – and do you know what *he* did?

SIR GEORGE: Yes. He laughed.

(*MRS STRITTON moves to the steps right centre.*)

CUDWORTH: Oh no, he didn't. He handed me over to a
kind of policeman.

MRS STRITTON: (*Astonished.*) Policeman! I didn't notice
any policeman. (*She mounts to the fifth step and looks over
the wall.*)

CUDWORTH: Well, this was a policeman of some sort.
And this old fellow explained to him, and this policeman
said, 'I'll have him analysed.' So I said, 'Look here, I'm a
stranger here. Nothing to do with you. Didn't even want
to come here. You leave me alone.' So they did.

SIR GEORGE: Well, Cudworth, I must say –

CUDWORTH: (*Angrily.*) I haven't finished yet. (*Rising, he
sits right of SIR GEORGE.*) I tell you, I've had a packet
down there today.

(*MRS STRITTON sits on the top step right centre by the wall.*)

This afternoon I saw a row of nice shops they'd just finished decorating, and there was a chap looking at 'em and making notes. So I asked him about them, and said they looked a valuable little property, and so on. He said they were going to build a similar row at the other side of the square. I asked him if everybody knew, and he said they didn't, it was still a secret. So I said, 'Well, what about the two of us forming a little syndicate and getting a quick option on the site? Then, with values soon going up and up, we'd make a nice thing out of it'. He didn't take that in at first, so I explained the idea.

SIR GEORGE: What happened? Another policeman?

CUDWORTH: No. Worse this time. There's a friend of his walking past, with a whole crowd of school kids. He calls this friend, and the kids swarm round us, so that I can't move. He tells his friend what I've suggested. This friend is some sort of schoolmaster – you can't tell properly what they all are down there – but he was some fancy kind of schoolmaster. Well, this schoolmaster chap asks me a question or two – and I gave him some sensible answers – as far as I can, because they're all so damned childish. And then what? *And then what?*

SIR GEORGE: I give it up.

CUDWORTH: (*Indignantly.*) This schoolmaster chap begins lecturing on me – yes, *on me* – while I'm there, and can't get out of this crowd of kids.

SIR GEORGE: Lecturing on you! D'you mean – as if you were a specimen or something?

CUDWORTH: (*Angrily.*) That's it. I *was* a specimen. He said so. Typical acquisitive mentality – or something. Said I used – now what's it? – genuine intuitive power anti-socially because – because – I wanted to compensate a feeling of inferiority! (*He rises.*)

MRS STRITTON: How insulting! What did he mean?

CUDWORTH: (*Faces MRS STRITTON.*) You can bet your boots that's what I asked him – sharp. I said, 'Look here, I started from nothing, just a little shaver of a clerk that nobody cared about, and I've worked hard and used my wits to get somewhere and be somebody – just to show 'em there are no flies on Fred Cudworth.'

SIR GEORGE: Quite! And what did he say to that?

CUDWORTH: Asked me to repeat it and then put it down in a notebook word for word. Then shook hands and said he was very grateful. I tell you, they're off their rockers. School kids! They're all like school kids. Why –

(But he is interrupted by ALICE, who appears in the doorway.)

ALICE: *(Breathlessly.)* Joe hasn't come up here, has he?

MRS STRITTON: No. I haven't seen him since I saw you both dancing.

ALICE: That's all right, then. *(She sits down, out of breath, on the second step left centre.)* I'll go back and find him when I've had a rest. Crikey – what a day we've had!

CUDWORTH: *(Sourly mounting to the top of the steps.)* What a day we've all had!

MRS STRITTON: Have you seen my husband?

ALICE: Yes, I passed him on the road. He's talking to some people there. He said he was looking for you.

MRS STRITTON: Oh – well – he'll be here soon, I suppose. *(She rises and looks over the wall from the fourth and fifth steps.)*

ALICE: I also passed Lady What's-it – creeping up the hill. I asked her how she'd got on, and she said she hated it.

CUDWORTH: Well, so do I. *(He moves to top left centre.)*

ALICE: You would. But I can't understand her – a woman –

MRS STRITTON: *(Turning, with sudden vehemence.)* But *I* hate it.

ALICE: *(Astonished.)* You don't! *(She faces MRS STRITTON, rising.)*

MRS STRITTON: *(With passion.)* Of course I do. I hate it, I hate it, I *hate it*. I wish to goodness I'd never set eyes on that beastly city. I loathe every bit of it. I'd like to – to – burn it down.

ALICE: *(Running up the steps, with quiet passion.)* I think I could kill you for saying that.

MRS STRITTON: And I loathe you too. You ought to have seen yourself – grinning and screeching and making a fool of yourself – down there!

ALICE: (*Slowly.*) I was having the best day of my life. I was
among people who were happy, and I was happy. I was
in a wonderful place at last. And all you can do is to spit
on it.

SIR GEORGE: (*Rising, faces ALICE, protesting.*) Here, I say,
young woman –

ALICE: (*Turning on him.*) I'm not talking to you. I wouldn't
know how to talk to you. I don't know what you mean.

SIR GEORGE: You don't know what I mean! I talk plain
English, don't I?

ALICE: When I say I don't know what you mean, I'm telling
you that I can't make head or tail of you and so can't talk
to you properly. To me you're like something stuffed and
in a glass case – both you and Lady What's-it.
(*SIR GEORGE sits on the stone seat.*)
And anyhow, I'm not talking to you, I'm talking to her.
(*Wheeling round on MRS STRITTON.*) Yes, you!
(*A slight pause.*)
And I'll tell you what's the matter with you. You're so
jealous you can hardly breathe. You're not only jealous of
your husband, you're jealous of everybody and
everything. You can't enjoy anything unless you grab it
for yourself. And you can't bear to see anyone enjoying
themselves. I saw you down there, hating it all, jealous of
it, trying to spoil your husband's pleasure, turning
everything sour –

MRS STRITTON: (*Furious.*) Shut up – don't – (*She bursts
into tears and turns away and sits down.*)

CUDWORTH: (*Angrily to ALICE.*) For two pins I'd box
your ears.

ALICE: (*Fiercely.*) You just try, that's all. (*Jeering, almost like a
street urchin, moving towards CUDWORTH.*) What about
that post office? Haven't you made any money today?
I met a man with a red beard who'd talked to you. (*She
laughs in his face, then moves to the top of the steps and faces
the door, speaking quietly now.*) I've always hoped, in a silly
sort of way, for something wonderful just round the
corner. But I never thought there was a place as good as

69

this. I didn't think people had it in them to build a city like this. I never really thought people could work and play together like these people can. I'd do anything for these people, I'd die for this place. (*She descends the steps and exits right, through the doorway.*)

(*MRS STRITTON is sobbing quietly, well apart from the two men, who look after ALICE and then at each other.*)

SIR GEORGE: (*After a pause, reflectively.*) Bloody rude.

CUDWORTH: (*Angrily.*) I wish I had her under my orders for a few weeks. (*Coming down to the second step, left centre.*)

SIR GEORGE: Dare say you do, Cudworth. But you're taking it a bit hard, aren't you? After all, she didn't tell you that you were stuffed and in a glass case, did she? Matter of fact, I rather like a gal with a bit of devil in her, y'know. Did you ever run across Buster Clayhorn – used to command the Blues?

CUDWORTH: (*Rather irritably.*) No, I never knew these Army men. I've spent my life in the City.

SIR GEORGE: I know, but I thought you might have run across Buster – might have lent him a few hundreds –

CUDWORTH: (*As before.*) I'm not a money-lender.

SIR GEORGE: (*Sincerely.*) No, of course not. Sorry! Well – (*He stops, and rises, because LADY LOXFIELD, looking worn, slowly enters through doorway. MRS STRITTON who is sitting, gives one look to see who it is, then looks away again.*) Ah – Lady Loxfield. Tirin' pull, isn't it? Come and sit down.

LADY LOXFIELD: Thank you. (*Crossing to left centre.*) I ought to have left much earlier, but I couldn't drag Philippa away. And at the end I had to come away without her, but she'll be here soon. (*Sitting on the stone seat right of SIR GEORGE.*)

SIR GEORGE: Enjoy yourself down there?

LADY LOXFIELD: (*Stiffly.*) Certainly not. Perhaps I care too much about certain standards. I've been used to being treated – well – in a certain way – you understand –

SIR GEORGE: Understand perfectly. Know just how you feel.

LADY LOXFIELD: Such impertinence everywhere too.
I enquired about charities, because I've done a good deal
of voluntary work in connection with various charities –
and the girl began laughing and made some most
impertinent remarks.

CUDWORTH: (*Grimly.*) She didn't give a lecture on you,
did she?

LADY LOXFIELD: No, of course not.

CUDWORTH: (*Descending the steps.*) You don't know them
here yet, then. This morning there was a chap with a red
beard...

SIR GEORGE: (*To stop CUDWORTH's story.*) I was talking
about Buster Clayhorn...
(*CUDWORTH moves right, then back to right centre.*)
...used to command the Blues – did you know him?

LADY LOXFIELD: There were some Dorset Clayhorns
I knew. Margery Clayhorn married an Australian and
they spent several days with us once in the residency at
Tago-Tago.
(*MRS STRITTON rises and looks over the wall.*)

SIR GEORGE: No, not the same. Buster was one of the
Leicester Clayhorns –

CUDWORTH: (*Sourly.*) Sounds as if you were talking about
cattle.

SIR GEORGE: Nonsense! Talkin' about an old friend of
mine.

CUDWORTH: (*Angrily.*) Well, go on then. But what does it
matter whether he's a Dorset Clayhorn or a Leicester
Clayhorn? I call it an idiotic way of talking about
people.

LADY LOXFIELD:. Really, Mr Cudworth, you seem to be
in an extremely bad temper this evening.

SIR GEORGE: (*Grinning.*) He's had a bad day.

LADY LOXFIELD: (*With a trace of malice.*) Oh – poor Mr
Cudworth.

CUDWORTH: Don't waste any pity on me. I don't want it.
Besides, you may need it for yourself soon.

LADY LOXFIELD. Indeed! Why?

CUDWORTH: (*Moving right.*) Well, for one thing your daughter isn't out of there yet, is she?

LADY LOXFIELD: She'll be here any minute now.

CUDWORTH: And when I saw her down there, she seemed to be having the time of her life –

LADY LOXFIELD: (*Annoyed.*) Well, really, Mr Cudworth. Philippa's young and naturally she enjoys a change. I can't see –

CUDWORTH: (*Cutting in, sharply, moving back to right centre.*) No, you can't, because you've missed my point. (*He points up.*) See that sun. Setting, isn't it? Well, when it *has* set, that door'll be shut, and nobody can get in, and nobody can come out.

LADY LOXFIELD: In other words, Philippa may be locked in. Thank you, Mr Cudworth.

CUDWORTH: (*Grimly.*) Not at all.

LADY LOXFIELD: I need hardly tell you that you're not behaving –

CUDWORTH: Like a gentleman? I'm not a gentleman. (*He mounts the steps to the back wall.*) Never pretended to be. Not interested. (*He looks over the wall.*)

LADY LOXFIELD: (*Turning to SIR GEORGE.*) I suppose they told you how you could get back home, didn't they?

SIR GEORGE: Yes, rather. Did they tell you?

LADY LOXFIELD: They did. I told them it was the *only* thing I really wanted to know. They didn't like that, of course.

MRS STRITTON: (*Coming to them.*) But they didn't tell me. (*She is on the first step left centre.*)

LADY LOXFIELD: Didn't they, Mrs Stritton? Perhaps they told your husband.

MRS STRITTON: I'm sure they didn't. And I don't think he'd ask. He – he – didn't want to go back.

SIR GEORGE: Disappointed in him? He dances in gardens!

LADY LOXFIELD: You don't want to stay in this absurd place, do you?

MRS STRITTON: No, I hate it.

(*CUDWORTH sits at the corner of the wall centre.*)

SIR GEORGE: Better stick to us, then. We know how to get back. Thunderin' good job too!
(*Enter JOE through the doorway slowly. The four look at him and he leans against the downstage door-post, looking at them, and smoking.*)

CUDWORTH: Didn't expect to see you coming out.

SIR GEORGE: (*With bantering tone.*) No, rather not. Thought this place would have been just your style.

JOE: (*Quietly.*) It *is* just my style. In fact, it's a lot better than my style.

MRS STRITTON: (*Sitting on the third step left centre.*) I hope there isn't going to be an argument. I'm getting rather tired of arguments.

JOE: That's all right with me. I don't want any arguing.

CUDWORTH: You seemed to me to like arguing.

JOE: So I do, as a rule. But, you see, today hasn't been an ordinary day for me. It's been a most extraordinary day. I've seen something I never expected to see, something I'd given up all hope of seeing.

SIR GEORGE: Really? What's that?

JOE: A city full of healthy people and busy people, and happy people. A really civilized city.

SIR GEORGE: You say that because you were enjoying yourself. I saw you.

JOE: Yes, I enjoyed myself. I had a good time. But that's because I'd seen a real city at last.

LADY LOXFIELD: If you don't want any argument, you'd better not say much more, because none of us here agrees with you.

JOE: (*Looking them over, quietly.*) No, I can believe that.

CUDWORTH: Depends partly on where one's come from and what one has to go back to.

JOE: True for you. And you can imagine where I came from and what I've got to go back to. Not much.

CUDWORTH: You said it. Not me.

JOE: (*Quietly.*) That's all right. I'm saying it for you. But there's another difference. You see, all you four – well, you're old-fashioned.

MRS STRITTON: (*Indignantly.*) What do you mean – old-fashioned? I'm not old-fashioned.

CUDWORTH: Neither am I. (*Rising.*) Pride myself on being up to date. Have to be, in fact, in my business.

JOE: (*Shaking his head.*) No, no, your minds work in the good old-fashioned style. What you say to yourselves all the time is, 'Damn you, Jack – I'm all right.'

LADY LOXFIELD: (*Indignantly.*) Certainly not!

SIR GEORGE: (*Hurriedly.*) No argument now.

JOE: No. No argument. Go on, lady.

LADY LOXFIELD: (*With dignity.*) All I wish to say is – that if you're implying that we – at least that I – am quite indifferent to the suffering and distress of other people, you're quite wrong. And I deeply resent the suggestion. I was saying only a few minutes ago that when I enquired about charities in this city, I was laughed at – why, I can't imagine. And I've done a great deal of voluntary charitable work. I've always felt it my duty.

JOE: That's okay. And I'm not saying you're hard-hearted. But in this city they don't believe in that kind of charity. They believe in social justice, and they've got it. That's what you people don't understand. You don't even like the look of it. And if you're sitting pretty yourselves, you don't mind being surrounded by people who are wondering where the next meal's coming from, when the next job'll turn up, how the kids are going to live, how you're going to keep up your strength to see 'em through. That's what I call being old-fashioned.

CUDWORTH: (*Sharply.*) Now wait a minute. I'm an individualist – (*Coming down to the second and third steps.*)

JOE: (*Sharply too.*) You're a little pirate – and you know it.

SIR GEORGE: (*Amused.*) That isn't what they called him here. Is it, Cudworth? What was it – a specimen – no –

CUDWORTH: (*Irritably.*) All right, we don't want that all over again. (*At the second step.*) Besides, I agree with him about *you*. You're old-fashioned all right.

SIR GEORGE: (*Comfortably.*) Never said I wasn't – I call that a compliment.

CUDWORTH: (*With malice.*) Even when stuffing and glass cases come into it?

LADY LOXFIELD: What on earth do you mean?

CUDWORTH: Oh – you came into it too. She mentioned you.

JOE: Who did?

MRS STRITTON: *Your* friend – the waitress.

JOE: Has Alice been up there? (*Moving forward, his foot on the first doorstep.*)

SIR GEORGE: Been and gone. After giving us all the rough edge of her tongue. You'll have to be careful there, young fella.

JOE: (*Anxiously.*) Was she looking for me?

MRS STRITTON: Yes. Everybody's been looking for somebody.

(*JOE steps back and looks through the doorway.*)

CUDWORTH: Well, I'm not. (*Coming down the steps to right.*) And I've had enough of this. Wasting time. No point in hanging about here. (*To SIR GEORGE.*) What about pushing off?

MRS STRITTON: (*Urgently.*) No, please wait, then we can all go back together. Much safer. (*She rises, standing on the second step.*)

CUDWORTH: Safer? There's no danger. Just as safe going back as it was coming here.

SIR GEORGE: (*To MRS STRITTON.*) Quite. Well, we can only give you a quarter of an hour. (*To LADY LOXFIELD and CUDWORTH, rising.*) Care for a stroll as far as the next tower?

LADY LOXFIELD: (*Rising hesitantly and coming down a pace.*) I'd like to – but I'm wondering about Philippa.

SIR GEORGE: She'll be here waiting for you. Do her good. (*He takes up his golf club.*) Coming, Cudworth? Better stretch our legs or we'll get stiff and that seat's extremely hard.

CUDWORTH: I've had enough traipsing round these damned walls.

(*The three go out left, sauntering slowly. LADY LOXFIELD followed by SIR GEORGE, then CUDWORTH.*)

JOE: (*Crossing to MRS STRITTON.*) But it won't be, y'know.

MRS STRITTON: (*Coming down one step.*) Won't be what?

JOE: As safe going back as it was coming here.

MRS STRITTON: Why not?

JOE: You wouldn't understand if I told you. (*He goes up the first step.*)

MRS STRITTON: (*Her left foot down one step.*) Are you trying to frighten me?

JOE: No. You'll be safe enough. You'd be still safer if you were dead.

MRS STRITTON: (*Indignantly.*) That's a nice thing to say! (*Stepping back.*)

JOE: Oh – I don't know. Haven't you ever wished you were nicely, safely dead, Mrs Stritton?

MRS STRITTON: (*In a low voice.*) Yes. Sometimes I have.

JOE: I thought you had.

MRS STRITTON: (*Turning on him.*) Well, haven't you?

JOE: No, not in that way. Not nicely and safely. But just dead. Once or twice, that's all. When I've felt –
(*He stops because MRS BATLEY slowly comes through the doorway, then halts, to look at them.*)
Ma, I thought some of these others would want to go back. But not you, Ma. Not you. I'm disappointed, Ma. I thought better of you.

MRS BATLEY. Now what are yer talkin' about, eh?

JOE: I'm talking about you, Ma. I'd hoped that you at least would want to stay down here and not come creeping back.

MRS BATLEY: (*Calmly, coming slowly down the doorsteps.*) Like to 'ear yerself talk, don't yer?

MRS STRITTON: Don't take any notice of him, Mrs Batley. (*She takes a step forward.*)

MRS BATLEY: I don't. (*She sits on the stone slab above the door.*)

MRS STRITTON: Did they tell you the way to get back?

MRS BATLEY: No. I never asked 'em.

MRS STRITTON: You'll have to come along with us then.

MRS BATLEY: Thank yer for the invitation, Mrs Stritton. But yer see I'm not going that way. I'm staying here.

I only came to get my basket. (*Picking up the basket.*)
I might as well 'ave it.

JOE: (*With enthusiasm.*) That's the girl. (*He sits on the second step centre.*)

MRS STRITTON: Mrs Batley, I'm surprised at you.

MRS BATLEY: 'Ow's that?

MRS STRITTON: I thought you said you had a lot of responsibilities – looking after people – keeping your home together – going out cleaning –

MRS BATLEY: That's it. 'Ad years and years of it. Could 'ave done with 'alf a dozen pairs of 'ands sometimes.

MRS STRITTON: Well then, you can't leave it all – to stay here –

MRS BATLEY: Can't I? 'Oo says I can't? As long as I can remember, they've been tellin' me what I can do an' what I can't do. An' no thanks for it neither when I did what I could do. Well, some of 'em can look after themselves for a change. It'll do 'em good.

MRS STRITTON: I don't like to hear you talking like that, Mrs Batley.

MRS BATLEY: (*Calmly.*) I dare say not. But today I feel like speaking me mind, for once.

JOE: That's right. Go on, Ma.

MRS BATLEY: Now, down there it was different. They said to me, 'Well, what d'yer think of it all, Mrs Batley?' An' I says, 'It's lovely. It's 'ow things should be,' I said. An' so it is. When I first saw all of them children comin' out o' them fine houses – an' all their mothers lookin' so nice an' smilin' – an' everything so clean an' pretty, I could 'ave cried. So I says to 'em, I says. 'There don't seem much 'ere for somebody like me to do, but whatever there is to do, let me do it,' I says. An' they says, 'Thank yer, Mrs Batley, thank yer very much,' they says. Just imagine that! As if it wouldn't be a pleasure. '*But*,' they says, 'you just take it easy a bit, Mrs Batley,' they says. 'Take it easy an' 'ave a look round an' enjoy yourself.' An' they've given me as nice a bedroom as ever yer saw. All to meself too. First I've ever 'ad all to

meself. (*She pauses.*) I fancy I dreamt of it once when
I was a girl... an' all them bright streets as well... an' the
gardens...an' the children's faces... I remember bein'
quite upset at the time...thinkin' it was nothin' but a
dream – just tormenting yerself, as yer might say. But it
ain't. It's real. It's 'ere (*She pauses, then rises.*) Well,
pleased to 'ave met yet, Mrs Stritton. Be'ave yerself,
young man. (*She nods and smiles and then goes calmly out.*)
(*They stare after her. MRS STRITTON crosses right, looks
out through the doorway, then turns to JOE.*)

MRS STRITTON: I suppose *you're* delighted.

JOE: Yes. I'm delighted.

MRS STRITTON: (*With sudden bitterness.*) Well, what are
you doing here, then? Why aren't you still down there?
Why aren't you having a lovely time too? (*She moves to
the stone slab above the door.*)

JOE: I have a reason.

MRS STRITTON: (*After waiting for it.*) Well – what is your
reason?

JOE: (*Shaking his head and smiling.*) Can't tell *you.*

MRS STRITTON: I wonder if there's anybody you *can* tell?

JOE: Yes. With any luck. That's not saying much because
I'm usually out o' luck.

MRS STRITTON: Most of us are.

JOE: But I have a feeling today that I might be lucky. (*He
pauses, then looks at her and rises.*) Mrs Stritton – this is
serious. (*Crossing to her.*) Are you going to give that chap
of yours a break? (*He stands on the third step.*)

MRS STRITTON: (*Coldly.*) I don't know what you mean.

JOE: (*Shrugging.*) All right. You don't know what I mean.
And you won't know what he means. Stonewalling. Well,
you'll win. Stonewalling always wins. Except, of course,
that it always loses. Because that's all you're left with in
the end – stone walls. You wouldn't know what I was
talking about, would you?

MRS STRITTON: (*Stubbornly.*) No. I haven't the slightest
idea. Something silly.

JOE: Some of you pick up any bit of happiness as if it was a
chicken – and then wring its neck.

MRS STRITTON: (*Suddenly stormily.*) Why do you keep on insulting me?

JOE: (*With equal sudden passion.*) Because I'm trying to save your life.

MRS STRITTON: My life isn't in danger.

JOE: You've got a knife in its throat now.

MRS STRITTON: Don't be so beastly. Besides, what's it to do with you? You don't even like me.

JOE: No, but I like life, and don't want to see it poured down the drain like dirty water. (*Looking off through the doorway.*) Your husband's coming now. (*He begins to move left, up the step.*) I hope when I get back, you'll have got rid of the body. They say that's the most difficult part. (*He goes out top left. MALCOLM appears through the doorway right.*)

MALCOLM: (*Eagerly.*) Dorothy, where have you been? (*He comes down the first doorstep.*)

MRS STRITTON: (*Coldly.*) I've been here, waiting for you.

MALCOLM: I wish you'd have stayed on. Honestly, Dorothy, I've had some most interesting –

MRS STRITTON: (*Cutting in, crossing to MALCOLM.*) I want to get away from here, I want to go home.

MALCOLM: But I don't even know the way –

MRS STRITTON: Some of the others do. We can go with them. And they'll be going soon.

MALCOLM: But why should we go? Y'know, if you'd only stayed down there a little longer, and seen –

MRS STRITTON: (*Angrily.*) I saw all I wanted to see. And I told you what I thought about it.

MALCOLM: Yes, but –

MRS STRITTON: (*Vehemently, crossing centre, her back to him.*) I tell you, I hate it, I hate it, I *loathe* it.

MALCOLM: (*Distressed.*) But why, Dorothy, why do you? (*Crossing to her.*)

MRS STRITTON: (*Turns to him, stormily.*) I suppose you think it's all so wonderful just because you saw that girl – that waitress woman – bouncing about and enjoying herself –

79

MALCOLM: No, of course I don't. I hardly noticed her. She's nothing to do with it. Surely you don't dislike this place simply because somebody else does like it?

MRS STRITTON: No, I don't. That's not the real reason, though the very sight of her romping round was enough to put me off.

MALCOLM: (*With timid persistence.*) Well then, what is it you don't like about it?

MRS STRITTON: Oh, don't let's start arguing –

MALCOLM: I don't want to start arguing. I only say – what is it you don't like here?

MRS STRITTON: And I told you before, I don't like any of it. It's silly. It's – common.

MALCOLM: Common? It seems to me very uncommon.

MRS STRITTON: You know what I mean, Malcolm. And all of them looking so pleased with themselves.

MALCOLM: Well, why shouldn't they look pleased with themselves? They've something to look pleased about. I was asking one chap –

MRS STRITTON: (*Cutting in.*) And then they've no decent manners. They don't know how to behave properly. And everybody pretending to be as good as everybody else!

MALCOLM: No, Dorothy, that's not quite true. They have some people – men and women – great thinkers, scientists, artists – that they admire and respect and look after better than we do any of our really great people. They –

MRS STRITTON: (*Cutting in.*) Oh, don't go on and on about them. I saw what they're like. I've got eyes and ears as well as you.

MALCOLM: (*Crosses left, after a slight pause.*) Not when you don't want to, you haven't.

MRS STRITTON: (*Turns to him before speaking.*) What does that mean?

MALCOLM: (*Moving back to left centre.*) It means that you made up your mind you wouldn't like this city and all the people in it. I don't know why. It was as strange to me at first as it was to you. But I wanted to find out about it, and you didn't. You'd made up your mind. (*He stops.*)

MRS STRITTON: (*After a pause.*) Well?

MALCOLM: And now you're ready to make up my mind
for me. You're trying to make *me* dislike it too. (*Suddenly
angry.*) And you can't do that, Dorothy, do you see?
I won't have it. I know – I *know* – you just closed your
mind, wouldn't try to learn anything, said the first stupid
thing that came into your head – anything – *anything* –
rather than ever admit you were wrong or try and
change yourself or open your heart and mind – and –
and be *generous* –

MRS STRITTON: (*Aghast.*) You hate me now, don't you,
Malcolm?

MALCOLM: (*Moving quickly to the top of the steps.*) No,
I don't. But I easily could. You've done this before. But
this is the worst. And I won't be bullied and cheated out
of what I think and feel. (*Shouting and pointing right.*) I
like that place and those people. It's a much better place
than we've ever known before. They're much better
people. They're *alive*. They're doing the things I've
always wanted people to do. (*Coming down.*) I'm going to
help them – (*He exits through the door.*)

MRS STRITTON: (*As he moves towards the doorway.*)
Malcolm!
(*She does not try to stop him but sits down on the second step
right centre of the steps and bursts into heavy sobs. He has
just got off, but now slowly and irresolutely returns, and
slowly goes nearer to her, finally sitting beside her, on the
stone slab, putting an arm round her.*)

MALCOLM: (*Gently.*) All right, Dorothy. Don't cry.

MRS STRITTON: (*Through her sobs.*) You were going to
leave me.

MALCOLM: Well, I haven't left you. I'm here.

MRS STRITTON: (*Subsiding now.*) You don't love me.

MALCOLM: Yes, I do.

MRS STRITTON: No, you don't. If you did, you couldn't
think of leaving me like that. I couldn't leave you.

MALCOLM: I haven't left you.

MRS STRITTON: (*Drying her eyes.*) I know I'm silly – and
sometimes I behave stupidly. Somehow I can't help it.

81

Sometimes I hate myself. Sometimes I wish I was dead.
(*Whispering.*) That man, Joe Dinmore, said that. Somehow
he knew. He said, 'Haven't you ever wished you were
nicely, safely dead, Mrs Stritton?' I don't see how he
could know that specially about me, but somehow he
did. And that upset me – that and one or two other
things he said. It's all been so queer, ever since we came
here. You didn't feel it so much as I did. Coming here –
and talking to all these people we didn't know – and then
going down there, and watching it taking you away from
me – and then coming back up here – and waiting. It's
been horrible, I think. You don't understand what I've
felt about it, Malcolm.

MALCOLM: Perhaps not. I can't see why – I mean, it's
seemed quite different to me. I don't think I'm going to
like it when we get back.

MRS STRITTON: (*Immensely relieved, happy.*) Oh – Malcolm
– you are coming back with me?

MALCOLM: (*Sadly.*) Yes, I'm going back with you.

MRS STRITTON: Oh – darling! (*Taking his arm.*) You *are*
good to me. Don't think I don't realize how good you
are to me. I think I'd have died if you'd left me.

MALCOLM: I wouldn't have left you. Yes, I know. I went in
there again, but I thought you might follow me in and
that then you might have changed your mind.

MRS STRITTON: No, I couldn't have done that.

MALCOLM: (*Sadly.*) No, you couldn't have done that. Well,
we'll go back. But I'm afraid I'm not going to like it.

MRS STRITTON: (*Eagerly.*) Yes, you will. You'll forget this.
And I'll do everything I can to make it better. We'll try
and see more people – the sort of people you like. I'll
make friends. No, I know I don't find it easy. But I will –
I'll make friends. It'll be different, you'll see. (*Warming
up to it.*) We might take that house in the Crescent. Or
perhaps you could leave the bank altogether. Malcolm, if
we went back with Mr Cudworth, you might ask him if
you could work for him. I'm sure he'd pay you much
better than the bank does. Shall I leave you together, or
would you like me to say something –

MALCOLM: (*With decision.*) I don't want to work for him.

MRS STRITTON: Oh – but – Malcolm –

MALCOLM: (*Fiercely.*) Drop it, Dorothy! I'm coming back. That's enough.

MRS STRITTON: (*Meekly.*) Yes, all right, dear.

(*They sit together, MALCOLM staring out bleakly, while she smiles, her hand on his left knee. JOE now enters slowly from top left and looks at them sardonically.*)

JOE: Timed it all right, haven't I? (*Moving along the top to left centre, above the stone seat.*)

MALCOLM: (*Exchanging a look with him.*) Yes.

MRS STRITTON: (*Brightly.*) We want to go back, and I don't know the way, and neither does my husband. Did you see the others?

JOE: Yes. Don't worry, they're coming along.

MALCOLM: I thought you liked it down there.

JOE: I did.

MALCOLM: Why come back here, then?

JOE: I've been asked that before. I have a reason.

MALCOLM: I hope it's a good one.

JOE: It is. (*To the top of the steps centre.*) I didn't know you were a comic.

MALCOLM: I'm not. Why?

JOE: Heard you making 'em shout with laughter down the road there. What was the big joke?

MALCOLM: (*Grimly.*) I was explaining our financial system.

(*Enter CUDWORTH from left briskly, on stage level. He comes to centre.*)

CUDWORTH: I'm going back. No sense in hanging about here. Waste of time. Not going to wait for those two, neither. Pair of snobs.

MRS STRITTON: (*Jumping up, standing on the first step.*) Can we come with you, Mr Cudworth?

CUDWORTH: Certainly. If you're ready now. (*He exits down left, at proscenium opening.*)

MRS STRITTON: Well, we are. Aren't we, Malcolm?

MALCOLM: (*Grimly, as he rises.*) Yes, but don't forget what I said, Dorothy. No asking for jobs.

MRS STRITTON: No, dear, of course not. (*She takes his arm, and they cross left.*)

JOE: (*To MALCOLM, coming down to the bottom of the steps.*) Well, I knew it would happen. But I'm sorry.

MALCOLM: Thank you. Good-bye.

JOE: Oh – you may see me again.

MALCOLM: (*Disengaging his arm and crossing to JOE.*) It would be all right if I did. But I don't think that's likely.

JOE: You never know. (*Dropping his voice.*) I might remind you then of what you've seen and heard today. Don't go cold and dead on it. Keep it warm and alive inside, pal. All the best!

MRS STRITTON: (*Calling.*) Malcolm!

MALCOLM: Yes, dear, I'm coming. (*To JOE, hurriedly.*) And all the best to you too – pal.

(*They shake hands. MALCOLM crosses to MRS STRITTON. They exit arm in arm down left, at proscenium opening. JOE watches them go, thoughtfully. PHILIPPA enters slowly at the doorway right. JOE turns to her, eagerly.*)

PHILIPPA: Hello!

JOE: (*Disappointed.*) Hello!

PHILIPPA: (*Crossing to left centre, looking off down left.*) That's not my mother who's just gone, is it?

JOE: No. Cudworth and the pair from Leamington wanted to be off.

PHILIPPA: (*Turning, mounts the steps.*) I'd have guessed they wanted to be off.

JOE: You'd have been right about two of 'em, but wrong about the third – Stritton. (*He moves up the doorsteps, leaning against the upstage doorpost.*) He's all right, or soon could be. Your mother's along there with Sir George. By this time they'll have got round to the Derbyshire Snookses or the Hampshire Higginses.

PHILIPPA: I wouldn't be surprised. (*Sitting at the corner of the wall, centre.*) Where's your girl?

JOE: If you mean Alice, she's still down there. But why d'you call her my girl?

PHILIPPA: Don't be silly. I saw what was on between you from the start. And I noticed the way she was looking at you down there this morning.

JOE. Well, you don't notice her looking at me now, do you?

PHILIPPA: Why don't you go down and find her?

JOE: Because I've got to stop up here and hope that she finds me.

PHILIPPA: Why should she do all the running about?

JOE: It's nothing to do with running about. I've got to keep out here, that's all.

PHILIPPA: Then I'm disappointed in you. I thought a man like you, once you'd found a place like that, wouldn't have let it go for anything. Do you remember what you said this morning? I mean when I told you to shut up and not spoil it. When Alice and I said it was all right. Then you said you wouldn't believe it was all right until you'd been inside the place because you'd been taken in before. Remember?

JOE: Sure I remember.

PHILIPPA: Now you've seen it for yourself, you come back here and say you've got to keep out. It seems to me you're all talk.

JOE: I'm mostly talk. But don't let that worry you.

PHILIPPA: It doesn't. Why should it? (*She rises and crosses to right wall.*) As a matter of fact, nothing's going to worry me now. Quite suddenly I feel I don't give a damn.

JOE: Save that for your mother. She's here too. (*He exits right, through the doorway.*)

(*Enter LADY LOXFIELD top left.*)

LADY LOXFIELD: (*Moving to centre.*) Well, darling, we're ready to go, and I expect you are too.

(*LADY LOXFIELD and PHILIPPA look at each other.*)

(*After a pause.*) Well, Philippa?

PHILIPPA: (*Moving to LADY LOXFIELD.*) Mother, I'm not coming back.

LADY LOXFIELD: Don't be absurd, darling.

PHILIPPA: I'm not coming back. I'm staying here. I came up to tell you I'm staying here.

LADY LOXFIELD: Quite impossible, darling. Nothing
would induce me to stay here. I told you what I thought
of the place this morning.

PHILIPPA: I'm not talking about *you,* Mother. I'm talking
about *me.* And I've made up my mind.

LADY LOXFIELD: You're tired, Philippa.

PHILIPPA: (*Flaring up.*) I'm *not* tired. And I'm not absurd.
I'm not any of those things you've been telling me I was
for years and years every time I've tried to find some life
of my own. I feel cool and calm and sensible, and I know
exactly what I want.

LADY LOXFIELD: You're talking to your own mother
now, darling. Not to a stranger. (*She sits at the corner of the
wall centre.*) You needn't glare and shout.

PHILIPPA: I'm sorry, Mother. I didn't mean to. But I can't
go back with you. I'd rather die. Going back there would
be only a kind of slow death. Those people in
Bournequay aren't *real.* (*She crosses left.*) They don't want
to do anything. They only want to keep on existing,
from one meal to the next, from one bit of gossip to the
next, from one bedtime to the next. (*She is left of LADY
LOXFIELD.*) You aren't really like that, Mother. (*She puts
her arm around her.*) Look what you said about going that
time to Venice. But now you're afraid of any sort of
change –

LADY LOXFIELD: And why not? I'm getting old. I've lost
your father. I've lost the life we had together. But I do
my best to keep what's left –

PHILIPPA: (*Rising and cutting in.*) Yes, but there isn't
anything left worth having. Not even for you there isn't.
(*To centre.*) And for me it's not living at all. And now that
I've seen this – been among those people down there – it
just wouldn't be possible for me to go back. (*She kneels
right of LADY LOXFIELD.*) The children, Mother, the
children! When I saw them this morning. I could feel
myself coming alive. It was as if something – in my
heart – suddenly snapped. I could have cried with
happiness. I said to those women who were looking after
them, 'Please let me stay, and I'll do anything – anything

– wash and scrub – I don't care what it is. Only let me
stay.' And they said I could. They were all so friendly –
and so *real.* Oh, Mother, can't you understand?

LADY LOXFIELD: I can see you're very excited and rather
overwrought, darling!

(*PHILIPPA rises impatiently and moves to right.*)

I know it's been very dull for you often, living with me.
I've tried – in more ways than you know, and often at
some self-sacrifice – to make it less dull, more amusing –

PHILIPPA: (*Turning to her.*) Yes, I'm sure you have. But it's
not a question of being dull or amused. It's more serious
than that. And I'm really a serious person, Mother.

LADY LOXFIELD: (*Rising, she moves to PHILIPPA, leaving
her bag on the wall.*) Then if you are, Philippa, I've a right
to remind you that serious people have a sense of duty,
and that you're my only child, that I've nobody else now
but you, and that you have some duty towards me.

PHILIPPA: And I don't simply want to get away from you.
It isn't that at all. Mother, why don't you stay here with
me? I've tried your kind of life. Why don't you try my
kind of life?

LADY LOXFIELD: (*Coldly.*) Because I don't think it's your
kind of life. And I'm certain it isn't mine. (*She moves a
few steps towards left.*) After all, I ought to know better
than you do –

PHILIPPA: (*Hotly.*) You oughtn't to know better than I do.
Why should you? I can't see any evidence of it. You
don't even really like what you say you like. You only
put up with it in a dim sort of way simply because you're
afraid of anything else. And I don't call that living.
I don't want to leave you, Mother. I hate to think of you
going back there – alone.

LADY LOXFIELD: (*Moving back to PHILIPPA.*) I'm glad of
that. And remember, I'm your mother. I brought you
into the world, I loved you and looked after you, I –

PHILIPPA: (*Cutting in, but gently.*) Yes, Mother, but you
didn't bring me into the world simply to keep me away
from the world. I must make my own life just as you

once made yours. And if now you want to prevent my doing that, Mother, then we must say good-bye – that's all.

LADY LOXFIELD: (*Distressed.*) No – Philippa – I'm too old to change – I –

PHILIPPA: Good-bye, Mother. (*She goes forward to kiss her.*)

LADY LOXFIELD: (*Clings to her, crying.*) No – no – darling – don't leave me – you can't leave me – I –

PHILIPPA: I must, Mother. (*She kisses her – and disengages herself.* Good-bye. (*She runs down the steps and hurries out through the doorway.*)

(*There is a pause, during which LADY LOXFIELD stands motionless, pulling herself together. Then slowly she turns towards SIR GEORGE as he enters at top left.*)

LADY LOXFIELD: I'm ready to go now, if you are, Sir George.

SIR GEORGE: Yes, certainly, Lady Loxfield. Great pleasure. Great pleasure.

(*JOE appears at the door right. SIR GEORGE turns to him.*)

Stayin' on, eh?

JOE: Looks like it.

(*LADY LOXFIELD picks up her bag, and dries her eyes.*)

SIR GEORGE: That door shuts at sunset, y'know, so better make up your mind soon whether you're going in or staying out.

JOE: I know. But thanks for mentioning it. 'Bye.

SIR GEORGE: 'Bye. (*To LADY LOXFIELD, indicating the proscenium opening down left.*) This way, I think.

LADY LOXFIELD: (*As they move down the steps together.*) I think you said you knew the Prescotts?

SIR GEORGE: Knew Tubby Prescott very well. Marv'lous shot, old Tubby Prescott.

(*They cross towards down left.*)

LADY LOXFIELD: He married one of the Murchison girls didn't he?

SIR GEORGE: Thought he married Jenny Fingleton's sister.

LADY LOXFIELD: Oh, it's *that* Prescott. But they were never in India.

SIR GEORGE: Tubby went to India – to shoot a tiger. But he didn't stay there long enough...

(*By this time they are both out of sight, having passed through the left proscenium opening. JOE runs to the top of the steps, and looks down over the wall right. The light though good enough for the action, is far less than it was earlier, and suggests the end of a sunset. We now hear a fanfare of distant trumpets from below like that heard at the end of Act One. JOE looks anxiously to top left, at the sunset. He then runs down the steps. As he starts to do so, the door begins to close slowly.*)

JOE: (*From centre, looking at the door, muttering.*) No – for God's sake!

(*As he says this, we see that the door is very slowly and massively beginning to close. We hear the sound of running footsteps and JOE hears them too and hurries forward to fling himself against the door. As he reaches it, ALICE desperately scrambles through to centre, and no sooner is she through than it closes with a decisive sound. JOE looks at her, grinning with nervous pleasure.*)

JOE: (*At the door.*) Well, Alice, you made it.

ALICE: (*Breathlessly.*) Don't stand there grinning at me, you damned great ape.

JOE: (*Down to right centre.*) What d'you want me to do, then?

ALICE: Get down on your knees.

JOE: Okay.

(*He begins to get down on his knees, but she furiously drags him to his feet.*)

ALICE: (*Furiously.*) I could kill you.

JOE: What for?

ALICE: For making me come out.

JOE: Why did you?

ALICE: Because I'm a woman and a damn fool.

JOE: Go on.

ALICE: I don't go on from there. I've said enough. (*She goes up the steps to the fourth step.*) Too much.

JOE: (*He goes to the third step left of ALICE.*) You liked it
   down there?

ALICE: You know I did.

JOE: It's good, isn't it?

ALICE: It's what I'd always hoped for, what I'd always
   believed was somewhere round the corner, if we could
   only find it. And there it is. I always hoped that men and
   women could live like that, if they tried. Life hadn't to
   be a dog-fight round a dustbin. We'd made it like that,
   but it needn't be like that. Here, they start every
   morning feeling as we only feel for about half an hour
   every two years, half-lit at somebody's birthday party.
   That's true, isn't it?

JOE: Yes, that's true, Alice.

ALICE: Here, they don't work to keep themselves out of the
   gutter. They work because they've got something big and
   exciting to do. They can see their life *growing*. They're
   building it up. And they're enjoying it all. They're not
   passing the time waiting for the undertaker. You told us
   this morning, before we went down there, that you didn't
   believe in this and that –

JOE: I know. I take it all back. I've seen it for myself.

ALICE: I saw it in your eyes, I heard it in your voice, when
   we were down there together. Those kids – d'you
   remember, Joe?

JOE: I shan't forget it, not for a single minute, as long as
   I live, Alice.

ALICE: I must sit down. My knees are going.
   (*She sits down on the fifth step against the wall right and he
   sits by her side on the top step.*)

JOE: Go on, Alice.

ALICE: Go on! Haven't I said enough! It's about time you
   started talking.

JOE: Not yet. I've plenty to say. But not yet. You've got to
   tell me.

ALICE: You make it hard for a girl, I must say, Joe.

JOE: I've taken the hard road too. You'll see. If you can
   behave like a woman, I can behave like a man. A real
   woman, a real man.

ALICE: Well if I hadn't been down there, been amongst those people, I couldn't talk like this. Before, I'd have been shot first. I've always been proud, though you mightn't think it.

JOE: I knew you had. I could see that. I know about you.

ALICE: All right, then. I'll tell it all. But be careful. If I hear anything from you that sounds like a laugh, I'll – I'll – kill you – or throw myself off that wall.

JOE: There won't be. What d'you take me for?

ALICE: Before that door opened, when we were all talking up here, I liked you a lot. Only I wish you'd believed in something. Remember how I lost my temper? That was because you weren't just what I wanted you to be. I don't know if that makes sense to a man but any woman would understand. I was angry with myself as well as with you. Then when we went down there and we saw what it was like, you were different. You were what I wanted you to be. Your mother must have seen you like that when you were a little boy. You were eager, you were happy, you believed everything you saw and heard. That's true, isn't it?

JOE: Yes, that's true enough.

ALICE: So then – I knew I loved you, Joe. It came in a flash. 'This is it,' I said to myself. And I knew it was, I hoped you loved me. You looked as if you did.

JOE: I did. I still do.

ALICE: Are you sure?

JOE: Certain.

ALICE: That's all right, then. (*She turns her face towards him, and they kiss. She remains in his arms.*) I don't know how you could, with those wonderful-looking women all round you down there. Made me feel like something that had crawled out of the dustbin.

JOE: You didn't look it. Besides, that's where I come from too. You looked – with your eyes all shining – what I felt. And that's something the rest of 'em wouldn't understand. They hadn't come here the way we'd come, Alice. So you were different.

ALICE: (*Happily.*) Oh – you do understand. (*Taking his hands.*) You see, Joe, I felt then that we'd started something between us it would take a long, long time to finish. So when you disappeared, I didn't think much of it. Thought you'd gone off to look at some machinery or whatever you like to look at. But I never thought you'd leave the place. I knew it was what you'd always wanted. It was our place. And we could stay there. They'd told us that. So I didn't worry about you, until it began to get late, and then I started looking for you and asking about you. And nobody seemed to know. Until I saw Mrs Batley – and she said you were up here – waiting for me, she said. So I ran and ran. I was blazing wild – you heard me – but I had to come out, if you'd come out. It wouldn't have been the same at all without you. I had to be with you, Joe.

JOE: That's what I'd hoped. That's why I waited and waited.

ALICE: But why?

JOE: I daren't go back once I'd made up my mind and come out. There were some nasty cracks about that, but I had to take 'em. You see, I felt if I went back, you'd persuade me to stay – or even if you didn't I'd never have guts enough to come out again.

ALICE: But what's the matter with you? (*Rising.*) Why shouldn't you stay? For God's sake, don't tell me now that this isn't what you wanted either.

JOE: (*Rising, with urgency, on the fourth and fifth steps.*) No, no. Don't you see – somebody's got to go back.

ALICE: No, I don't see. Some of them have gone back, haven't they?

JOE: Of course they have. I expected that. Cudworth's gone back. Mrs Stritton's gone back and taken her husband with her – poor devil. Sir George and Lady What's-it have gone, even though Lady What's-it had to lose her precious daughter. Yes, they've all gone. And what good is it going to do anybody that they have gone? If they ever say a word about this place, they'll swear blind that it's terrible. So somebody's got to go back and tell the truth about it.

ALICE: (*To the right end of the stone slab.*) And that must be the bloke I go and fall for and tack myself on to. It just would have to be.

JOE: Yes, it must. That's just what it must be.

ALICE: All right, I was trying to be funny. Tell me what you mean?

JOE: I mean, you wouldn't want a chap who could keep this to himself.

ALICE: I see.

JOE: You said you had to come out because I'd come out –

ALICE: Yes, because I'm a woman. That's how it takes you.

JOE: And I say, because I'm a man – and not just a monkey – I've got to go back and tell them all what we've seen here. Before, I knew what was wrong – you heard me – but what was the use of me getting up and spouting about it when I didn't know if it could ever be put right?

ALICE: And because you know now –

JOE: I've got to tell them. I've got to keep on telling 'em – day and night – wherever I am –

ALICE: Wherever *we* are –

JOE: Wherever *we* are, I've got to tell them.

ALICE: (*She runs to him, at the third or fourth steps, grasping his arms.*) We've got to tell them. But, Joe, how do we get back?

JOE: How did we come here? Some kind of miracle got us here to give us a test, and if we've passed that test and we're ready to go it'll get us back all right. But it's not going to be easy, when we *are* back, y'know Alice. It'll be a hard road. Some of 'em'll laugh and jeer just because they don't *want* anything different. They're frightened of losing some miserable little advantage they've schemed and worked for. They think they can't enjoy their own health unless they know that a lot of other people are dying on their feet. They don't want to lose the whip-hand they've got over somebody. They'd rather have their little privilege and prestige in an ashpit than take a chance and share alike in a new world. Some of 'em, poor creatures, are so twisted and tormented inside themselves that they envy and hate other people's happiness. And we'll have to talk to plenty of them.

ALICE: I can see this isn't going to be easy, Joe. It's going to be tough. (*She crouches on the third step, looking out to the front.*)

JOE: You don't know the half of it yet. Then there are all the smart boys – the kind I was – who've had to take plenty and know it's all rotten, but won't have it that you can see anything any better. They get big laughs at your expense. I know. I've been one of 'em. And there are plenty of them too. (*He crouches behind ALICE.*) And that's not all, Alice. There'll be days – rainy days – dark days – when nobody wants to listen, when the butcher hasn't been paid and the grocer looks at you sideways and you've nothing to smoke and they're asking you when you're moving on to the next town – and *then* – we shan't be sure ourselves we were ever here –

ALICE: Joe – the light's going. We must have one last look. (*They rise, and look over the wall right, ALICE right of JOE on the fifth step.*)

All the lights are coming up along the terraces and in the gardens. Joe, we could never forget the gardens.

JOE: We'll not forget any of it.

ALICE: (*After a pause.*) Joe – couldn't we stay after all?

JOE: *You* could. (*He steps back.*) I must go.

ALICE: You're not going without me.

JOE: Then you can't stay.

ALICE: (*Calling down quietly.*) Good-bye, my lovely city. I don't know when I'll ever see you again. (*She breaks down.*)

JOE: (*Comforting her.*) Now, Alice – take it easy, kid – (*Taking her in his arms.*)

ALICE: (*Through her sobs.*) I don't want to go… And it'll seem worse than ever when we get back.

JOE: No, it won't. Because, to begin with, we'll remember. That's why we've got to go back – because we're the ones who've been – and seen it all… And then we'll hope. And keep on hoping. And every time we find a spark of hope and vision in anybody, we'll blow it into a blaze… (*Holding her at arm's length.*) They will tell us we can't change human nature. That's one of the oldest excuses in the world for doing nothing. And it isn't true. We've been changing human nature for thousands of years. But what you *can't* change in it, Alice – no, not with guns or whips or red-hot bars – is man's eternal desire and vision and hope of making this world a better place to live in. (*Looking out front.*) And wherever you go now – up and down and across the Seven Seas – from Poplar to Chungking – you can see this desire and vision and hope, bigger and stronger than ever beginning to light up men's faces, giving a lift to their voices. Not every man, not every woman, wants to cry for it – but there's one here, one there, a few down this street, some more down that street – (*Pointing out front.*) – until you begin to see there are millions of us – yes, armies and armies of us – enough to build ten thousand new cities –

ALICE: (*Looking up.*) Like our city?

JOE: (*Triumphantly.*) Yes, like our city. (*He takes her by the shoulders.*) Where men and women don't work for machines and money, but machines and money work for men and women – where greed and envy and hate have no place – where want and disease and fear have vanished for ever – where nobody carries a whip and nobody rattles a chain. Where men have at last stopped mumbling and gnawing and scratching in dark caves and have come out into the sunlight. And nobody can ever darken it for them again. They're out and free at last. (*They look back to the City.*)

'I dreamt in a dream I saw a city invincible to the attacks of the whole earth, I dreamt that was the new city of Friends,'

ALICE: (*Quietly, taking his hand.*) Come on, Joe, let's get going…

(*As they move, and the last light begins to fade, we hear the fanfare again. They go down left of the steps and off. Curtain.*)

The End.

SUMMER DAY'S DREAM

Author's Preface

*S*ummer *Day's Dream*: I took a great deal of time and trouble over this play, which was re-written several times. As its title suggests, it is really a fantastic comedy, in which, however, certain values come up for discussion; and it is not, as some weekly reviewers appeared to think, a political-economic manifesto. With an interesting cast, grandly led by Herbert Lomas as 'Stephen Dawlish', the play had four good weeks out of London, opened in the early autumn at the St Martin's Theatre, and was withdrawn just before it reached its fiftieth West End performance. But it had not been a failure in the sense that *Home Tomorrow*, was a failure. It had been enthusiastically praised by most sections of the Press, and our audiences were very warm and demonstrative in their appreciation of it. It played to figures that would have ensured it a long run before the War. But we were in a small but expensive theatre; our running costs, which included heavy charges for handling two elaborate sets, were much too high; and although we could have kept going on 'smash hit' business, anything less than this meant a piling up of losses we could not afford. The whole economic background to this play seemed to me so monstrous that I did not even want to make a fight of it, as I might have done earlier.

J B Priestley
Brook, Isle of Wight
December, 1949

Characters

STEPHEN DAWLISH
an old man

FRED VOLES
a farm bailiff

MARGARET DAWLISH
Stephen's daughter-in-law

ROSALIE DAWLISH
Stephen's grand-daughter

FRANKLYN HEIMER
an American industrialist

MADAME IRINA SHESTOVA
a Russian official

CHRISTOPHER DAWLISH
Stephen's grandson

DR BAHRU
an Indian research chemist

Summer Day's Dream was first produced at the St Martin's Theatre, London, on 8 September, 1949, with the following cast:

STEPHEN DAWLISH, Herbert Lomas

FRED VOLES, Charles Lamb

MARGARET DAWLISH, Eileen Thorndike

ROSALIE DAWLISH, Adrienne Corri

FRANKLYN HEIMER, John Salew

MADAME IRINA SHESTOVA, Adina Mandlova

CHRISTOPHER DAWLISH, John Westbrook

DR BAHRU, Olaf Pooley

Director, Michael Macowan

SYNOPSIS OF SCENES

The action of the play takes place at Larks Lea, an old country house on the South Downs; and the time is around Midsummer, 1975.

ACT ONE

Scene 1

The entrance hall of Larks Lea, an old country house on the South Downs. Early afternoon around Midsummer, 1975.

The house was originally a stately early eighteenth century mansion. Everything is clean and well-kept in the place, but its original grandeur has obviously gone for ever, and it has an air of cheerful ruin. Sections of the wood panelling are missing, revealing the bricks underneath, and it is clear that the entrance hall is now used as an all-purpose room and has a farmhouse look about it. The front entrance, with large double doors with a decorative fanlight over them, are in an alcove up right centre. When the doors are open the remains of a stone balustrade can be seen, and a glimpse is had of a lush, overgrown, neglected garden in high summer. There are windows in the right and left sides of the alcove. There is a large window right also overlooking part of the garden. A once fine, broad shallow staircase, now sadly dilapidated, leads from up left to the first floor. There is tall narrow window in the back wall where the staircase turns at a small landing. A door down left leads to the kitchen and the rest of the ground floor of the house. The stairs are uncarpeted and two mats, one by the doors up centre, and one centre, only partially cover the stone-flagged floor. There are no curtains to the windows. The furniture is nondescript. A large sofa, with a drop end, stands under the window right. A circular, rough wood table stands centre, with an upright chair above it and kitchen-type elbow chairs right and left of it. A small wood stool stands underneath the table. A small plain refectory table with a wood bench right of it, stands against the wall left. Small stools at each end of the refectory table complete the furniture. Left of the doors up centre there are two or three hooks on the wall on which a raincoat is hanging. Other coats and a fishing basket hang on some hooks left of the staircase window. Shot-guns and other odds and ends generally found about a farmhouse, occupy various corners. An old coat hangs over the bannister rail, and a pair of gum-boots stand at the foot of the stairs. There are no pictures. Shaded electric pendants hang right centre and left centre, but at night the actual source of light, which is soft and mellow, falls in localised areas from two hessian shaded lights, one over the foot of the stairs, and the other over the table centre. They are controlled from switches on the left wall of the alcove up centre.

When the curtain rises, it is a bright, hot summer day. The doors up centre are wide open. STEPHEN DAWLISH, who is very old, but still a tremendous character, is asleep in the chair right of the table centre. He is snoring gently and peacefully. He is dressed in very old patched tweeds. All the English characters are dressed very simply and rather shabbily, though the young people have a good deal of colour in their clothes. All of them look very healthy, as if they spent most of their time out of doors. After some moments – for the scene should be very slow in opening, to suit the mood of the time – FRED VOLES enters up centre. He is a man of about sixty, a slow, dependable rural type. He carries a trug basket full of potatoes. He moves above the table centre, sees STEPHEN is asleep, laughs gently but does not disturb him. He then moves quietly to the table left, puts the basket on it, sits on the bench left, takes an old pipe, a pouch of tobacco and some matches from his pocket, and fills and lights the pipe. STEPHEN slowly wakes up and sniffs carefully at FRED's smoke.

STEPHEN: Fred?

FRED: Yes, Mr Dawlish?

STEPHEN: (*Sniffing; almost accusingly.*) There's some real tobacco in that pipe.

FRED: There is. But I've still mixed it with some coltsfoot – about half and half. (*He rises and moves to left of STEPHEN.*) Try some? (*He hands his pouch to STEPHEN.*)

STEPHEN: (*Taking the pouch.*) Thank you, Fred. (*He takes a pipe from his pocket and begins to fill it.*) Where did the tobacco come from?

FRED: Frank Waterhouse. His lad, the one who's at sea, brought him some, and when we sold them two heifers to him the other day, Frank gave me about a pound.
(*STEPHEN returns the pouch to FRED, and lights his pipe.*)
Some's for you, of course, Mr Dawlish, if you want it.

STEPHEN: Certainly I want it, Fred. All you can spare. (*His pipe is going now, and he tastes it.*) Not bad. Not bad at all.

FRED: 'Tisn't, is it? I'll bring yours up tonight. You've got some coltsfoot to mix in with it, eh?

STEPHEN: Plenty. (*He sighs with satisfaction and smokes comfortably.*) I was dreaming, Fred. Sixty years back. Nineteen-fifteen – first World War. About the time you were born.

FRED: (*Sitting in the chair above the table centre.*) That's right. Nineteen-fifteen. I'm sixty this year.

STEPHEN: (*Slowly.*) I was in the trenches again – near Neuve Chapelle – splashing about in gum-boots in a foot or two of water. (*He pauses.*) I could see the rotting sandbags, as plain as I can see you – after sixty years. By thunder, Fred, I've been through something in my time – and it's all here somewhere, even the sandbags. I'm a miracle, Fred, and nothing less.

FRED: Right, Mr Dawlish. And maybe we all are.

STEPHEN: Certainly. Only I'm more of one.

(*FRED laughs.*)

Is the hay in?

FRED: Finished this noon. I came to tell you. But I've had to send the big cart up to Longbarrow Down.

STEPHEN: Why? You're not lending it to Joe Watson again, are you?

FRED: No. Joe doesn't need it this year.

STEPHEN: Then why send it up to Longbarrow Down?

FRED: Joe sent his boy down with a message that them three foreigners up there have had an accident with their helicopter or whatever it is – and they look like being stuck here for a day or two. So Christopher and Miss Rosalie said these foreigners had better come and stay with you.

STEPHEN: (*Grumbling humorously.*) Oh, they did, did they?

FRED: It'll be all right, won't it, Mr Dawlish?

STEPHEN: I don't know, Fred. I've arrived now at an age when I've stopped knowing – or really caring – whether things are all right. But I don't mind them coming here.

FRED: (*Grinning.*) That's a good job, because they're on their way here now.

(*MARGARET DAWLISH enters down left. She is a tall striking-looking woman in her forties. She has obviously been cooking, but nevertheless retains an impressive air of dignity. She has a rather slow, deep voice, and a strange, searching look. She carries two pillows.*)

MARGARET: (*Moving to the foot of the stairs.*) Good afternoon, Fred.

FRED: (*Rising.*) Afternoon, Mrs Dawlish. (*He moves left.*)

STEPHEN: The big cart's on its way here with three foreigners who've been asked to stay here.

MARGARET: Well, I think we ought to have them. The dark one – Indian or something – has hurt himself.

STEPHEN: What's this, Margaret? More witchcraft?

MARGARET: Not this time. Gladys Watson brought me some eggs in exchange for some butter, and she told me. One of the three is a woman – a Russian.

STEPHEN: (*Grumbling humorously.*) Worse and worse.

MARGARET: (*Moving above the table, centre.*) We can manage for a day or two. (*She places the pillows on the chair above the table, centre.*) And it'll be a nice change for you, Father.

STEPHEN: I don't want a nice change. I don't want any more changes, nice or otherwise. I've seen too many. Where are we going to put them?

MARGARET: I've worked that out nicely. Christopher's still sleeping outside, so one of them can have his room. Rosalie can share with me...

STEPHEN: Yes, yes, my dear. You've worked it out...

MARGARET: As for meals – I'm baking that lovely piece of ham – and a big rabbit pie – and then there's plenty of...

STEPHEN: (*Interrupting.*) All right, Margaret. I don't really want to know. And it's none of Fred's business. Is it, Fred?

FRED: (*Grinning.*) No, Mr Dawlish. (*He sits on the bench left.*)

STEPHEN: (*Slyly.*) All Fred wants is a glass of beer – to go with his pipe. And so do I.

MARGARET: (*Moving to the table left.*) He can have one, but I'm not sure about you, Father. (*She examines the basket of potatoes.*) This last brewing is very strong.

STEPHEN: Well, that's how I like it – *strong*. You forget
   I wasn't born in nineteen twenty-five like you – but in
   eighteen ninety-five. I'm a Victorian, I am. And when
   I first started drinking beer, you could still buy a pint of
   the best ale – the best – for three-pence – and it was *ale*.
   After you'd spent a shilling you began to feel muzzy.

MARGARET: And what good did that do you?

STEPHEN: Well, you seemed to be living in a better world,
   among much nicer people.
   (*MARGARET picks up the basket of potatoes and moves to
   the door down left.*)
   Make it a glass each, please, Margaret.

MARGARET: Just this once, then. (*She exits down left.*)
   (*The two men grin at each other.*)

STEPHEN: (*After a pause.*) When are you picking up the
   potatoes?

FRED: Next week. I thought we might all take it easy a bit
   the rest of this week – after the hay.

STEPHEN: Certainly. Take it easy. I spent more than half
   my life, when I ought to have been enjoying myself,
   arguing and planning and running round like a maniac,
   all to sell a lot of things to people I didn't know, so that
   I could buy a lot of things I never had time to use. Sheer
   lunacy. And it took nothing less than an atom bomb to
   blow me out of it.

FRED: Your two young folk are feeling 'creative', they tell
   me. Bursting to write some more music and poetry and
   all that.

STEPHEN: That's how it should be, at their age. Nice
   weather for it, too. Hotter than it used to be, Fred,
   though why it should be, I don't know. There seems to
   be more and more I don't know.
   (*MARGARET enters down left. She carries two mugs of beer.*)

MARGARET: (*Handing a mug of beer to FRED; with mock
   indignation.*) Why should I wait on you two men when
   I'm busy in the kitchen? (*She moves to STEPHEN and
   hands him a mug of beer.*)

STEPHEN: Because you're a good woman, my dear, and
   all good women like waiting on men. Now tell *me*

something. What were these strangers doing up on Longbarrow Down?

MARGARET: (*Gravely.*) Bringing trouble to us. (*She moves to the stairs and picks up the coat from the bannister rail.*) But I also know that it's better we should have them here.

STEPHEN: I see. But what were they doing up there?

MARGARET: (*Moving up centre and hanging the coat on the hooks left of the doors.*) Gladys Watson said they seemed to be looking at the chalk. (*She moves to the foot of the stairs, picks up the pair of boots, moves and places them on the floor left of the doors up centre.*)

FRED: Somebody came to look at it about three months ago. You remember – I told you, Mr Dawlish?

STEPHEN: Yes. And I said then I thought they must be archaeologists. Probably this lot are, too.

FRED: Would a Russian woman be a – what's it?

STEPHEN: Archaeologist? She might. The sexes seem to share everything there – except sexual life. But what about the second chap – the one who isn't dark and Indian and hasn't hurt himself, we hope?

MARGARET: (*Moving above the table, centre.*) Gladys Watson thought he was an American. (*She picks up the pillows and moves to the stairs.*)

STEPHEN: Fred, it looks as if we're about to entertain the rulers of the world.

MARGARET: (*Going up the stairs; quite calmly.*) Perhaps that is why I am feeling rather frightened.

FRED: You don't look frightened, Mrs Dawlish.

MARGARET: But I am, though. (She exits at the top of the stairs.)

FRED: (*Rises, moves to the foot of the stairs and glances up after her. Lowering his voice a little.*) She's usually right, too, isn't she ? (*He moves left of the table, centre.*)

STEPHEN: Yes. It's annoying – but she is. (*He raises his mug.*) Well – your health, Fred.

FRED: (*Raising his mug.*) Thank you, Mr Dawlish. All the best.

(*They drink, with obvious satisfaction.*)

STEPHEN: Have you said anything yet to Frank
Waterhouse about joining us to do some real line-
breeding with the Guernseys?

FRED: Not yet. Brown'll come in with us, but I thought
you'd better talk to Frank Waterhouse. He still fancies
that old bull of his – and that bull's not good enough for
this job.

STEPHEN: Of course it isn't. Must have something better
than Frank's bull. I'll have a word with him. He'll
probably be calling tomorrow. (*He ponders for a moment.
Slowly.*) It's funny we never spotted it years ago.

FRED: Spotted what, Mr Dawlish ? (*He finishes his drink and
puts the mug on the table centre.*)

STEPHEN: That God designed this island, not for factories
but for cattle-breeding. I overlooked it myself for sixty-
five years. Don't forget that tobacco, Fred.

FRED: (*Moving to left of the doors up centre.*) I'll bring it up
tonight.

(*ROSALIE DAWLISH enters up centre. She is an eager,
lively and very attractive young girl. She wears a simple but
effective brightly-coloured working dress. She is rather tired
and hot at the moment, but clearly in radiant health and
good spirits.*)

ROSALIE: (*Nodding to FRED and moving above the table
centre.*) The cart's coming up with those people.
Christopher stayed behind to help with it. Phew! I'm hot.

FRED: I'd better lend a hand.

ROSALIE: Yes, please do, Fred.

(*FRED exits up centre.*)

STEPHEN: I suppose you came ahead to make yourself
look beautiful.

ROSALIE: (*Moving to the sofa.*) Yes; of course. (*She perches
herself on the upstage end of the sofa.*) But I must rest a
minute first. And I'm terribly thirsty.

STEPHEN: (*Handing her his mug.*) Finish this. I only had it
to keep Fred company.

ROSALIE: (*Taking the mug.*) Thank you. (*She drinks, then
regards him affectionately.*) Don't you think I ought to try
to look beautiful?

STEPHEN: Yes, I do. And if I knew how to do it, I'd make myself look beautiful too.

ROSALIE: Well, you have a kind of rugged grandeur – like an old king or even a mountain.

STEPHEN: Good! Though you've never seen a real mountain.

ROSALIE: I dream of them often. Colossal mountains, shining white with deep blue precipices. Granddad, I've begun working on a new poem.

STEPHEN: I know. The rumour has run around.

ROSALIE: I thought I might try some of it on you tonight, but now these people will be here.

STEPHEN: Then they can hear it too.

ROSALIE: Perhaps they don't like poetry. They're not English.

STEPHEN: Well, we can see, my dear. There was a time when I didn't care for it.

ROSALIE: (*Smiling.*) What was wrong with you?

STEPHEN: I think I was ill. Most of us were. But I didn't know it.

ROSALIE: (*Rising and moving above the table centre.*) But now you're all right.

STEPHEN: Yes – except that I'm very old.

ROSALIE: (*Perching herself on the upstage edge of the table centre.*) What does it feel like inside – being very old?

STEPHEN: Not as bad as you'd think. You enjoy things a bit at a time, and aren't waiting for life really to begin three weeks on Saturday. And you don't care any more what people think about you.

ROSALIE: Don't you care what *I* think about you?

STEPHEN: Yes, my dear. But you're not people. I mean – people like these three who are coming here.

ROSALIE: (*Smiling thoughtfully.*) I'd like them to think that I'm very strange and fascinating.

STEPHEN: Quite right. But *I* don't care if they think I'm just a barmy old idiot. And probably they will.

ROSALIE: Of course they won't. (*She drinks.*) Aunt Margaret won't care what they think about her, either, and that makes her so impressive. (*She places the mug on the table centre.*)

STEPHEN: She says she feels frightened.

ROSALIE: About these people?

STEPHEN: Yes.

ROSALIE: Was she serious?

STEPHEN: Very.

ROSALIE: Oh dear!

STEPHEN: It may be just nothing – a mere fancy. I don't know. By thunder! The longer I live the less I know.

ROSALIE: (*Thoughtfully.*) Perhaps I'd better not bother trying to be strange and fascinating. I'll be simple and natural – and dullish. Outside, I mean. Inside, I'm very exciting – but that only comes out in poetry.

STEPHEN: (*With mock gravity.*) Certainly. But even outside I wouldn't say you were dullish, my dear. So just be yourself, and let it rip.

(*ROSALIE rises and moves to the door down left.*)

And you must find out from Margaret where she's putting these people. They may be here soon.

ROSALIE: Any moment. (*She exits quickly down left.*)

(*STEPHEN closes his eyes and seems to doze. After a few moments, FRANKLYN HEIMER enters up centre. He is a middle-aged American of the industrialist-executive type, and may be either the round-bodied or tall gaunt type, but should be one of these. He wears a light suit made of some plastic material, and a gaudy tie, all in sharp contrast with STEPHEN's shabby tweeds. He carries a briefcase. In his opening speeches he talks very slowly and distinctly, with great politeness. He pauses in the doorway for a moment, then moves to the table left and puts his briefcase down on it. STEPHEN wakes.*)

HEIMER: Mr Stephen Dawlish?

STEPHEN: (*Rising.*) Yes, sir. (*He moves below the table, centre, to HEIMER.*)

HEIMER: (*Holding out his hand.*) I'm Franklyn Heimer, Vice-President of the American Synthetic Products Corporation.

111

STEPHEN: (*Shaking hands with HEIMER.*) How d'you do?

HEIMER: Glad to know you, Mr Dawlish. I walked right in because your grandson told me that was just what I had to do. Those were my instructions, Mr Dawlish, to walk right in.

STEPHEN: Quite so. And the others...?

HEIMER: Coming right along, Mr Dawlish.

STEPHEN: Then sit down, won't you, Mr Heimer? My granddaughter will take you up to your room shortly. (*HEIMER, clearly glad of the rest, crosses STEPHEN and sits in the chair left of the table, centre, breathing rather hard.*)

(*He sits on the bench left.*) Three of you, aren't there?

HEIMER: (*Impressively.*) Yes, sir. Madame Shestova, who represents the Synthetic Products Department of the Soviet Foreign Trade Commission, and Dr Bahru, who is a research chemist employed by the South Asia Federation – and a mighty nice clever young fellow, though Asiatic, of course.

STEPHEN: (*Amused.*) And this Madame Shestova – is she nice, too?

HEIMER: (*Solemnly and weightily.*) I wouldn't know, Mr Dawlish. I've had dealings with her before in my business, and she's a young woman with brains and plenty of looks. But she's one of their refrigerated products, I guess. So I just wouldn't know. (*He pauses.*) Well, we've had a little trouble with our transportation, sir, as you may have heard.

STEPHEN: Yes. What happened?

HEIMER: We concluded our business up on the chalk hill there, and then when we were taking off, Dr Bahru found one of the controls jammed on his helicopter and had to crash-land us. Dr Bahru hurt his foot, but otherwise we're all okay. But we broke the T-V-Com, so that cut us off. And your grandson tells me you have no T-V-Com here.

STEPHEN: (*Dryly.*) No, we haven't. I'm afraid you'll find us very much behind the times these days, Mr Heimer.

HEIMER: (*Amused.*) Still stick to the old-fashioned telephone, eh?

STEPHEN: No, we haven't a telephone either. When the system broke down round here, we never bothered to repair it.

HEIMER: (*Astounded.*) But how do you talk to people?

STEPHEN: We just go up to them – open our mouths – and start talking. It works pretty well.

HEIMER: But wastes a lot of valuable time, I guess.

STEPHEN: It saves a lot of time, too. After all, if a man isn't worth a visit or a letter, probably he isn't worth talking to. I was in industry once, Mr Heimer, and I can remember how I used to be surrounded by batteries of telephones all ringing and buzzing all day, and then when I'd rush home to try to rest, the things would start ringing and buzzing there. I didn't like it then. Now, looking back on it, I'd call it just plain hell.

HEIMER: Sure. Often felt it myself. But – of course…

STEPHEN: (*Smiling.*) This is a little backwater of a country, no longer busy doing the world's work.

HEIMER: Now, Mr Dawlish, I didn't say that.

STEPHEN: (*Smiling.*) No, I said it. Let the people who are doing the world's work have the telephones and T-V-Coms – and the nervous breakdowns. We don't need 'em any more. (*He rises.*) But I'm neglecting my duties as a host. (*He eases to the stairs.*) Naturally you want to get some message through.

HEIMER: (Rising; briskly.) I surely do, Mr Dawlish. (*He moves left and turns.*) And I've been thinking. We still keep a small branch office in your largest town – Shrewsbury, isn't it?

STEPHEN: Probably. But Shrewsbury's a long way from here. You can still telegraph, of course, but I'm told the service is very unreliable these days. I'd write a letter if I were you.

HEIMER: I thought if we couldn't find a helicopter or even a land atomicar…

STEPHEN: We haven't any atomicars. Not since we decided to leave the atoms alone.

HEIMER: That's what they told me down there. So I thought we might hire an old-fashioned automobile.

STEPHEN: (*Shaking his head.*) There aren't any round here. We no longer use them. No petrol, you see.

HEIMER: (*Astounded.*) Not even any gasoline?

STEPHEN: (*Moving above the table centre; solemnly.*) Not even any gasoline.

HEIMER: (*Moving to left of STEPHEN.*) But what about your tractors?

STEPHEN: We don't use tractors, either. We prefer animals, horses chiefly. That was a horse in the cart we sent for you and your companions. They're pleasant creatures, and very useful. (*He moves down right.*) Unlike tractors, they learn our ways, they reproduce themselves, they help to manure the soil, and now we haven't to work in factories to produce goods for export, to pay for the petrol we used to have to import. It's more fun and much healthier looking after horses than working in a factory. And I've tried both.

HEIMER: Sure thing – but hell! Horses are so slow.

STEPHEN: In this part of the world, Mr Heimer, nature is slow too. So now we're all slow together.

ROSALIE: (*Enters down left. To HEIMER; smiling.*) Hello.

HEIMER: (*Smiling.*) Hello, there.

STEPHEN: This is my granddaughter, Rosalie Dawlish. Mr Heimer.

HEIMER: (*Moving left of the table centre and shaking hands with ROSALIE.*) Very glad to know you, Miss Dawlish.

ROSALIE: (*Smiling.*) I'm glad to know you too, Mr Heimer. (*She moves to the foot of the stairs.*) Would you like me to show you your room?

HEIMER: I certainly would. And it's very kind of you, Miss Dawlish. (*He looks around the hall.*) I guess this is one of your fine old country mansions I used to read about.

(*STEPHEN moves to the doors up centre and stands gazing out into the garden.*)

ROSALIE: Grandfather bought it when he was rich, years ago, but now it's really a farmhouse, of course. I've always lived here. I love it.

STEPHEN: (*Calling over his shoulder.*) Better apologize to Mr Heimer in advance for the lack of all the comforts and conveniences he's used to at home.

HEIMER: (*Protesting.*) Say...

ROSALIE: (*Interrupting; prettily.*) I don't know what they are, Mr Heimer, as I've probably never even seen them, but I'm terribly sorry – for your sake – we haven't any of them.

HEIMER: Now – now – now. You're talking to a man who likes to take a camping trip every year. Yes, sir. Never miss it if I can help it.

STEPHEN: (*Over his shoulder; dryly.*) When was the last one?

HEIMER: (*Ruefully.*) Well – three or four years ago, I guess.

STEPHEN: (*Dryly.*) Been out of luck lately then, haven't you?

HEIMER: Well – synthetic products... (*He collects his briefcase.*)

STEPHEN: (*Interrupting; still over his shoulder.*) I'd do some camping – and to hell with synthetic products.

ROSALIE: Granddad, you're not to tease Mr Heimer. (*To HEIMER.*) I must warn you about him. He'll try to tease you all the time. He does us, but of course we're used to it. (*She moves slowly up the stairs.*) There's a marvellous blackbird sings just outside your room, and the rose-garden looks enchanting from your window.

HEIMER: (*Moving to the stairs.*) It sounds swell. (*He follows ROSALIE up the stairs.*)

STEPHEN: (*Looking out across the garden.*) This must be the Russian woman.

ROSALIE: (*Hastily.*) Come on, Mr Heimer. I ought to change.

HEIMER: You know, I'm going to *like* it here.

ROSALIE: (*As she exits.*) Of course you are.

> (*ROSALIE and HEIMER exit at the top of the stairs. STEPHEN eases above the chair right of the table centre. MADAME IRINA SHESTOVA enters up centre. She is about thirty, fair, but in the Slavonic style, with wide cheekbones and rather slanting eyes. She is severely dressed in a feminine*

variation of a uniform, which is made of some light material.
She wears several ribbons, like medal ribbons, to show that
she has been decorated by her government. She is obviously
handsome, though at first she seems stiff and cold. Her English
is careful and correct, with not too strong a Russian accent,
but it is limited in expression. She carries a briefcase.)

STEPHEN: You must be Madame Shestova.

IRINA: (*Not smiling.*) Yes.

STEPHEN: I am Stephen Dawlish, and I think you've
already met my grandson, Christopher.

IRINA: Yes. And I thank you for inviting us to your house.

STEPHEN: It's a pleasure, Madame Shestova. If you don't
find it too uncomfortable, then I hope you can spend
several days with us.

IRINA: (*Not smiling.*) Thank you, but for me that will not be
possible. I am an official of the Soviet Government –
here on duty.

STEPHEN: (*Indicating the chair right of the table centre.*) Do
sit down.
(*IRINA moves to the chair indicated and sits.*)
(*He moves to the sofa and sits at the upstage end of it. He*
smiles. With marked charm.) My dear young lady – if you
will allow an old man the privilege of calling you a dear
young lady – forget you're an official and take a little
holiday. We'll put some roses into those pretty cheeks of
yours.

IRINA: (*Bewildered.*) Some roses? Into my cheeks? Oh –
I see – it is a poetical image.

STEPHEN: (*Dryly.*) Well, I suppose it was once.
(*IRINA, looking at him, smiles for the first time and her face*
lights up wonderfully.)
(*He smiles.*) That's better. You've probably no idea the
difference it makes. Before, it was like seeing a garden
with frost in May. One of my womenfolk will be down
soon, to show you your room.

IRINA: (*Looking around.*) Thank you. (*She rises.*) This is
interesting to me.
(*STEPHEN rises.*)

(*She moves below the table centre to left of it.*) At the
university I studied English language and literature, as
well as economics. This is like the houses in so many of
your old novels.

STEPHEN: (*Moving above the table centre.*) It was rather like
them – once. Not now.

IRINA: But you are not a lord?

STEPHEN: No, no. I started as an engineer, and then
became a successful industrialist, making textile
machinery. I bought this place and a few hundred acres
of land, but I had to work myself almost blind and daft
to find time to spend a few days here. Then came –
catastrophe and ruin – and since then I've been able to
stay here all the time – and eat well, sleep well, enjoy my
surroundings and have plenty of time to think.

(*MARGARET enters at the top of the stairs and comes down.
She has changed her dress or at least taken off an apron or
overall.*)

It's been wonderful – only I started forty years too late.
(*He looks up and sees MARGARET coming down the stairs.*)
Madame Shestova, this is my daughter-in-law, Mrs
Dawlish, who looks after this house for us all.

(*MARGARET moves above the chair left of the table, centre.
The two women look searchingly at each other.*)

IRINA: (*Crossing MARGARET to left; politely but coldly.*)
I hope this will not be a great trouble to you.

MARGARET: (*Looking gravely at IRINA.*) No, we are pleased
to have you here.

IRINA: (*Stiffly.*) Thank you.

MARGARET: I think you could be very happy here.

IRINA: (*Turning away down left; politely indifferent.*) I hope so.

MARGARET: (*Softly.*) I mean – really happy. In a new way.

IRINA: (*Turning; bewildered and rather annoyed.*) I do not
understand.

MARGARET: No, not yet, of course.

(*IRINA, puzzled, looks enquiringly at STEPHEN.*)

STEPHEN: (*Crossing above MARGARET to right of IRINA;
confidentially.*) There are some people, Madame Shestova,

who don't seem to be so firmly clamped on to time and space as the rest of us are. They wander on the border between the known and the unknown. They see round corners. They can taste tomorrow night this afternoon. And Margaret's one of these people.

IRINA: (*Distastefully.*) That is mysticism.

STEPHEN: I'm afraid it is. And I believe we used to have some kind of law against it, but now we don't bother.

(*IRINA looks at him, puzzled. Then she looks at MARGARET, who smiles at her. She manages a tiny smile in reply. At the end of this little scene, CHRISTOPHER DAWLISH and DOCTOR BAHRU enter up centre, followed by FRED, who is carrying two light cases. CHRIS, who is left of BAHRU is supporting him. BAHRU is a pleasant, slim Indian, about thirty-five, dressed in light plastic clothes like his two colleagues. He speaks carefully in a small, precise voice, in sharp contrast to CHRIS's rich, exuberant manner. He is hopping on one foot, the other being shoeless. CHRIS, aged about thirty, is a big, handsome, romantic-looking chap, dressed in an open coloured shirt and old corduroy trousers. It should be obvious from the first that he is strongly attracted by IRINA, who is aware of this and very much aware of him, to her annoyance. FRED puts the cases down on the floor left of the door up centre and stands by them. IRINA moves to the bench left and sits. This entrance scene, in contrast to those that have just passed, should be rather bustling and noisy, with a certain amount of overlapping lines, etc.*)

(*Heartily.*) Well – well – well.

CHRIS: This is Dr Bahru. My grandfather.

STEPHEN: How d'you do? You'd better rest that foot, hadn't you?

CHRIS: Unless you want to go straight to bed.

BAHRU: (*Protestingly.*) No – no – please.

CHRIS (*Leading BAHRU to the chair right of the table centre.*) Then we'll settle you down here for a time.

MARGARET: (*Moving left of the chair right of the table centre.*) Sit in this chair.

CHRIS: This is my aunt – Mrs Dawlish.

BAHRU: How do you do?

MARGARET: (*Drawing the stool out from under the table centre.*) Don't bother about being polite, please.

BAHRU: Thank you so much.

(*CHRIS assists BAHRU into the chair.*)

MARGARET: (*Arranging the stool.*) Put your foot on this stool. (*BAHRU puts his foot up on the stool.*) There.

STEPHEN: All right now, Dr Bahru?

BAHRU: Yes, of course, thank you.

(*MARGARET takes a cushion from the sofa and puts it on the stool under BAHRU's foot. CHRIS moves above the table centre to right of IRINA.*)

You are all very kind. But it is really nothing at all, this foot.

CHRIS: (*Smiling.*) Hello, Madame Shestova. I told you, didn't I, that you'd find yourself now a castaway on a mad island?

IRINA: (*Thawing just a little.*) You did tell me. But how do you know I think so?

CHRIS: I can see it in your eyes.

IRINA: (*Stiffly.*) That is not true.

CHRIS: Yes, yes. I can see in them Northern Lights, flashing across a thousand question marks made of ice.

STEPHEN: (*Above the foot of the stairs.*) That'll do, Christopher. And don't listen to anything this young man says, Madame Shestova.

CHRIS: (*Moving up centre.*) You want your case, don't you? (*He picks up one of the suitcases.*)

MARGARET: (*Moving to CHRIS.*) I'm so sorry – I should have taken you to your room. Give me the case, Christopher. (*She takes the case from CHRIS.*)

IRINA: (*Rising and moving to the foot of the stairs.*) No, please, I can take it.

(*MARGARET ushers IRINA up the stairs and they exit at the top. CHRIS stands at the foot of the stairs, watching them.*)

STEPHEN: (*Moving left of BAHRU.*) Well, Dr Bahru, I told your two colleagues they ought to spend a few days here with us, and now I'm saying the same thing to you. What about this foot of yours?

BAHRU: If I do not use it for a day or two, it will be all right.

STEPHEN: You ought to explain that to Madame Shestova and Mr Heimer, and then they might not be in such a hurry.

BAHRU: (*Smiling.*) I will try to persuade them. But being Russian and American, they have much to do and many responsibilities. They feel they have the whole world on their shoulders.

STEPHEN: (*Moving up left centre.*) It's an illusion, but one of the oldest. Well, we'll do our best to look after you.

BAHRU: You are very kind.

STEPHEN: Fred, we'll go out through the kitchen. See you later, Dr Bahru.

(*FRED and STEPHEN move to the door down left and exit.*)

BAHRU: (*As they go.*) Yes, please.

(*CHRIS moves down left.*

He takes out a cigarette case and offers it to CHRIS.

CHRIS, smiling, shakes his head.)

But I may smoke?

CHRIS: (*Crossing below the table centre to the sofa.*) Yes, of course. (*He sits.*)

(*BAHRU takes a cigarette from his case and lights it.*)

Most of our older people – like my grandfather and Fred Voles – still smoke, but very few of us younger people do. In our time, tobacco has been so scarce that it didn't seem worth while acquiring the habit. But we enjoy our food and drink all the more – and now we have plenty to eat, plenty to drink – and live like kings.

BAHRU: (*After a pause.*) Yes, it is nice here.

CHRIS: We think it is. I'm glad you do.

BAHRU: So very green, so beautiful. So many flowers, so many birds.

CHRIS: My grandfather says we always had more than our share of flowers and birds, and more than we used to deserve to have. But now, he says, there are more flowers, more birds, than ever before.

BAHRU: You do not travel yourself?

CHRIS: (*Smiling.*) Only between here and Arcturus.
(*ROSALIE enters at the top of the stairs and comes down. She has changed her dress.*)
Hello, Rosalie.

ROSALIE: Hello.

CHRIS: This is Dr Bahru. My sister Rosalie.

ROSALIE: Hello.

BAHRU: How do you do?

ROSALIE: (*Moving above the table centre.*) Oh – your foot.

BAHRU: It is not badly hurt, thank you.

ROSALIE: (*Perching herself on the upstage edge of the table centre.*) Good. (*To CHRIS.*) I met Madame What's-it – the Russian – upstairs. She looks like the Snow Queen in uniform.

CHRIS: That's it, Rosalie. That's why I felt I'd known her since I was eight.

ROSALIE: Are you going to fall in love with her?

CHRIS: Yes.

ROSALIE: That's what I thought when I saw her. I said to myself: 'We shall have Snow Queen music from poor Chris for the rest of this year.'
(*BAHRU smiles.*)
(*To BAHRU.*) Christopher writes music. Did he tell you?

BAHRU: Yes. And you write poetry. Is that right?

ROSALIE: Yes. And very clever of you to remember. We only do it in our spare time, you know, but we manage to have a lot of spare time, especially in winter.

BAHRU: You have always been an artistic family – no doubt?

ROSALIE: I don't think so – have we, Chris?

CHRIS: No. Our parents weren't like that at all. It's because we've grown up in a poor country with few things to distract us. So my grandfather says. We've had to use our own minds to entertain ourselves.

ROSALIE: (*After a pause.*) I said some of my new poem to Mr Heimer on the landing upstairs – he asked me to, so I did – and he told me it was hard to follow, but (*In an American accent.*) all very fine and dandy.

CHRIS: I call that pretty sound criticism.

ROSALIE: Then he told me about his synthetic products, and when I said I didn't think I'd care for them very much, he seemed quite hurt.

BAHRU: (*Amused.*) Yes, I think Mr Heimer would be quite hurt.

ROSALIE. So I said I probably would like them if I saw them. Now he's going to send me a huge case full of them when he gets back to America. (*She pauses.*) I like Mr Heimer.

BAHRU: Tell me why, Miss Dawlish. Because he is an important executive, a powerful personality?

ROSALIE: (*Surprised.*) Oh, no! There's something innocent and lost about him – like a sort of old baby, puzzled but still hopeful.

(*BAHRU laughs appreciatively.*)

(*She rises.*) Aunt Margaret said you might like some tea. We have some, though most of us don't drink it much now.

BAHRU: Tea would be very nice, thank you, Miss Dawlish.

ROSALIE: (*Moving to the door down left.*) I'll make some. (*She starts to sing.*) 'Where the bee sucks…'

(*She exits down left, still singing. The two men listen a moment. IRINA enters at the top of the stairs, and unnoticed by the two men, comes quietly down and stands at the foot, listening. She carries her briefcase.*)

CHRIS: (*Smiling at BAHRU; with delicate over-emphasis.*)
'Be not afeared; the isle is full of noises,
Sounds and sweet airs, that give delight and hurt not.
Sometimes a thousand twangling instruments
Will hum about mine ears…'

(*He sees IRINA and breaks off. He looks hard at her. She returns his look, but with no expression on her face.*)

BAHRU: Go on, please.

CHRIS: (*Rising and crossing to the foot of the stairs; with a touch of irony.*) Here's Madame Shestova, who probably wants to talk about more serious things.

IRINA: That was Shakespeare, I think?

CHRIS: Yes. Caliban, in *The Tempest*.

IRINA: We Russians can appreciate Shakespeare. And Dr
  Bahru wishes you to continue the speech.
  (*CHRIS continues with the quotation. As he does so he moves
  above the table centre to right, then down right, turns, crosses
  to the chair left of the table centre and sits. IRINA moves
  down left.*)

CHRIS: (*Still with delicate over-emphasis.*)
  'Sometimes a thousand twangling instruments
  Will hum about mine ears; and sometimes voices,
  That, if I then had waked after long sleep,
  Will make me sleep again; and then, in dreaming,
  The clouds methought would open, and show riches
  Ready to drop upon me; that, when I waked,
  I cried to dream again...'

IRINA: (*Coldly.*) This Caliban is presented as a victim of
  British Imperialism.

CHRIS: I don't think so.

IRINA: (*Sitting on the bench left.*) Yes. But you recite his
  speech as if it were mysticism.

CHRIS: So it is. The whole play is.

IRINA: (*Severely.*) That is not so.

CHRIS: (*Rises impulsively, takes a pace towards IRINA and
  looks her hard in the eyes.*) It's like looking at a cheap little
  textbook bound in silver and gold..

IRINA: (*Coldly.*) I do not understand what you are saying,
  but please do not look at me in this way.

CHRIS: I beg your pardon, Madame Shestova. I realize
  I am behaving very badly to a guest. Please forgive me.
  I'm not quite myself. I was up early this morning and
  worked very hard, because we were hay-making. So I'm
  tired. I'm also bewildered, baffled, and light in the head.
  Sorry. (*He turns and moves quickly towards the doors up
  centre, but then suddenly wheels round, and stares at IRINA.
  With an exasperated warmth.*) You are the most beautiful
  woman I have ever seen – and yet nothing I do or say
  touches you at all. As if a man tried to pluck the flower
  of the world, and found it was made of steel and ice. It's

blue mid-summer here, and yet you stare at me out of a Siberian winter.

(*He turns and exits quickly up centre. IRINA watches him go, astonished, and more moved than she will allow. Then she turns and meets BAHRU's glance. He is amused, but tries to hide it.*)

IRINA: (*Trying to be coldly indignant.*) He has no right to say such things to me.

BAHRU: (*With a touch of irony.*) No, he has not. But then he said he was sorry.

IRINA: (*Indignantly; almost to herself.*) I am a responsible official of the Foreign Trade Commission of the Soviet Union, and I have a difficult task which must be completed as soon as possible. I do not like this place, or these people. Now that they no longer have world power, these people, they lose themselves in a decadent romanticism.

BAHRU: (*A little too politely.*) That is probably quite correct, Madame Shestova.

IRINA: (*Rising and moving left of the table centre.*) That is what I came down to say to you, Dr Bahru. With Mr Heimer we must have a conference, to decide what can be done.

BAHRU: I must leave that decision to you and Mr Heimer. But we shall have to stay here tonight.

IRINA: But no longer. I must report to my department.

BAHRU: At once?

IRINA: As soon as possible.

BAHRU: Surely a few days will not matter. You are not Americans, who are always in such a hurry.

IRINA: (*Moving to the doors up centre.*) No. But – (*With a flash of feminine temper.*) I do not wish to stay here.

BAHRU: (*Smiling.*) Now you talk like a woman.

IRINA: (*Turning; annoyed.*) I do not talk like a woman. That has nothing to do with this decision… (*She breaks off.*) (*MARGARET enters at the top of the stairs and comes down to them.*)

(*She moves right of MARGARET.*) Where is Mr Heimer, please?

MARGARET: (*Smiling slightly.*) He's in his room. I know,
because as I came past just now, I could hear him
snoring.

IRINA: It is important we should have a conference here.
Please tell him that Dr Bahru and I are waiting for him
here. Or if you will show me his room, I will tell him.

MARGARET: (*Looking at her searchingly.*) No, I can tell him.

IRINA: (*Stiffly.*) Thank you.

MARGARET: But why are you so angry?

IRINA: (*Turning away up centre.*) I am not angry.

MARGARET: Yes, you are. Was it Christopher?
(*IRINA shrugs her shoulders.*)
He's falling in love with you, and now, I suppose, you
don't know what to do or say. But it had to happen some
time to you. So why not here – now? I'll give your
message to Mr Heimer.
(*She turns, goes up the stairs and exits at the top. IRINA,
stiffly angry, moves to the chair left of the table centre, sits,
opens her briefcase, takes out some papers and starts to read
them. BAHRU stares at her speculatively. After a few moments
IRINA looks up, annoyed.*)

IRINA: (*Coldly.*) The portable T-V-Com you carried in the
helicopter – can it be repaired?

BAHRU: I might be able to repair it, but that will take
time.

IRINA: How long?

BAHRU: I cannot tell yet. Not until I have examined it
properly.

IRINA: Mr Heimer said he would ask about
communications here. Also possible transport.

BAHRU: Yes. But I imagine everything will be difficult.

IRINA: These people will make it difficult. Because they
are no longer interested in progress. They are decadent.
(*MARGARET, followed by HEIMER, enters at the top of
the stairs. He looks rather sleepy and tousled. He carries his
briefcase.*)

HEIMER: (*As he comes downstairs.*) Yes, Mrs Dawlish, there
I was – a boy again – wearing torn old blue cotton pants

– and *fishing* – yes, sir. And there was the old creek, with the sun on it, the way I haven't seen it for forty years. That certainly was a swell little dream… (*He breaks off, to greet the other two.*) Well, well, here we are. (*He moves to the chair above the table centre and sits.*) And Mrs Dawlish tells me you'd like to talk things over.

IRINA: (*Stiffly.*) If you please, yes. (*She glances at MARGARET.*) A private conference.

(*MARGARET eases left of HEIMER.*)

HEIMER: (*Heartily.*) Suits me.

(*They all look at MARGARET.*)

MARGARET: (*Dryly.*) I hope you will not be disturbed.

HEIMER: (*With BAHRU; rather embarrassed.*) That's all right, Mrs Dawlish.

BAHRU: (*With HEIMER; rather embarrassed.*) Please do not worry.

ROSALIE: (*Enters gaily down left. She carries a tray of tea-things.*) Tea. Tea. Who wants tea?

MARGARET: (*Moving to ROSALIE and taking the tray from her.*) Thank you, Rosalie. Will you help me in the kitchen?

ROSALIE: Yes, of course. (*She turns and exits down left.*)
(*MARGARET places the tray on the table centre, near to IRINA.*)

BAHRU: It is very kind of you, Mrs Dawlish.

IRINA: (*Stiffly.*) Thank you.

MARGARET: (*Having put down the tray, surveys them sombrely. Gravely.*) I should like to say something to you.

HEIMER: (*Heartily.*) Why sure. Go ahead, Mrs Dawlish.

MARGARET: (*Slowly.*) You left us nothing but the bare thorn and our bleeding hands; but now our hands are healed, and the thorn is beginning to flower. (*She picks up the two beer mugs from the table, turns and moves towards the door down left.*) Remember that.

HEIMER: (*Rising and moving left centre; embarrassed.*) Say, wait a minute, Mrs Dawlish. Why are you telling us this?

MARGARET: (*Slowly.*) I don't know – yet. (*Turns abruptly and exits down left.*)

(*There is an awkward silence, during which HEIMER takes out a cigar and lights it.*)

HEIMER: (*Moving right above the table centre and gazing out of the window right; musingly.*) Don't quite get on to that one, Mrs Dawlish – but the other – the kid Rosalie – she's a cute little trick. Started reciting her poem to me up there before she showed me my room. (*He turns.*) Darned nice room, too – made me feel relaxed right away...

IRINA: (*Interrupting; coldly.*) It is necessary, I think, that we have a conference.

HEIMER: (*Moving to the chair above the table centre; hastily.*) Certainly is. (*He sits.*) We got business to attend to.

(*IRINA pours out cups of tea for herself and BAHRU.*)

BAHRU: (*With a touch of mischief.*) And Madame Shestova says she does not like this place, or these people.

HEIMER: Is that so?

IRINA: (*Grimly.*) Yes, that is so.

HEIMER: (*Confidentially.*) Well –

(*IRINA passes a cup of tea to HEIMER.*)

– (*He passes the cup to BAHRU.*) it's a run-down, old-fashioned sort of place, I guess, and I imagine the folks are just as queer – what you'd expect.

(*IRINA looks enquiringly at HEIMER, the tea pot poised.*) Never take it, thanks. But – maybe because I'm feeling relaxed right now, I kind of like it here. However – (*He changes his tone.*) we got business to attend to. Go ahead, Madame Shestova.

IRINA: You have enquired about sending messages?

HEIMER: Asked the old gentleman, Mr Dawlish. No T-V-Com. Not even an old-fashioned telephone.

IRINA: It is very bad. Just decadence.

HEIMER: (*Grinning.*) Try telling that to the old gentleman. Now about transportation. No helicopters. And the only big airport they use in this country for the stratosphere ships must be two or three hundred miles from here. That right, Dr Bahru?

BAHRU: Yes, I enquired about that earlier.

HEIMER: No atomicars. Thought if we could find an old automobile we might hire it, but the old gentleman says they no longer import gasoline into this neck o' the woods. Prefer horses. Say! He might be kidding at that. We'd better talk to the young fellow...

IRINA: (*Sharply.*) He will be worse than his grandfather. And these women are useless.

BAHRU: (*Ruefully.*) So, too, unfortunately, is my foot just now.

HEIMER: (*Apologetically.*) Now – I was just going to ask about that.

BAHRU: I must rest it for a day or two.

HEIMER: Sure thing. Say – (*He rises and eases left centre.*) listen – let's just relax till tomorrow morning. And you needn't look at me like that, Madame Shestova. It'll take all of six months to erect the plant and build the camps up there, so don't think I'm going to try to slip a fast one over your Foreign Trade Commission during the next eighteen hours. Hell's bells! Let's relax.

IRINA: (*Coldly.*) I am trying to do my duty, that is all, Mr Heimer. If you wish to postpone any decision about messages or transport because we have not enough information – I will agree. But as we are all three here, in private conference, there is important work we can do. (*She glances at her notes.*)

HEIMER: (*Moving above the table centre, opening his briefcase and extracting some papers.*) Okay. (*He sits and glances at his own notes.*) This is as far as we got this morning. (*He is now very crisp and business-like.*) We've agreed to accept Dr Bahru's report on the chalk itself. It's what we want. I suggest – and he agrees – that we ship from Europe here all the other raw material we need, so that we use the chalk on the spot, taking it through the first two processes, giving us Mixture B. My Corporation can take all the Mixture B that can be produced here. But, of course, working on the usual World Settlement terms, the Soviet Government can claim up to thirty-seven and a half per cent of the annual output.

IRINA: I do not know, of course, if the Commission will exercise its right to a share of the product.

HEIMER: I hope you don't. We can do with it all.

BAHRU: I am certain that on the basis of my report, when they see it, the Soviet Government will demand its share.

HEIMER: And I'd say you're right. Now – (*He glances at his notes*) about the labour force. I had a word about that with our West European Labour Directorate. They say we can still pick up a few minor executives and technicians here in England, or bring in some Dutch and Germans – good steady fellows. But for a general labour force, especially at first, we can't depend on the British. They don't want the jobs, not even for good money. (*He looks at them solemnly.*) I didn't believe 'em, when they told me that, but from what I've noticed round here today, I guess they're right.

BAHRU: I think so.

HEIMER: (*With growing enthusiasm.*) Okay. Suppose they are. Our mobile labour unit can dump five to ten thousand Chinese on these hills as soon as we give 'em the word to go. Our construction boys – and there aren't any better, believe me – will tear the guts out of these Downs, and in six months you won't know the place. Big plant, landing grounds, rows of hutments, bungalows for the technicians, cafes, dance halls. T-V-Palaces, bright lights, gambling joints if we use the Chinks, and – er...

IRINA: (*Calmly.*) Brothels.

HEIMER: Maybe. But you said it – not me. (*He looks around him.*) This old place, when it's got real plumbing in, and some up-to-date fixings, wouldn't be bad for one of the executives. Know a nice young fellow I might send over here who'd jump at it. I'll make a note to remind myself. (*He makes a note on his papers, then looks up at BAHRU and IRINA. Slower.*) Better not let on to these folks what's going to happen. All for the best, of course. (*He rises and moves to the sofa.*) We've got to make progress. (*He sits.*) Just because they've dropped behind – kind of lost heart, I guess – that doesn't mean the rest of us must lie down on the job – no, sir. All the same – we better not let on.

IRINA: I am not afraid to tell them what will happen here.

BAHRU: Perhaps you will enjoy telling them.

IRINA: (*Rising and breaking down left; sharply.*) That is not true.

BAHRU: (*Suddenly annoyed.*) You will not use this tone of voice with me, please, Madame Shestova. I am a scientist, and my position is at least as good as yours. I am not one of your servants.

IRINA: (*Turning and moving up centre.*) I have no servants. In my country we are all free citizens.

BAHRU: That is not true.

(*IRINA turns angrily and moves to left of BAHRU, but before she can speak HEIMER intervenes.*)

HEIMER: (*Rising; bluffly.*) Hey – what is this? We've all been friendly up to now – don't let's spoil it. Relax – relax.

BAHRU: I am sorry. My foot is rather painful.

IRINA: (*Picking up her briefcase and papers.*) And I have a headache. (*She moves to the stairs.*) I must rest in my room. (*As she reaches the foot of the stairs, CHRIS enters up centre. He carries a large bunch of red roses.*)

CHRIS: (*As he enters; grandly.*) Red roses for the Snow Queen. Madame Shestova – see how our English earth has bled for you.

(*IRINA pauses on the second stair and turns. CHRIS hands her the flowers. She takes them and, without thinking, like any woman, plunges her face into them. When she raises her head, she sees him staring at her. He speaks softly, intimately.*) Now you look as I knew you could look. I had a vision of you looking like that when I gathered the roses.

IRINA: (*Sharply and coldly.*) No. Take them, please. (*She holds out the flowers to CHRIS.*)

CHRIS: They're yours. I gathered them for you.

IRINA: (*Dropping the flowers on the floor.*) I do not want them.

(*She turns and exits up the stairs. CHRIS watches her in silence.*)

HEIMER: (*Softly.*) Y'know, if she's not careful, she'll start behaving like a woman.

BAHRU: She has been reminded this afternoon that she *is* a woman.

HEIMER: (*Solemnly.*) If she was an American, my friends, she'd be quite a dish.

CHRIS: (*With quiet fervour.*) She is better than a dish. (*He crosses to left of HEIMER.*) She is a woman – and the face she raised from these roses was a spring morning in some strange, beautiful country – and I shall never forget it.

HEIMER: Young man, you ought to tell *her* that – not us.

CHRIS: I shall, but when I say it to her, I shall put it better – that was just the first rough draft.

HEIMER: And I thought you meant it.

CHRIS: Of course I mean it. That's why it's worth saying over and over again, and improving every time.
(*ROSALIE and MARGARET enter down left. MARGARET moves to the table centre and stacks the tea-things on to the tray.*)

ROSALIE: (*Moving to the foot of the stairs.*) Oh – look at these roses.

CHRIS: The Snow Queen flung them down.

ROSALIE: Then either you're losing badly – or winning.
(*ROSALIE picks up the roses, takes them to the table left and puts them in the jug. MARGARET picks up the tray and exits with it down left. STEPHEN enters down left.*)

STEPHEN: (*As he enters.*) We shall be having supper in about two hours' time, gentlemen. (*He moves above the table centre.*) I don't know what you want to do until then...

BAHRU: I think perhaps I should like to go up to my room now, please.

STEPHEN: Certainly.
(*CHRIS moves to BAHRU and assists him to rise.*)
And if you're wise, you'll stay there and give that foot a good rest. We'll send up your supper and anything else you want.

CHRIS: (*Helping BAHRU to the stairs.*) I know where your room is, and I'll look after you. Now then...

(*They go carefully up the stairs and exit at the top. ROSALIE picks up the jug of roses, moves and places it on the table centre.*)

STEPHEN: What about you, Mr Heimer?

HEIMER: Well, we just finished our little conference…

(*MARGARET enters down left and moves to the stairs.*)

STEPHEN: And you wouldn't like to tell me what it's been about – um?

HEIMER: No, couldn't do that, Mr Dawlish. Sorry.

(*MARGARET pauses at the foot of the stairs.*)

STEPHEN: (*Dryly.*) No, I thought not.

HEIMER: How about showing me round?

STEPHEN: I wish I could, but I must sit down. But Rosalie will show you round.

HEIMER: Fine. How about it, Miss Rosalie?

ROSALIE: Yes, of course.

STEPHEN: (*Crossing to the bench left and sitting.*) And you'll see some of the finest land you ever set eyes on. And remember we're not just living off it. We're living with it. We love it – and we think it's beginning to love us. Eh, Rosalie?

HEIMER: (*Moving to the door up centre; uneasily.*) I get you. Well, let's go.

(*ROSALIE follows HEIMER up centre.*)

MARGARET: (*Moving left of HEIMER.*) Mr Heimer…

HEIMER: (*Stooping and turning.*) Yeah?

(*MARGARET looks steadily at him.*)

What is it, Mrs Dawlish?

MARGARET: (*Softly.*) Nothing.

ROSALIE: Come on, Mr Heimer. (*She exits up centre.*)

(*HEIMER turns and follows her off.*)

STEPHEN: (*Quietly.*) Why did you stop him like that?

MARGARET: (Softly.) There was something in his voice – uneasiness, a sense of shame, a guilty feeling – and I wanted to see if it was in his eyes too.

STEPHEN: And was it?

MARGARET: (*Moving to right of STEPHEN.*) Yes, it was.

STEPHEN: (*Reaching out and touching her hands; gently.*) Your hands are trembling, my dear. Are you still feeling frightened of something?

MARGARET: Yes. I am *still* afraid.

(*She crosses STEPHEN to the door down left and exits as the curtain slowly falls.*)

Scene 2

Scene – the same. Evening. The same day.

When the curtain rises, the daylight still lingers, and a golden dusk shines through the windows and the open doors up centre. MARGARET enters down left. She carries a tray on which there is a plate of cake, a jug of milk, a jug of beer and some mugs. She puts the tray on the upstage end of the table left, then goes up the stairs and exits. As she does so, FRED strolls in up centre, at ease and smoking his pipe. MARGARET re-enters at the top of the stairs. She carries a work-basket.

FRED: (*Easing centre.*) Good evening, Mrs Dawlish.

MARGARET: (*Coming down the stairs.*) Good evening, Fred.

FRED: Just looked in to give Mr Dawlish some tobacco I promised him.

MARGARET: (*Moving to the table left and putting the work-basket on it.*) Sit down, then, and have a glass of beer.

FRED: (*Moving to the stool below the table left.*) Quiet up here. (*He sits.*)

MARGARET: (*Pouring out a mug of beer.*) Yes. Everybody's scattered about. The Indian, Dr Bahru, went up to bed, and I'm just going to take some tea up to him presently and have a talk. (*She hands the mug of beer to FRED.*) Mr Dawlish is sitting in the garden with Mr Heimer, the American. And Madame Shestova is wandering round the garden by herself. And Christopher and Rosalie went down to the village hall to rehearse the play.

FRED: Yes, I know about them. Don't forget, I'm in that play, too. I'm Peter Quince, the Carpenter. But I'd soon finished my bit tonight.

MARGARET: Of course. (*She pauses.*) Fred, I think these people will be staying here rather longer than they imagine. (*She moves the stool from above the table left to right of the bench and sits.*) We shall need more food for them. I was wondering if you could find me a good joint of mutton. (*During the ensuing dialogue she arranges the work-basket on the bench, and commences to patch a blouse.*)

FRED: Can you spare a couple of cockerels, Mrs Dawlish?

MARGARET: Yes, I think so. Why?

FRED: George Watson, Joe's cousin, is killing a sheep, and he'd like some cockerels 'cos they're having a do this weekend. His daughter's getting married.

MARGARET: Is that the girl with red hair and huge freckles?

FRED: That's the one.

MARGARET: She's a lively handful. Who's marrying her?

FRED: Chap who comes from Wiltshire way – breeds pigs. George says he's no size at all – she'd make two of him – but he's a bossy little runt an' he'll master her in no time. Seen him do it already once or twice, George has.

MARGARET: Um – we'll see. Just wait a year or two. Who's making any cheese now? We could do with some.

FRED: I'll find out tomorrow. Had a nice piece up at Frank Waterhouse's, the other day. Oh – I heard one or two of 'em saying at the village hall tonight that Charlie Newman got a bustard today on Longbarrow Down.

MARGARET: (*Eagerly.*) A bustard. That would be wonderful, so long as it's not an old bird.

FRED: They told me Charlie said it wasn't. And weighs about twenty-five pounds, they said. Lovely eating.

MARGARET: Ask him what he wants for it, Fred. A bustard would be a pleasant surprise for these visitors of ours.

FRED: It's not so long since they were a surprise to us – is it? Never set eyes on one till after the Third War. I remember Mr Dawlish saying they used to be here – and people liked 'em better than any other bird for eating – and then for a hundred and fifty years they vanished – just not a sign of 'em.

MARGARET: (*Smiling.*) Yes, and then when we were all broken up and ruined, the bustards came back.

FRED: I know. But what made 'em come back?

MARGARET: Perhaps God did.

(*IRINA enters up centre. She is dressed as in the previous scene. She is smoking a long Russian cigarette, and she looks more human, more at ease, than before.*)

IRINA: Good evening.

FRED: (*Rising.*) Good evening.

MARGARET: (*Smiling.*) Have you been looking at the garden?

IRINA: (*Moving right of MARGARET.*) Yes, it is very beautiful.

MARGARET: I'm glad you think so. (*She indicates the cakes, etc.*) I've just brought these things in so that people can help themselves whenever they want to. Beer in that jug. Milk in that. Or you could have some tea – I'm just going to take some up to Dr Bahru.

IRINA: (*Moving below the table centre.*) No, thank you. Later perhaps I will take a glass of milk. (*She moves right of the table centre and looks out of the window right.*) Mr Dawlish and Mr Heimer are there in the garden discussing. But for once I did not want to discuss, or to listen to discussion.

MARGARET: (*Enigmatically.*) No, I can understand that.

IRINA: (*Turning; rather puzzled.*) Can you?

MARGARET: Yes. I saw you walking about by yourself, looking at the flowers. Probably some of them are strange to you.

(*FRED resumes his seat on the stool below the table left.*)

IRINA: (*Moving up left centre.*) Yes, they are. And I should like to know their names. I was born and brought up in Moscow, where my father was an engineer. But the brother of my mother – my – my –

MARGARET: (*Prompting her.*) Uncle.

IRINA: – yes, my uncle – was the director of a *kolkos* – collective farm – in the Ukraine – and nearly every year, in summer, when I was young I would stay with him. And now I have been remembering all that.

MARGARET: Yet this is quite different, isn't it?

135

IRINA: Quite different. (*She moves above the table to right of it and looks again through the window.*) Yet when I was alone in your garden, hearing so many birds sing, looking at so many flowers, I began to remember those times when I was younger – and deep inside I felt something – something – oh – it is difficult for me to describe. My English has not been used to describe such feelings, but only for official and trade discussions and negotiations. And now – when I do not want to discuss and negotiate – when I walk in a beautiful wild garden in the evening – and I feel so many things at once – so happy – so sad – so much strange aliveness inside – I have no words in English – (*She sits in the chair right of the table centre.*) only in Russian, which no one here can understand.

FRED: No, that's hard luck, miss.

IRINA: You must not call me 'miss'. I am Madame, because I am married.

FRED: I'm sorry. But somehow – you don't... (*He hesitates.*)

IRINA: Yes?

MARGARET: (*Calmly.*) You don't seem married. That's what Fred meant to say. Have you any children?

IRINA: (*Curtly.*) No.

MARGARET: (*Rising.*) I must get Dr Bahru his tea. Wait here for Mr Dawlish, Fred. (*She moves to the door down left.*) He won't stay out much longer now.

FRED: Right, Mrs Dawlish.

(*MARGARET exits down left. FRED remains quietly with his pipe and beer. There is a pause. When IRINA speaks, she is in a different mood, the Soviet official again.*)

IRINA: Tell me, please – for this interests me very much – what is your position here? You do not seem like a servant.

FRED: I'm not. I'm a sort of bailiff, I suppose.

IRINA: (*Rising.*) You are paid wages? (*She moves to the chair left of the table centre, turns it and sits in it facing FRED.*)

FRED: I have a share in the farm. When there's any money, I get my share of it. But it's all different here to what it used to be. Money doesn't mean so much. There's a lot of swapping round of stuff you need. And you work with people you like to work with, almost a kind of family affair. We'd never have got anywhere if it hadn't been.

IRINA: But is it a Capitalist or Socialist system?

FRED: It isn't a system at all, far as I can see. We just get along as best we can. We aren't bothering with systems.

IRINA: But this old Mr Dawlish – he represents a ruling class?

FRED: In this room he might, but in the kitchen his daughter-in-law – she's the ruling class, and in the barns and cowsheds and fields I'm the ruling class. Christopher? On the farm I boss him, but up here he bosses me, makes me sing and try to act in his plays.

IRINA: Is the cultural life organized from a centre?

FRED: (*Seriously.*) Say that again, please – miss. I didn't quite catch it.

IRINA: (*Slowly.*) Is the cultural life organized from a centre?

FRED: No. We don't have anything organized from centres. When all the centres were blown to bits, we decided we wouldn't bother with centres any more. Seems to work all right.

IRINA: (*Frowning.*) It seems to me very primitive.

FRED: (*Disinterestedly.*) I dare say.

IRINA: But you read newspapers, technical journals, cultural periodicals – you try to educate yourself and to keep yourself well informed?

FRED: No. Gave it up a long time since.

IRINA: (*Gravely.*) But that is very bad.

FRED: Is it? Oh – I know what's going on round here, of course. We have a little weekly paper – with plenty of local news in. I have a look at that.

IRINA: (*Worried.*) I did not realize you were now so backward.

FRED: (*Simply.*) No, I don't suppose we do neither.

IRINA: Would you call it a democracy here?

FRED: To tell you the truth – and no offence – I don't know and I don't care.

IRINA: (*Indignantly.*) Then you are politically uneducated.

FRED: (*Cheerfully.*) That's right.

(*STEPHEN enters up centre. He stumps in, looking ruffled and rather angry.*)

STEPHEN: (*Angrily.*) I've gone and lost my temper. (*He moves above the chair left of the table centre.*) At my time of life. It's a beautiful evening. I've never seen the garden looking better. I'm entertaining a guest – Mr Heimer – nice fellow, too. We begin talking. Then we begin arguing. Then I go and lose my temper. Whew! (*He blows his breath out impatiently, and stumps to right of the table left.*)

IRINA: And – Mr Heimer – what about him?

STEPHEN: Lost his temper too. So he's cooling off out there, and I'm cooling off in here. Glass of beer, Fred, please. Did you bring me that tobacco?

FRED: (*Rising.*) Yes, Mr Dawlish. (*He pours out a mug of beer.*)

STEPHEN: Good man. Madame Shestova – beer – milk?

IRINA: (*Rising.*) Some milk, please. (*She crosses down left.*)

STEPHEN: And some milk, Fred. (*He moves below the chair left of the table centre and turns.*) What the blue blazes is the use of a man trying to argue if he loses his temper? (*He shouts angrily.*) A reasonable man ought to behave like a reasonable man.

(*FRED pours out a mug of milk and hands it to IRINA.*)

IRINA: (*Smiling.*) Are you referring now to yourself or to Mr Heimer?

STEPHEN: To both of us. He lost his temper first. But I'm a lot older and never ought to have lost mine at all. We're a pair of braying asses – but I'm the older donkey and ought to have known better. (*He sits in the chair left of the table centre.*)

(*FRED hands STEPHEN a mug of beer.*)

Thanks, Fred. (*He takes a good pull at the beer.*) Ah – that's better. Don't deserve it, though – silly old fool.

IRINA: This is wonderful milk.

STEPHEN: It's the best there is. Eh, Fred?

FRED: (*Moving above the table centre.*) Just about. And I'll be getting along. Jim's a bit worried about one of the Guernseys, and I promised I'd have a look at her tonight

with him. (*He takes a small package from his pocket.*) Here's
the tobacco, Mr Dawlish. (*He hands the package to
STEPHEN.*)

STEPHEN: (*Taking the package and putting it in his pocket.*)
Thank you, Fred. And thank Waterhouse for me, will
you? And just switch some light on at the door for us.

FRED: (*Moving up centre.*) I will. (*He switches on the lights.*)
Good night.

IRINA: Good night.

STEPHEN: Good night.

    (*FRED exits up centre. STEPHEN, mug in hand, looks
smilingly at IRINA.*)

IRINA: Why are you looking at me like this?'

STEPHEN: (*Softly.*) Let me tell you something, my dear.
I can see the beauty of that wild ruined garden of ours,
with the flowers blazing through the dusk, reflected in
your face. You look very beautiful, my dear.

IRINA: (*Embarrassed, but pleased.*) That is a nice thing to say
to me.

STEPHEN: It's true. And you be careful, now. We're
impressionable round here.

IRINA: (*Puzzled.*) Impressionable?

STEPHEN: Give us half a chance – and we fall in love. I'm
warning you, my dear.

HEIMER: (*Enters up centre. Indicating the electric lights;
angrily.*) Well, Mr Dawlish, I see you don't turn up your
noses at electricity.

STEPHEN: (*Rising, moving to HEIMER and shouting angrily.*)
Mr Heimer, we don't turn up our noses at anything that's
really useful, pleasant, and won't make slaves out of us.
(*His manner quickly changes to one of comical despair.*) My
God! Now we're off again. Sorry, Mr Heimer.

HEIMER: (*Cordially.*) So am I, Mr Dawlish. My fault...

STEPHEN: No, no, my fault. And old enough to know better.
(*IRINA moves to the chair left of the table centre and sits.
She takes a drink of milk, then places her mug on the table
centre.*)

HEIMER: It won't happen again, Mr Dawlish.

STEPHEN: We'll make sure it doesn't, Mr Heimer.

HEIMER: Fine. Shake. (*He offers his hand to STEPHEN.*)

STEPHEN: (*Shaking HEIMER's hand.*) Spoken like a man. Now let me give you some beer. (*He turns, moves to the table left and pours out a mug of beer.*)

HEIMER: (*Moving down left.*) Thanks a lot, Mr Dawlish.

STEPHEN: We make this supply of electricity locally, with a couple of wind vanes up on the down. I had a hand in it so I know all about it. It's a sketchy weak supply, but it does what we want it to do. (*He hands a mug of beer to HEIMER.*) Now – try that.

HEIMER: (*Taking the mug.*) Thanks. And here she goes. (*He takes a good drink. He smiles.*) This kind of beer's new to me – but it's a mighty good drink and it's got quite a punch. You make it round here?

STEPHEN: Yes, it's brewed by a local man who likes beer.

HEIMER: (*Sitting on the downstage end of the bench; expansively.*) You know – I feel fine. Yes, *sir.* All loosened up.

STEPHEN: (*Sitting on the upstage end of the bench.*) Good. You just stay loosened up, Mr Heimer. And if your business doesn't like it, then let your business lump it. (*To IRINA.*) Any questions?

IRINA: That man – Fred, you call him. I like him, but he seems to be uneducated.

STEPHEN: He can milk a cow, shear a sheep, feed a pig, shoe a horse, grow wheat, barley, oats, roots and vegetables, make a rabbit pie, play the double bass and sing a tenor solo – what more do you want?

IRINA: No, I meant politically uneducated. He said he did not know or care whether this was a democracy or not.

STEPHEN: That's because it is one. We achieved it by accident. It's due to the fact that we're now a small and poor society. We aren't big and powerful any longer. Real democracy doesn't come in large sizes.

IRINA: (*Firmly.*) I cannot agree with this.

HEIMER: (*Angrily.*) And I say – *shucks!* Now listen – Mr Dawlish.

STEPHEN: (*Holding up a finger.*) Mr Heimer – remember. We don't start again, do we?

HEIMER: Oh, no. Sure thing. Sorry.

STEPHEN: Easy does it, eh?

HEIMER: Easy does it, Mr Dawlish. Go ahead.

STEPHEN: (*Mildly.*) I was only going to say that to make anything big work properly, you have to have a tremendous concentration of power. And where you have this concentration of power, there's no democracy. You may have something you prefer to democracy, but in that case don't go on talking about democracy. You know what happened to us?

HEIMER: Well, everything broke down here after the Third War, and then you had the big emigrations that were part of the World Settlement Plan.

STEPHEN: Right. And the remnant of us who were left had to start almost from scratch again. So there couldn't be any more concentration of power. We all had to improvise just to live at all.

IRINA: Like primitive peoples.

STEPHEN: No doubt. Well, politicians jockeying for power and officials issuing directives were useless. They couldn't plough a field or mend a roof. We had to begin again with families and small friendly groups of neighbours, people who knew and understood each other. The man who knew most about the particular job in hand became the boss, just for that job. And we said good-bye – and I hope for ever – to the self-appointed bosses who knew more about everything than everybody else. Now we all have our own little bits of responsibility. And that's what I call democracy. You call it what you like. Another glass of milk, Madame Shestova?

IRINA: No, thank you.

STEPHEN: More beer, Mr Heimer?

HEIMER: (*Rising.*) Thanks, I'll do it. (*He refills his mug.*) But, as you say, Mr Dawlish, now you're a small impoverished community, you can simplify your problems.

STEPHEN: They've been simplified for us. We work for what we need – and that's satisfying and not frustrating –

and then when we're not working we enjoy ourselves in our own way. We don't look after machines all day to pay for other machines to entertain us half the night. We find we can do without a lot of things that were beginning to make slaves of us.

HEIMER: It sounds *okay,* but they could talk like that on the Congo.

STEPHEN: I've never been on the Congo, but probably they had some good sensible ideas about life there.

HEIMER: Maybe, but however you look at it – it's a narrow life.

STEPHEN: Perhaps life is best when it's narrow – but deep and high. The spirit expands upwards, not sideways.

IRINA: (*Reproachfully.*) That sounds like mysticism.

STEPHEN: All right, then, let's have some mysticism, though I'd say I'm about as mystical myself as a rat-catcher's terrier.

HEIMER: (*Chuckling.*) Well, don't make me the rat any more tonight.

STEPHEN: (*To IRINA.*) Don't mind me, my dear young lady. I'm just an old man who's seen too many changes.

IRINA: (*Simply.*) I like you very much.

STEPHEN: Thank you, my dear. Now what's worrying you about us?

IRINA: I do not understand this point of view.

STEPHEN: Well, you see, we've had to drop a lot of stuff clean out of our lives. We haven't time for anything that doesn't either feed our bodies or refresh and rejoice our spirits. You might say we have two main problems – what to get for dinner, and what to do after dinner. So we grow things and raise stock – swap eggs for cheese, chickens for mutton – that's one level and it keeps us busy and interested. On the other level, what you might call after dinner, we write and sing songs, draw a bit, act plays, wonder and philosophize in our own way. But a whole lot of dusty stuff has dropped out.

IRINA: What is this 'dusty stuff'?

HEIMER: Now we're coming to it.

STEPHEN: Why, I know now that I spent at least half of my life worrying myself sick about a lot of things that seem to me now so much idle nonsense, rubbish and muck. All that dreary unrewarding middle level – trends of this and that, relations between this and that. (*He rises.*) For instance, now that we're not a world power and nobody cares tuppence about us, we no longer have to bother our heads about all the ridiculous intrigues of foreign ministers. No more foreign affairs. (*With fervour.*) No more wondering if Russia does this, will America do that. What a relief. I don't know and I don't care. We no longer have to waste our attention and energy on every gang of intriguers and power-seekers. So now we have attention and energy and emotion to spare for other and more rewarding matters. We have time to love and enjoy life and to praise God for it.

HEIMER: Good for you. But what about me getting a word in, Mr Dawlish?

STEPHEN: Quite right, Mr Heimer. But we take it easy, eh?

HEIMER: (*Holding up a finger; solemnly.*) We take it easy. (*IRINA suddenly bursts into laughter.*) What's this, Madame Shestova?

IRINA: (*Rising and moving to the doors up centre.*) I am sorry. But suddenly I think – men are so funny. (*She stands for a few moments, gazing out into the garden.*)

STEPHEN: (*Moving right of the table centre.*) You be careful if that's what you're beginning to think. But go on, Mr Heimer. (*He sits in the chair right of the table centre.*)

HEIMER: (*Solemnly.*) Far as I'm concerned – and I can say this for quite a lot of us Americans anyhow – it isn't just the power, or the dollars we earn, or even the damned excitement of making something big – but – well, I guess we got a sense of responsibility and duty to the world.
(*IRINA turns and moves above the table centre.*)
Yes, sir, don't forget that – responsibility and duty. (*He looks from STEPHEN to IRINA.*)

(*STEPHEN nods.*)

IRINA: (*Sitting in the chair above the table centre.*) Yes, Mr Heimer. This is very interesting to me.

(*HEIMER nods, then turns to STEPHEN.*)

HEIMER: You folks had it once. Then things got too tough for you. Well, you're making the best of it right now, I guess, doing what you can. But somebody's got to feel that responsibility and duty – and get busy. That's a real man's life, the way I see it. And if it takes more than you want to give it, if you can't go on camping trips the way I like to do, if you can't grow roses and read poetry, well, that's just too bad – but there's the big job, there's your responsibility, your duty, just the same. Yes, *sir*.

IRINA: (*Respectfully.*) That is how we Russians feel. But I did not know you Americans felt like that, Mr Heimer.

HEIMER: (*Moving and sitting left of the table centre; with modest pride.*) We certainly do, most of us, Madame Shestova.

STEPHEN: (*Smiling.*) There spoke the sound Puritan heart of America, that has kept it from becoming a vaster and more terrifying Babylon. The old gospel of duty and work. Eh, Mr Heimer?

HEIMER: Yes, Mr Dawlish. And if you ask me, it means as much today as it did to our folks two hundred years ago. We're still pioneers.

STEPHEN: (*Sharply.*) But you're not – and that's the trouble.

HEIMER: (*Sharply.*) And I say we are – though the job might be different.

STEPHEN: (*Loudly.*) And that's the point, my friend. When the tasks were simple pioneering tasks – clearing the forest, tilling your land – the gospel of duty and work did no harm and did much good.

HEIMER: (*Rather angrily.*) And I say it still does no harm and does much good.

STEPHEN: (*Vehemently.*) And I say you're mistaken, my friend. (*He rises.*) You carry your sense of duty and responsibility into enterprises that are very different from those simple old tasks. You still do – without asking yourselves what you are doing.

HEIMER: (*Rising and shouting.*) We know what we are doing.

IRINA: (*Holding up her finger; half-laughing.*) Please – please – where is this *take it easy?*

(*HEIMER moves down left.*)

STEPHEN: (*Ignoring IRINA.*) I say, that just as the armies of mad conquerors blindly marched, so, blindly and with furious mad energy, you tear down, lay waste, build, set machines in motion – produce, produce, produce – littering the world with things men might be happier without.

HEIMER: (*Turning and shouting.*) You try 'em, brother, that's all, just you try 'em. You could do with some of our products here right now.

STEPHEN: (*Shouting.*) Of course we could. We all like gadgets and toys. But the price we have to pay, sooner or later, is too high…

HEIMER: (*Moving left of the table centre; angrily.*) Who says it's too high?

IRINA: (*Rising; loudly.*) Please – please – take it easy – take it easy.

STEPHEN: (*Shouting.*) I *am* taking it easy. I say, you find yourself dragged in the dust behind the runaway chariot of commercial production, of your sense of responsibility and duty gone mad…

HEIMER: (*Shouting angrily.*) It's the one thing that *can't* go mad…

STEPHEN: (*Still shouting.*) It all ends in other people's confusion and misery, in a hopeless muddle of values. If you want to throw your life away for the sake of plastic ashtrays, that's your affair, but don't…

HEIMER: (*Still shouting.*) Who's talking about throwing lives away – and what's wrong with ashtrays anyhow…

STEPHEN: But – I say – don't ask us to do it or to admire you for doing it…

IRINA: (*Banging on the table.*) And I say – please – please – will you not take it easy?

STEPHEN: (*Mildly.*) Why, of course, Madame Shestova. Mr Heimer, you ought to apologise to Madame Shestova.

HEIMER: (*Rather startled.*) Why – sure – sorry... (*He resumes his seat left of the table centre.*)

IRINA: (*Turning and moving up left; with mock severity.*) You have both been very bad.

STEPHEN: (*Crossing to the table left.*) Quite right. And it's high time I stopped talking. And time too those youngsters were back from the village.

HEIMER: Rehearsing a play, aren't they?

STEPHEN: (*Refilling his mug with beer.*) Yes. *Midsummer Night's Dream.* You ever seen it, Madame Shestova?

IRINA: (*Moving right of STEPHEN.*) Once – in Moscow. When I was still a student – quite young in fact.

STEPHEN: (*Sitting on the bench; smiling.*) You're quite young still, my dear, though I suppose you don't think so.

IRINA: No, sometimes I feel quite old. Tonight in the garden, when I was reminded of the holidays I spent with my mother's brother – my uncle – as a child, suddenly I felt that life had gone past, that already I was old.

HEIMER: (*Heartily.*) You'll get over that all right. I can give you twenty-five years, I guess, and I don't feel old – not me.

IRINA: You are a man, it may be different.

HEIMER: (*Chuckling.*) Now that's the first time I ever heard you admit that there might be a difference. You just be careful.

STEPHEN: (*Gently.*) Often, when you feel as you do tonight, my dear, when you tell yourself that life has gone past, the very opposite is true. Some great blazing lump of life is just arriving – and you're only clearing a space for it.

IRINA: I have not known such a thing.

STEPHEN: Give yourself time.

(*The voices of CHRIS and ROSALIE are heard off up centre. They are saying lines from the play.*)

CHRIS: (*Off.*) 'Take thee well, nymph – '

STEPHEN: And you may not need much.

(*CHRIS and ROSALIE appear in the doorway up centre. CHRIS is left of ROSALIE. IRINA leans on the bannister post.*)

CHRIS: ' – ere he do leave this grove,
Thou shalt fly him, and he shall seek thy love.
Has thou the flower there? Welcome, wanderer.'

ROSALIE: 'Ay, there it is.'

CHRIS: 'I pray thee give it to me.
I know a bank whereon the wild thyme blows,
Where ox-lips and the nodding violet grows;
Quite over-canopied with luscious woodbine,
With sweet musk-roses, and with eglantine:
There sleeps Titania, sometime of the night –
Lull'd in these flowers with dances and delight...'
(*HEIMER claps.*)
Sorry, we were doing lines on the way up. Any beer left?
(*ROSALIE moves down right.*)

HEIMER: (*Rising.*) Plenty. (*He moves to the table left, picks up the tray of drinks and food, moves and places it on the table centre.*) What about you, Miss Rosalie?

ROSALIE: Milk for me. Lord! I'm thirsty – hungry, too.

HEIMER: (*Standing above the table centre, he pours out a mug of milk, moves to ROSALIE, and hands it to her.*) How's the play coming along?
(*CHRIS moves to the table centre and pours himself out a mug of beer.*)

ROSALIE: It's in the messy stage at present, and not enough people to choose from, really.
(*HEIMER passes the plate of cake to ROSALIE.*)
(*She takes a piece of cake.*) My part's Puck. I did it once before. If you two had been staying longer, you could have been in it.
(*HEIMER replaces the plate of cake on the table centre.*)

CHRIS: Of course they could. Mr Heimer would knock spots off old Bucket as Bully Bottom.

ROSALIE: (*Pointing to IRINA.*) And there's the perfect Titania.

IRINA: (*Easing left centre; shyly.*) Oh – no...

ROSALIE: Just look at her, Chris.

CHRIS: I am looking.

ROSALIE: (*Emphatically.*) She has the perfect lovely strange fairy look.

CHRIS: (*Fervently.*) She *has*. (*He quotes with mock anger.*) 'Ill
met by moonlight, proud Titania.' (*He looks steadily at
IRINA.*) It would have been so good for your English
too, Madame Shestova. Think of all the enchanting lines
you'd have had to say. (*He quotes.*) 'Hoary-headed frosts
fall in the fresh lap of the crimson rose.' (*He looks at the
red roses on the table left.*)
(*IRINA turns as if to go upstairs.*)
(*He looks at IRINA. Softly.*) Running away?

IRINA: (*Turning; proudly.*) No.

HEIMER: (*Moving to the chair right of the table centre and
sitting; heartily.*) Looks like we've missed something.

CHRIS: (*Moving to the sofa and sitting.*) Of course you have,
Mr Heimer.

ROSALIE: (*Moving to right of HEIMER; smiling.*) Yes, just
think of all the things Titania has to say to you. (*She
strokes his head with her left hand as she quotes.*)
'Come, sit thee down upon this flowery bed,
While I thy amiable cheeks do coy,
And stick musk-roses in thy sleek smooth head,
and kiss thy fair large ears, my gentle Joy...'

HEIMER: (*Protesting jovially.*) Here, wait a minute, young
woman. I remember it now. This fellow's got a donkey's
head on him, hasn't he?

ROSALIE: (*Perching herself on the upstage arm of the sofa.*) Yes,
but it's a *wonderful* part.

HEIMER: (*Laughing.*) Wait till I tell 'em this back home.
My – my – my!
(*The others laugh, more in sympathy than from genuine
amusement.*)
(*He continues in the same vein.*) That's what they wanted
me to be, I'll tell 'em. Bully Bottom – the one with the
donkey's head – Bottom – the – what is he?

ROSALIE: (*Laughing.*) The weaver.

HEIMER: (*Laughing.*) The weaver – that's the fellow –
comedy man. Say – I'll read it with Mrs Heimer and my
two youngsters. Just a private performance. *Midsummer
Night's Dream.* And that's just where I am – yes, sir, slap

in the middle of it. In a midsummer night's dream just where it belongs – midsummer in old England. Don't look at me like that, Madame Shestova. I know I sound crazy, but I'm not.

IRINA: (*Moving above the table centre; clearly and seriously.*) But no, I was not thinking of that. Because I feel it too – as if I was in a dream – a midsummer dream. (*She sits in the chair above the table centre.*)

HEIMER: (*Laughing again.*) What d'you know about that, eh? It's got her too. Mr Dawlish, you and I could argue till all's blue, I guess, and we'd never agree. But I want to tell you again – I like it here. I certainly do. I feel fine. All loosened up and relaxed – yes, sir. I wouldn't have missed it for ten thousand dollars. Midsummer Night's Dream – we had a little crash and then walked right into it – yes, sir, slap into the middle of it.

(*He laughs, and the others laugh with him. MARGARET enters at the top of the stairs and comes slowly down. She looks pale and angry. CHRIS sees her first, stops laughing and stares. The others gradually follow his example. ROSALIE rises.*)

CHRIS: What's the matter?

MARGARET: (*Standing on the bottom stair.*) I know now why these three came here. Dr Bahru has just told me.

HEIMER: (*Rising quickly; indignantly.*) Now that's too bad. Spoiling everything.

MARGARET: (*Bitterly.*) Yes. Spoiling everything. (*With growing urgency.*) But I knew in my heart you had come to do that. When I saw you three together this afternoon, what did I say to you then? That once you left us nothing but the bare thorn and our bleeding hands. And I asked you to remember that now our hands are healed and the thorn is beginning to flower.

STEPHEN: (*Quietly.*) What is this, my dear? What have you learnt?

MARGARET: (*Slowly and quietly.*) Dr Bahru discovered that the chalk in our Downs could be used for making some new synthetic substance. He brought Mr Heimer and Madame Shestova here to show them how much of it there is, and now they have decided to manufacture the new substance here, to dig out the chalk, to erect a manufacturing plant, to build a whole industrial town...

ROSALIE: (*Horrified.*) No. No.

MARGARET: Yes. (*To HEIMER.*) That is true, isn't it?

HEIMER: (*Defiantly.*) Certainly is. And why not? You've got something here the whole world needs, so we're going to make use of it. Nothing new about that. You British used to do it all over the world.

(*MARGARET moves silently to the door down left and exits.*)

ROSALIE: (*Crossing to the door down left; distressed.*) Oh – Aunt Margaret.

(*She exits quickly. HEIMER looks defiantly at STEPHEN, who finally meets his glance.*)

STEPHEN: (*Steadily.*) It's true we used to do it ourselves. In fact we led the way. And in the end we paid a heavy price. After that we had to find another way out. I think we were beginning to find it. And now you come here.

HEIMER: (*Crossing to right of STEPHEN.*) Now look, Mr Dawlish. If this thing's worked right – and I'll see it is – you can get a whole heap of dollars for your land here – and then if you don't like it here any more – why, you can go some place – buy more land...

STEPHEN: (*Rising abruptly.*) No, I can't. (*He moves to the doors up centre.*)

HEIMER: Well, you're old I guess – but...

CHRIS: (*Interrupting.*) I'm not old, Mr Heimer. But I know what my grandfather means, and I feel as he does. You don't understand. This isn't just a piece of land, just something to pull a living out of. It's our home. It's part of us. We love it. To us it's just as if you proposed to excavate our bones and nerves, to tap our lifeblood, and then mash them all up with chemicals to make your synthetic muck.

HEIMER: That's just fanciful, young man.

STEPHEN: (*Moving right of HEIMER; gravely.*) No, it isn't, Mr Heimer. Those of us who were left here, after you had all finished with us, had nothing but the land – the patient outraged land – a few old implements, our hands, and what remained of faith, hope and love. We had to find a new way to live. Without it we couldn't have existed at all during these last fifteen years. We found that new way. And at last we began to live, not merely to exist. And now you want to destroy it.

HEIMER: (*Rather impatiently.*) Sure, you've had a tough time. But we're not out to destroy anything. You've been in industry yourself in your time, Mr Dawlish...

STEPHEN: (*Interrupting; very sharply.*) I have. And now I wouldn't turn a dozen sheep off the bare top of a down for all the synthetic products in the world.

HEIMER: (*Crossing to right below the table centre; annoyed.*) And if you ask me, that's childish. And this is serious, it's important business. (*He moves up right and turns.*) I can clown around with the next fellow, but, as I warned you when we were arguing earlier tonight, I've got a sense of responsibility and duty to the world.

STEPHEN: (*Sharply.*) And as I told you then – you carry your sense of responsibility and duty, without thinking, into the wrong enterprises. You drive blindly on and drag the rest of us choking in the dust behind you. (*He breaks off. With a change of tone.*) It's past my usual bedtime, and I'm tired. Madame Shestova – will you excuse me? I hope you will not find it too uncomfortable here. We will do our best...

IRINA: (*Rising and moving to right of STEPHEN.*) Oh – no – please...

CHRIS: (*Rising and looking steadily at IRINA.*) Madame Shestova hasn't said anything yet.

IRINA: (*Looking at CHRIS.*) No. (*She looks at STEPHEN.*) Because now – I'm too tired. And if you will excuse me – please. (*She moves to the stairs, hesitates and turns.*) Good night. (*She turns and exits quickly up the stairs.*)
(*There is a pause, then STEPHEN moves slowly towards the stairs.*)

STEPHEN: (*Softly.*) I think our Russian friend is not feeling very happy.

CHRIS: (*Quietly.*) No, she isn't.

HEIMER: (*To CHRIS; rather explosively.*) Hell! I'm not feeling happy either – and don't imagine I am.

STEPHEN: (*With grave courtesy.*) If there is anything you need, Mr Heimer, that we can supply, I hope you will tell Christopher. Good night. (*He moves slowly up the stairs.*)

HEIMER: Good night, Mr Dawlish. Nice of you to have us here.

CHRIS: Good night, Grandfather.

(*STEPHEN exits at the top of the stairs.*)

HEIMER: (*Sitting in the chair right of the table centre; quietly.*) I'll just let him get up there, then I'll follow. I might have a word with Bahru at that. Talks too much, that Asiatic.

CHRIS: (*Dryly.*) You mustn't blame him. My Aunt Margaret is a very difficult person to hide anything from. She has special ways of her own of knowing.

HEIMER: One of these rather unbalanced psychic types, I guess.

CHRIS: She's the best balanced of us all, and the one we depend on when things are bad, but she doesn't really live in our kind of world.

HEIMER: (*Mildly, but firmly.*) I'll risk saying it again. I think that's just fanciful, young man.

CHRIS: (*Coolly.*) It could be. I'm inclined that way. But even the idea of synthetic products was once thought to be fanciful.

HEIMER: (*Complacently.*) I'll grant you that. But now we make 'em by the million. So they were wrong. You can't prove me wrong. That's the difference.

(*MARGARET and ROSALIE enter down left. MARGARET is grave and composed, but ROSALIE looks as if she has been crying. MARGARET moves to the table left, picks up her work-basket, takes it and sits left of the table centre.*)

Oh. Hello there.

ROSALIE: (*Moving above the table centre.*) I don't want to be rude, Mr Heimer, but I think you ought to go to bed.

I'm horribly disappointed in you, and I can't talk to you any more.

HEIMER: (*Rising.*) Now, listen, Rosalie, you and I were getting to be great pals...

(*CHRIS sits on the sofa. MARGARET resumes her sewing.*)

ROSALIE: And all the time you knew what was going to happen to us...

HEIMER: (*Protesting.*) But I don't see it the way you do.

ROSALIE: No, please. I can't talk about it any more – not to you. (*She moves to the doors up centre.*) Say good night. (*She stands in the doorway, gazing out over the garden.*)

HEIMER: You bet. (*He eases to the stairs.*) I was just going, anyway. But – well, I'm disappointed in you too. (*He lingers for a moment, rather wistfully, a friendly man, looking at them.*) Well – good night all.

(*They murmur good night. HEIMER turns and exits up the stairs. ROSALIE turns, moves above the table centre, pours herself out a mug of milk and helps herself to some cake.*)

ROSALIE: I know it's all wrong, but I always want to eat and drink when something terrible has happened. (*She sits in the chair right of the table centre.*) And then I feel sick afterwards.

CHRIS: I hope you two aren't going to stay up. I feel like writing some music.

MARGARET: Aren't you tired now?

CHRIS: No. I was earlier, but after I put my bed under the beeches, before supper, I had a little sleep. So now I feel in grand form.

MARGARET: (*Calmly.*) Because you are in love.

ROSALIE: (*Fiercely.*) With that woman? I hate her now.

MARGARET: She is only doing what she thinks is her duty. And she is not happy. I saw that from the first. I think her marriage means nothing to her. She lives in a cold desert of duty.

ROSALIE: (*After a slight pause.*) I don't understand you, Chris. Writing music now. Don't you realize what these people are going to do to us?

CHRIS: Why not?

ROSALIE: Because I can't see how you can sit there like that – not caring – talking about writing music – if you did. It'll be the end of everything.

CHRIS: (*Rising; carefully.*) If these people were going tonight – or even early in the morning, I'd feel about it as you do. Perhaps more so. (*He takes his violin case from the window sill right.*) But they haven't gone yet.

ROSALIE: But we can't stop them going, whenever they're ready. And when they do go, they'll take this foul plan with them, and very soon... Oh – I can't talk about it. But Margaret will tell you what is going to happen. She got it out of Dr Bahru.

(*CHRIS places the violin case on the sofa, opens the case and takes out his violin and bow.*)

CHRIS: (*Carefully.*) It's not been decided yet when or how they go. They haven't even sent any messages yet. Nobody knows they are here or what is happening.

ROSALIE: (*Eagerly.*) You think...

CHRIS: (*Interrupting.*) No. I'm not even thinking – yet.

MARGARET: (*Folding her sewing and placing it in the work-basket.*) Chris is right. Why should we give up hope – when nothing has happened? (*She rises.*) Let's go, Rosalie.

ROSALIE: Not yet. I'm too excited and miserable to sleep. I want to talk.

MARGARET: (*Moving to the stairs.*) We can talk upstairs. Chris wants us to leave him. And he's right. This is his time.

ROSALIE: (*Rising.*) Why – his time?

MARGARET: (*Moving up the stairs.*) Come on. Good night, Chris.

CHRIS: Good night, Margaret. Good night, Rosalie.

ROSALIE: (*Moving to the stairs.*) Good night.

(*MARGARET and ROSALIE exit up the stairs. CHRIS takes some sheets of music manuscript from the violin case and places them on the table centre. He then moves up centre, switches off the light over the stairs and opens the doors up centre to their fullest extent. The moonlight streams in. He gazes out over the garden for a few moments, tunes his violin very quietly, holding it to his ear, then moves to the table centre, glances at the music he has already written and whistling softly, makes a correction or two. He plays a tiny snatch or two of melody, then stops, and moves restlessly and impatiently to the doors up centre. He pauses for a moment, then steps outside the doors and begins to play, very softly, with a mute on his strings, some passages from the composition heard in Act Two, Scene Two. As he plays, IRINA enters at the top of the stairs and comes slowly and quietly down into the room. She wears slippers and pyjamas, and over her pyjamas a long, pale-coloured wrap or dressing-gown made of plastic material similar to that of her uniform. Her hair is looser and her whole appearance softer and more feminine than before. She moves to the table centre, glances at the manuscript, then moves up centre and stands left of the alcove, listening to CHRIS. After a few moments CHRIS stops playing, turns and re-enters.)*

CHRIS: (*Quietly.*) What can I call you now?

IRINA: (*Softly.*) Irina.

CHRIS: (*Softly to himself.*) Irina. Irina.

IRINA: (*Softly.*) I could not sleep or rest. And then
    I thought I heard far away the bird that sings at night...

CHRIS: (*Quoting smilingly.*)
    'The nightingale that in the branches sang,
    Ah, whence, and whither flown again, who knows.'
    Most of them have stopped singing now, Irina, but
    I heard one still singing last night – a little hoarse and
    rusty now – but a nightingale.

IRINA: (*Moving to the bench left.*) I do not know why I am
    here talking to you.

CHRIS: (*Moving to the table centre and putting his violin and
    bow on it.*) Because for years and years I have been
    waiting for you, at the rising of every moon.

IRINA: (*Sitting on the bench.*) That is not true. (*She laughs
    softly.*) No, I must not say that now – must I?

CHRIS: (*Easing left of the table centre.*) No, Irina, not now. In
    the morning perhaps – but then only once or twice.

IRINA: Did you hear me say, when Mr Heimer was
    laughing, that I felt as if I was in a dream – a
    midsummer dream?

CHRIS: (*Moving and sitting on the bench, upstage of IRINA.*) Yes, I heard you – and have been happy ever since.

IRINA: It was true. That is how I feel – in a dream. I do not understand myself. What can you think of me?

CHRIS: It is quite simple – I love you.

IRINA: (*Rising and crossing above the table centre; gravely.*) Oh, no. Listen, please. There is something I must tell you. My husband is an engineer. He was my father's chief assistant and friend. He is much older than I am – a good man – I respect him very much.

CHRIS: (*Very softly.*) But you don't love him.

IRINA: (*Very softly.*) No. I read of this love in novels and saw it played in the theatre and opera. I did not think it was a real thing.

CHRIS: (*Rising.*) And now?

IRINA: (*Moving towards the doors up centre; slowly.*) I do not know. I am wandering in a dream – with strange feelings in my heart. All day I have been like a child again – and yet not a child. After I threw down the flowers you gave me and went to my room – I cried, and yet did not know why I was crying. All like a dream.

CHRIS: (*Moving to IRINA.*) And how is it with you in this dream of yours, Irina?

IRINA: (*Turning to CHRIS.*) It seems the same as it is with you – Christopher. I seem to love you.

(*She moves into his arms, and with a kind of slow dreamy intensity, they kiss. After a moment or two, while they are still embracing, the song of a nightingale can be heard from outside.*)

(*She turns in his arms. She whispers.*) Listen – it is there now – the magic bird.

CHRIS: (*Quoting; half-playfully.*) 'Believe me, love, it is the nightingale...'

(*IRINA leans against CHRIS and they stand looking out into the garden, listening to the song of the bird, as the curtain slowly falls.*)

End of Act One.

ACT TWO

Scene 1

Scene – The terrace of Larks Lea. Afternoon. Three days later.

The scene is dominated by a large and deep-pillared porch which is approached by four broad and wide steps, running from centre to the wall left. The steps are flanked right by a short low section of balustrade, and left by the grey stone outside wall of the house, the entrance to which is in the left wall under the porch at the top of the steps. In the wall of the house left there is a recess that at one time or other held a small statue. Its base is about two feet from the ground and it is now occupied by a portable T-V-Com. This apparatus is a person-to-person television, worked on some much simpler principle than our television. The set is like a portable transmitting-and-receiving radio set with sight added. It has a rather shiny screen, about eighteen inches square, framed and heavily shaded. The set has various mysterious and impressive controls, dials, etc. Attached to it, by a flexible lead, there is a small hand microphone-cum-camera device. It is so placed on the stage that the effect can be worked, at the discretion of the producer, either with a small talking film, preferably in colour, projected from behind the screen, or by using actors flickeringly lit behind the screen, which must then be a transparency. Neither sound nor image need be very clear, and there should be various cracklings, flickerings, etc., as it is established that the set is not working well. The T-V-Com can of course be placed so that it is overshadowed by foliage and is never seen in full stage light. The recess has a small stone bench or seat beneath it. The garden, right, is approached by a rustic arch down right. The whole place is thick with climbing plants, lush flowers and foliage, giving the impression of being rather uncared for, but all rich and grand in a natural fashion, and looking rather more sub-tropical than the usual English scene. The plinth of a broken pillar stands right centre, and a few feet of the broken pillar itself lies left centre. These pieces of stone are used as seats. A wheelbarrow, containing a sack of earth and a shovel, stands above the arch down right. A sieve hangs on the wall above the door up left, and a trug basket stands on the ground under it. Various articles used about the farm, such as fruit baskets, sacks of lime, et cetera, are stacked against the walls of the house and porch. The scene should be reasonably convincing, as the outside of an English country house in a state of decay. The stonework of the porch and house is worn and weather-beaten, but the whole effect suggests a certain dreamlike feeling.

When the curtain rises, it is a bright hot afternoon, and a rich golden light floods the scene. IRINA is seated on the balustrade centre and CHRIS is lying across the steps with his head on her lap. He is dressed as before, but IRINA has changed her plastic uniform for a coloured dress similar to that worn by ROSALIE. Her hair is worn looser. She is blooming and relaxed and both she and CHRIS have the dreamy preoccupation of satisfied lovers.

CHRIS: I was in love with you long, long before you came here. Then, as soon as I saw you the other afternoon I fell ten thousand fathoms deeper in love with you. And I'm still falling, at least ten fathoms a minute.

IRINA: My darling, you should not say such things to me.

CHRIS: Why? Because you don't believe me?

IRINA: (*With half a sigh.*) No, because I do.

CHRIS: (*Teasingly.*) And perhaps there is a special order forbidding you to listen.

IRINA: There is. It is a directive of the Central Council commanding Soviet Officials abroad not to enter into such relationships. And until I met you, Christopher, I found it easy to obey this order. But now...

CHRIS: (*Turning to her.*) My darling, my golden love.

BAHRU: (*Enters up left. Standing at the top of the steps left.*) You have done some agricultural work this afternoon?

CHRIS: Yes.

IRINA: (*Teasingly and lovingly.*) But I have done more work than he has. He is rather lazy, I think.

BAHRU: (*Smiling.*) I am not surprised.

CHRIS: We English *are* a bit lazy – an old fault of ours – if it is a fault. And I'm not sure it is.

IRINA: He is really thinking about his music – not about farm work.

(*BAHRU moves to the T-V-Com.*)

CHRIS: It's possible to do both at once.

IRINA: (*Rather troubled.*) Is – the T-V-Com working now?

BAHRU: No, I stopped to have a little rest, but I think
I shall have it ready quite soon.

IRINA: (*With a hint of sadness.*) I see.

CHRIS: (*Looking at BAHRU.*) My own belief is – everybody
here would be happier, including yourselves, if you
found you couldn't make it work – yet.
(*IRINA looks hopefully at BAHRU.*)

BAHRU: (*Shaking his head; gravely.*) I understand why you
say that – you have my sympathy, I do assure you – but
such a thing is not possible. (*He sits on the bench down
left.*) I must put this T-V-Com in working order as soon
as I can.
(*IRINA rises, and goes up the steps.*)
I have my duty to attend to. We all have our duties to
attend to – eh, Madame Shestova?

IRINA: (*Pausing on the top step and turning; steadily.*) Yes.
I have not forgotten.

BAHRU: To dream is very pleasant – I enjoy it myself, and
last night I dreamt of being in my little garden with my
dear wife and our two beautiful children – but the time
comes when we must wake up.

CHRIS: (*Rising and moving up the steps; rather hastily.*) Let's
find something to drink, Irina. (*He exits up left.*)
(*IRINA and BAHRU exchange a long sober look, then IRINA
turns and exits up left. BAHRU gives his attention to the
T-V-Com, makes some final adjustments, then switches it on.
A light flickers on the screen and the set crackles. After a few
moments, MARGARET enters slowly up left and stands at
the top of the steps, looking curiously at BAHRU.*)

MARGARET: (*Picking up the trug basket.*) Well, Dr Bahru,
how are you getting on with that instrument?

BAHRU: (*Switching off the T-V-Com.*) It is nearly ready,
thank you, Mrs Dawlish. But it will not have much
power. We shall have to use it very carefully.

MARGARET: (*Taking the sieve from the wall.*) You will be
able to see people – and to talk to them?

BAHRU: (*Rising.*) Yes. But of course as it is only a small portable one, it is very crude. And it has been damaged. (*He eases centre.*) Have you never seen the big T-V-Coms?

MARGARET: No. Nor the little T-V-Coms neither. (*She comes down the steps.*)

(*BAHRU laughs gently.*)

Why do you laugh? (*She leans the sieve against the right side of the balustrade and places the trug basket on the down stage end of it.*)

BAHRU: Excuse me, please, Mrs Dawlish, but I was thinking how curious it is that I – an Indian – should be here in England explaining a scientific invention to you. Forty years ago – even thirty years ago – it would still have been you English who would have been explaining these modern marvels to us ignorant Indians. Now – well, it is very different.

MARGARET: (*Cheerfully.*) I see no harm in that. Once it was our turn, now it is your turn. (*She opens the sack on the wheel-barrow.*) But who are you going to see and talk to with that thing – your wife?

BAHRU: (*Sitting on the upstage end of the balustrade; sadly.*) No, unfortunately. I should like very much to see my wife and to talk to her. But that is not possible. She is not allowed a T-V-Com. This can only be used for official business. In a few minutes I shall try to get through to the head of my department.

MARGARET: And do you like him? (*She begins to fill the trug basket with earth from the sack.*)

BAHRU: No, I dislike him very much. And he dislikes me. But still we shall be able to see each other and to talk. You must admit that is very wonderful.

MARGARET: (*Calmly.*) It seems rather absurd to me.

BAHRU: Absurd? Why?

MARGARET: You can't see your wife and talk to her. All it gives you is somebody who dislikes you, and you don't want to see and talk to. So why bother?

BAHRU: (*Nonplussed.*) But you do not appear to understand, Mrs Dawlish. If you have important business to discuss...

MARGARET: If it is so important, it will keep until you get home. (*She closes the sack.*) And that will give you more time to decide if it really *is* important. And perhaps it isn't.

BAHRU: But of course it is.

MARGARET: Do you love your wife?

BAHRU: (*Surprised.*) Yes, very much.

MARGARET: Then seeing and talking to her really *is* important. And you should never have let anybody decide that it wasn't. (*She picks up the trug basket and the sieve. Very gently.*) There must be something wrong with the values in your world, Dr Bahru. (*She exits down right.*) (*BAHRU stares after her for a moment, rather taken aback, then with a shrug rises, crosses to the bench down left and sits at the T-V-Com. After a few more adjustments, he switches it on. On the screen there are vague flashes, like a television set before it is properly tuned in, and there are various noises, including sounds of voices, male and female, talking vague gibberish. He picks up the microphone and speaks into it.*)

BAHRU: (*Into the microphone.*) Dr Bahru for Dr Rockfeller Chen. Dr Bahru for Dr Rockfeller Chen. Dr Bahru for Dr Rockfeller Chen

(*After a few moments a flickering image of a middle-aged American-cum-Chinese type in tropical clothes appears on the screen. He looks hot and angry and speaks with a loud, unpleasant voice.*)

CHEN: (*Through the T-V-Com.*) This is Rockfeller Chen. It is very late. Who is that?

BAHRU: Dr Bahru.

CHEN: Dr Bahru?

BAHRU: Yes, Dr Chen.

CHEN: (*Angrily.*) This is Dr Chen,

BAHRU: Yes, I know. And this is Dr Bahru.

CHEN: Oh yes – I see you now, Dr Bahru, Where are you?

BAHRU: Southern England.

CHEN: (*Fussily.*) Where? Can't see you well. Can't hear you properly. Something wrong with your set.

BAHRU: It's only a small portable set, Dr Chen, and has been damaged. Wait a moment, please, and I'll try to make it better.

(*As he fiddles with the controls, the voice of DR CHEN comes through without the image, but it is somewhat faint. At the same time IRINA enters up left and stops dead, alarmed, when she sees what is happening.*)

CHEN: Hurry up, Dr Bahru. Make it snappy. Another call is coming through – very important.

(*BAHRU faces the screen again, and the image of CHEN re-appears.*)

BAHRU: Is that better, Dr Chen?

CHEN: A little better, but still very bad. Where did you say you were, Dr Bahru?

BAHRU: Southern England.

CHEN: Southern England?

BAHRU: Yes.

CHEN: Oh – yes – the report for the American Synthetic Products people. Is it ready?

BAHRU: Yes, my report is quite ready.

IRINA: (*Moving down one step and interrupting; urgently.*) No. No. Please, Dr Bahru.

(*BAHRU lowers the microphone, rises, turns away from the T-V-Com, then takes a step or two towards IRINA as she confronts him. The image on the screen becomes vague, and more flickering.*)

CHEN: (*Angrily and faintly.*) Where are you, Dr Bahru? Make it snappy. No time to waste. Dr Bahru.

BAHRU: (*Turning and raising the microphone; desperately.*) Yes, I'm here, Dr Chen.

(*He is too late. The image and voice of CHEN are rapidly fading.*)

CHEN: (*Just audibly.*) No time to waste. Another call coming through…

(*CHEN's image and voice fade out, BAHRU switches off the T-V-Com, puts down the microphone then turns to IRINA, who is looking unhappy.*)

BAHRU: Madame Shestova, that was my chief, Dr Rockfeller Chen, and I was about to make my report to him. It may take hours before I can get through to him again. Why did you interrupt me like that?

IRINA: (*Unhappily.*) I do not know, Dr Bahru. I spoke
before I thought.

BAHRU: You and I and Mr Heimer have agreed that
although we are sorry for these people here, we must do
our duty. And you yourself have said that their attitude
is reactionary, unscientific, and undemocratic.

IRINA: Yes, that is true.

BAHRU: But now, Madame Shestova, you prevent me from
doing my duty.

IRINA: (*Moving to the broken column left centre; distressed.*) No,
Dr Bahru. I did not mean to speak. (*She sits on the right
end of the broken column and faces right.*) It – it – came out.
I am sorry.

BAHRU: (*After a pause.*) I will tell you why you interrupted
me, Madame Shestova.
(*IRINA looks at him rather dreamily over her right shoulder,
but does not speak.*)
The reason is that you do not want me to make my
report.

IRINA: (*Faintly.*) No – please. That is not true. As you said
– we have our duty.

BAHRU: (*Softly, but carefully.*) You still say it, but you no
longer feel it, my dear colleague. And again, I will tell
you why. (*He moves down left centre.*) You are no longer an
official of the U.S.S.R. Foreign Trade Commission. You
are a woman lost – drowned – in love.

IRINA: (*Distressed.*) Please. You must not say such a thing.

BAHRU: I say it only to you, Madame Shestova. But
I know about such things. I have a wife, who loves me
very much. And I have watched you these last two days
sinking deeper and deeper – drowned in love. All of us
here – all except this terrible wonderful young man,
Christopher – are ghosts. Now you live only in his eyes,
his voice, his touch. You are caught in a blinding dream.
You...

IRINA: (*Turning to him; interrupting, distressed.*) No – no –
please, Dr Bahru.

BAHRU: (*With a touch of complacency.*) I have finished. But
you see, I am not only a scientist – I could have been a

poet too, (*He breaks down left and turns.*) only that was too old-fashioned. I have been reminded of that fact several times. It is something in the atmosphere, perhaps. (*He pauses, then moves to the broken column and sits on it, left of IRINA.*) But what I say about you is true, isn't it?

IRINA: (*In a low troubled tone.*) Yes. Before, I never thought such things possible. Now I understand. It is life in another world. There is no past – no future. (*She pauses.*) There are moments when I wish to die – of shame, of happiness. As you said of Christopher – it is terrible – it is wonderful.

(*MARGARET enters down right. She carries a trug basket of fruit and some light garden netting over her shoulder. BAHRU rises. MARGARET glances at IRINA, looks at BAHRU, then places the basket on the ground below the balustrade.*)

MARGARET: Have you used your machine yet?

BAHRU: Yes – for a minute or two.

MARGARET: And what did it offer you beside anger and confusion?

BAHRU: I tried to talk to my chief – Dr Rockfeller Chen – in Singapore. But – we were interrupted. Soon I will try again.

MARGARET: (*Sitting on the balustrade.*) Ask him what he can make out of our chalk that will be better than the life you will murder here.

BAHRU: (*Crossing to MARGARET; sharply.*) I do not like this way of talking. It has nothing to do with him – or with me. We are scientists...

MARGARET: (*Interrupting.*) And so it has nothing to do with you. (*She starts to straighten out the netting.*) You are not responsible – you are scientists. Dr Bahru, we have stopped believing that dangerous lie.

BAHRU: (*Angrily.*) Mrs Dawlish, in these days I doubt if you have any scientists here.

MARGARET: (*Sharply.*) Then all the better. Now we can all be responsible for what we do, and nobody can any longer say, 'It has nothing to do with me.'

BAHRU: (*Turning and crossing angrily to left; loudly.*) And that is a foolish argument.

(*CHRIS enters up left. IRINA looks around at him and smiles.*)

CHRIS: (*Standing at the top of the steps left; easily.*) Probably all arguments are foolish, I know mine always are. Irina.

IRINA: (*Rising.*) Yes, Christopher?

(*IRINA and CHRIS stand looking at each other, oblivious of the other two.*)

CHRIS: (*Smiling.*) I promised to go down to the Dutch Barn. (*He comes down the steps and moves to IRINA.*) And you promised to help.

IRINA: (*Smiling.*) Yes, of course.

CHRIS: Come on, then.

(*CHRIS and IRINA, smiling and dreamy, move as in a trance and exit down right. The other two watch them go in silence. There is a pause.*)

BAHRU: (*Softly.*) Those two – they are lost in a dream.

MARGARET: (*Softly.*) And it is better to be lost there than to be found anywhere else.

BAHRU: (*Moving to MARGARET.*) I am glad Christopher appeared then, because I am afraid I was angry with you, Mrs Dawlish. (*He takes one end of the netting and helps MARGARET to straighten it out.*) I am sorry. I do not know why I was angry so suddenly.

MARGARET: (*Mildly.*) Perhaps because you felt uncertain, and wanted to convince yourself.

BAHRU: No, I need no convincing. You cannot understand what science and industry have meant to us in India. (*He sits on the steps.*) There was so much ignorance, filth, superstition, poverty. I am proud to be an Indian scientist, Mrs Dawlish.

MARGARET: (*Looking hard at him; slowly.*) And yet – I think you feel uncertain.

BAHRU: (*Uneasily.*) It is only here that I may feel a little uncertain, not when I am in the East. There is something here – an atmosphere, and influence. Madame Shestova and Mr Heimer do not say anything to me, but I think they feel it too.

MARGARET: (*Rising.*) This has always been a strange island, Dr Bahru.

(*BAHRU rises and moves centre, holding one end of the netting.*)

It was once famous for its magic.

(*BAHRU assists MARGARET to fold the netting.*)

The Celts were great poets and magicians. And the Celts have never died. They were only silent for a little time while the smoke was thick over the cities. And now it has cleared again.

BAHRU: (*Quietly.*) And you cannot forgive me because you think I wish to bring it back.

(*There is a pause. MARGARET looks hard at him.*)

MARGARET: (*Slowly.*) No, what I am wondering now – is whether you will forgive yourself, Dr Bahru. (*She moves with the net and hangs it on the wall above the door up left.*)

BAHRU: You cannot talk to me like that, Mrs Dawlish, I am a research chemist – a scientist – with an official position – with certain duties to perform – certain obligations. And I have had to conquer thousands of years of superstition and ignorance – you do not understand. And anyhow, this is not a reasonable sensible talk. I cannot listen any more. (*He breaks down right.*) I tell you, I will not listen...

(*He breaks off as ROSALIE enters down right. She is carrying a bunch of lavender and some bay leaves.*)

ROSALIE: (*With chilly humour.*) You don't sound to me as if you were listening, Dr Bahru. What's the matter with you?

BAHRU: (*Turning and moving left; embarrassed.*) I am sorry. It is nothing. We were having a discussion.

MARGARET: (*Descending the steps and crossing to ROSALIE.*) It is probably my fault, Rosalie.

BAHRU: (*Rather sharply.*) You do not believe that.

(*MARGARET sits on the balustrade.*)

ROSALIE: (*Crossing to the steps; coldly.*) Don't start all over again. (*She indicates the T-V-Com.*) I suppose this is the famous machine we have heard so much about?

BAHRU: Yes. It is ready to be used now.

ROSALIE: (*Moving up the steps and turning.*) So at any moment it will be telling you and Mr Heimer what you have to do next. Where are the next places you have to ruin to manufacture your bits of rubbish?

(*HEIMER enters down right. He is hot and breathless, and gives the impression that he has been hurrying to catch up with ROSALIE.*)

HEIMER: (*As he enters.*) Say – listen – Rosalie…

ROSALIE: (*In a cold, clear tone.*) Your machine's waiting for you, Mr Heimer. Hurry up and attend to it. (*She hangs the bay leaves and lavender on the wall in the porch.*) There must be lots of other people's homes and lives you can turn into cigarette cases and ashtrays.

HEIMER: (*Crossing to the foot of the steps; protestingly.*) Now – don't be that way. Have a heart.

ROSALIE: (*With immense scorn.*) Why – what will you make that into – (*She turns and moves to the door up left.*) a cup and saucer? (*She exits up left.*)

(*HEIMER moves to the bench down left and sits, mopping himself and groaning a little, glad of a rest.*)

BAHRU: (*Easing centre and turning.*) Mr Heimer, the T-V-Com is working now, though it is not very good of course. But I got through for a minute or two to my chief in Singapore…

HEIMER: (*Interrupting; sharply.*) What did you tell him?

BAHRU: Nothing. Madame Shestova interrupted me before I could make my report, and then some other call cut us off. Should I try again or would you like to use it first?

HEIMER: (*Rather impatiently.*) No need to decide that now. Let me get my breath and relax. (*He puffs and blows a little.*) I tried to catch up with Rosalie all the way up the hill.

MARGARET: (*Amused.*) And why did you do that, Mr Heimer?

(*BAHRU moves to the wheel-barrow and perches himself on it.*)

HEIMER: (*Gloomily.*) That's what I keep asking myself. I keep following her round like a lost dog, trying to get a friendly word out of the kid, I guess.

MARGARET: Yes – but why?

HEIMER: (*Rising; exasperated.*) I don't know why. (*He crosses to left of MARGARET.*) I don't know what's got into me.

(*He glares at her.*) And don't get me wrong. Don't think sex comes into it, because it doesn't. I can tell. It's on the level. (*He turns and faces front.*) I'd feel just the same if Mrs Heimer and my own girls were here. I just want to be pals with Rosalie, the way we were the first night here. And now that I can't be, because she won't let me – hell! I'm worried to death, can't relax, can't have any fun, and half the time feel as low as a snake's under-carriage. (*He turns to MARGARET.*) I can't understand this poetry she writes – doesn't mean a thing to me – but if she came out now and took me off to read some to me – gosh! – I'd feel a mile high. (*He sits on the steps.*) But no, Sir – not a chance.

MARGARET: (*Rising and easing centre; smiling and cool.*) I'm sorry, Mr Heimer,

HEIMER: (*Bluffly.*) Oh – nothing for you to be sorry about.

MARGARET: No. Except that now you may be haunted for years.

HEIMER: (*Taken aback.*) Haunted for years?

MARGARET: (*Moving up the steps to the door up left.*) Yes. (*She gives HEIMER a cool smile, turns and exits up left. HEIMER rubs his chin in an exasperated fashion, then looks at BAHRU. BAHRU takes a cigarette case from his pocket and lights a cigarette.*)

HEIMER: (*Gloomily.*) After what happened to 'em – and the way they live now, cut off from everything – these folks might easily be nuts. If you ask me, Bahru, we never ought to have stayed here.

BAHRU: That is what I think too. We ought to leave now as soon as possible.

HEIMER: I'm waiting for a message about transportation. Should be here any time now. What was that about our Russian colleague interrupting you?

BAHRU: (*Rising.*) It is because she is madly in love with this young man, Christopher. (*He moves and sits on the balustrade.*)

HEIMER: I'll say she is. And you've got to hand it to that girl, Bahru. Once she found out about love, she found it

out in a big way. Ever since the first night here – and
what happened then is anybody's guess – she's just been
floating around starry-eyed. If the boys in the Kremlin
knew half of it, they'd have her off this Foreign Trade
Commission, and serving hash in a truck-drivers'
canteen before you could say vodka.

BAHRU: (*Seriously.*) She would certainly be in trouble,
I think. Therefore, I shall say nothing about this.

HEIMER: Hell – no – we'd all better make up our minds
to say nothing about anything. Check?

BAHRU: Yes. We must all agree to say nothing.

HEIMER: You bet. (*He pauses and broods.*)

BAHRU: (*Dreamily.*) Once I am away from here, I shall feel
differently. But there is something here…

HEIMER: It's like I said that first night. We're wandering
around in a midsummer night's dream. You remember?
Oh, no, you'd gone to bed.

BAHRU: (*Dreamily.*) Yes – I had gone to bed, and afterwards
I heard the nightingale singing in the moonlight – and in
the morning there was a pale gold sunlight among the
roses. It was different – yet I remembered how my wife
and I, not long after we were married, had spent our days
in an old garden among the foothills of Kashmir.

HEIMER: (*After a pause; with a sudden effort.*) Here, let's
snap out of this. (*He rises.*) We got business to attend to.
(*He eases centre.*)

BAHRU: (*Rising.*) Yes, certainly, Mr Heimer. (*He crosses to
the T-V-Com.*) Shall I try the T-V-Com again?

HEIMER: Why not? Wait a minute, though – what about
the time?

BAHRU: Mr Heimer, it shows how stupid I am becoming
here in this place. Why – it must have been about eleven
o'clock at night in Singapore when I spoke to Dr
Rockfeller Chen. No wonder he was so impatient. I dare
not disturb him again now.

HEIMER: (*Moving to BAHRU.*) Well – let's see. (*He glances
at his watch.*) Yep. If I can get through to my chief – old
G. J. Copplestone – it'll be just about the middle of the
morning with him. That's fine.

(*BAHRU adjusts the controls of the T-V-Com.*)
Let's go ahead and try. Old G.J.'s got one of the finest
sets in America – so it ought to be okay at his end. Got
through to him all right when we were in Germany –
remember? Think you said you'd never met G.J., eh?

BAHRU: No, I have never met him. But I have often heard
of him, of course.

(*STEPHEN enters up left. He is smoking his pipe and stands
at the top of the steps.*)

HEIMER: Greatest manufacturer and seller of synthetic
products in the whole wide world. Must be worth close
on fifty million dollars – and is sitting right on top of
the heap – except that he can't eat, can't sleep, can't keep
a wife, and has quarrelled with all his three children. But
a man can't have everything – and after all he's got
plenty – yes, sir. About a quarter of the homes in North
America take old G.J.'s T-V news and entertainment
programmes. Likes to look after 'em himself too, to give
the people his philosophy of life.

STEPHEN: And what is his philosophy of life, Mr Heimer?

HEIMER: (*Turning.*) Oh – hello there, Mr Dawlish. We're
trying to get through to my chief – old G. J. Copplestone.

STEPHEN: Who gives millions and millions of people his
philosophy of life.

(*BAHRU sits on the bench left.*)

HEIMER: That's so.

STEPHEN: Well, what is his philosophy of life?

HEIMER: Well – it's a hundred-per-cent American. And
nothing highbrow about it. I guess you'd call it plain
thinking for decent plain folks.

STEPHEN: Plain thinking about what?

HEIMER: Oh – well – how to work – how to spend your
dollars – how to raise a family – how to live. The old
man's mighty fond of giving advice.

STEPHEN: (*Coming down the steps and sitting on the
balustrade; dryly.*) We old men are. It's a weakness of mine
too, though I only do it in one home, where they can
always tell me to shut up. And I'd say that your Mr

Copplestone is still dishing out more than his fair share
of advice. However…

(*BAHRU switches on the T-V-Com. There are flickerings on
the screen and the set crackles.*)

BAHRU: We are getting through, I think, Mr Heimer.

HEIMER: (*Picking up the microphone.*) Excuse me, Mr
Dawlish. (*Into the microphone.*) Franklyn Heimer for
Mr G. J. Copplestone. Franklyn Heimer for Mr G. J.
Copplestone. Full person-to-person call – Number One
Priority. Franklyn Heimer for Mr Copplestone. Full
person-to-person call – Number One Priority. Yes,
Franklyn Heimer here.

(*Morse signals come from the T-V-Com. BAHRU adjusts the
controls.*)

(*To BAHRU.*) Hold it now, G.J.'s coming through. There's
his signal.

(*A flickering image of a thin, miserable, angry elderly American
appears on the screen.*)

Franklyn here, G.J.

COPPLESTONE: (*Angrily.*) Can't see you properly. Can't
hear you properly.

HEIMER: Sorry, G.J. We had a little accident here in
England – G.J.…

COPPLESTONE: Never mind England. Get over to
Sweden tonight – then back here tomorrow night. Get
busy. Don't loiter.

HEIMER: (*Apologetically.*) Now, look – G.J.…

COPPLESTONE: Don't interrupt. No time. Need you here.
Joe Steinberg's had another nervous breakdown. I've had
young Wardle sent back to that alcoholics' camp. Elmer's
down with ulcers again. There's no dam' co-operation
round here. Get started – but take in the Swedes tonight.
And get a grip on yourself, Franklyn – you're slipping.

HEIMER: (*Desperately.*) Now – just a minute G.J. You want
to know about this British set-up…

COPPLESTONE: Chickenfeed. Don't bother me with that.
My blood pressure's up again. American Synthetic
Products stands to win or lose fifteen million in the next
week. Think big for once…

HEIMER: (*Suddenly exasperated.*) Think big about what, you old crackpot? (*He is appalled by what he has said. To BAHRU.*) Switch it off – for Pete's sake – switch if off. (*He puts the microphone down.*)
(*BAHRU switches off the T-V-Com, HEIMER steps back exhausted and mops his forehead.*)

BAHRU: (*Solemnly.*) Mr Heimer, I am afraid he heard you.

STEPHEN: (*Chuckling.*) I hope he did.

HEIMER: (*Ruefully.*) Well – I guess it had to come out. It's not so bad at that. He wasn't receiving the call too well, and if he remembers what I said, I'll swear the set was so lousy he mistook what I was saying. But – boy! – I never talked to the old man like that before.

STEPHEN: (*Chuckling.*) Perhaps he was right, Mr Heimer – and you are slipping. But there's one consolation.

HEIMER: What's that?

STEPHEN: You're not suffering yet from a nervous breakdown, delirium tremens, ulcers, or a high blood pressure. (*With a kind of mischievous dreaminess.*) And it looks like being a lovely evening.

BAHRU: (*Rising and moving up the steps.*) Excuse me, please.

STEPHEN: (*Gravely.*) Certainly, Dr Bahru. But one question first – if you don't mind.

BAHRU: (*Pausing and turning.*) Of course.

STEPHEN: You're not feeling very happy about this business of yours, are you?

BAHRU: (*Gravely.*) No, Mr Dawlish, I am not. Excuse me. (*He turns and exits up left. STEPHEN looks at HEIMER, who is staring at him.*)

STEPHEN: Yes?

HEIMER: I'm going to say this for the last time, Mr Dawlish, I can fix it with the Corporation so that you can get a whole heap of dollars for the use of your land here. We're not trying to cheat you. And with any luck I ought to be able to get you enough so that you can go where you like and live as you like. And what's wrong with that?

STEPHEN: Everything. We can't buy anywhere what you want to destroy here. You can't go shopping for a good

life. You have to live it. And it's far better to be versatile
– to go from the field to the book, the desk to the
workshop.

HEIMER: That's no way to get to the top.

STEPHEN: There isn't a top, so it's no use racing to find it.

HEIMER: (*Sitting on the steps.*) It looks to me as if you're
settling down to small-time and small-town stuff.

STEPHEN: Nearly as small as the Florence of Leonardo
and the London of Shakespeare and Bacon, Mr Heimer.
But you've met some of our young folks. What's wrong
with 'em? Oh – I know – they haven't got this, they can't
get that. But – Mr Heimer – look me in the eye – and
tell me – *what's wrong with 'em?*

HEIMER: (*Slowly.*) I'll admit it, Mr Dawlish. There isn't
one gol-darned thing wrong with 'em.

STEPHEN: (*Softly.*) And now you want to shove 'em into
the ovens and ash-cans of your G. J. Copplestone...

HEIMER: (*Rising; angrily.*) No, I don't.

STEPHEN: What do you want, then?

HEIMER: (*Moving to the bench down left and taking a cigar
from his pocket.*) I want to smoke this cigar – and think.
(*He sits.*) Hell! You've got me going round in circles. (*He
lights his cigar and broods.*)
(*CHRIS and IRINA enter down right. They saunter on,
smiling and dreamy. HEIMER, brooding, ignores them, but
STEPHEN surveys them smilingly.*)

STEPHEN: Been down to the big barn?

CHRIS: (*Easing centre.*) Yes.

STEPHEN: How much work did you do?

CHRIS: (*Sitting on the plinth right centre.*) Not much.

IRINA: (*Moving close to CHRIS; happily.*) He is very lazy.
I do more work than he does. He is thinking of his
music for tonight.

STEPHEN: (*Gently.*) Come here, my dear, and let's have a
good look at you.
(*IRINA moves to right of STEPHEN.*)
(*He looks up at her, smiling, and takes her hand.*) My dear,
when you came here, you were a handsome woman. Now

you're a beautiful woman. If my heart wasn't so old and tough – if it was only ten years younger – why, you could take it and break it.

IRINA: (*Shyly.*) Thank you. You promised at the very first, you remember, if I stayed – to put roses in my cheeks.

STEPHEN: (*Softly and half-sadly.*) Yes, my dear, but not that blue moonlight in your eyes.

(*IRINA turns her face away, meets CHRIS's eyes, and they stare at each other for a moment. STEPHEN does not look at them, but it is obvious he is aware of them.*)

HEIMER: (*Exasperated in thought.*) Hell's bells – I dunno.

CHRIS: (*Amused.*) What's the matter, Mr Heimer?

STEPHEN: (*Quickly.*) No, no, Christopher – leave him alone. He wants to think. He's been talking to his boss.

(*IRINA breaks down right.*)

(*To IRINA. Softly.*) You'll have to be putting on that uniform of yours again soon, Madame Shestova.

(*IRINA does not speak, but her distress shows in her face, and CHRIS, noticing this, makes haste to cut in.*)

CHRIS: (*Rising; protestingly.*) Grandfather. (*He moves to right of IRINA.*) Irina knows. It's cruel to remind her...

IRINA: (*Moving to the broken column; embarrassed and distressed.*) Christopher – please say nothing. (*She sits on the broken column, facing right.*)

(*CHRIS sits on the wheel-barrow.*)

STEPHEN: (*Impressively.*) My boy, there are times when a man must speak plain words –

(*BAHRU and MARGARET enter up left.*)

– even though they may seem to some of his listeners as sharp and cruel as knives. They may be the knives of the surgeon.

(*BAHRU moves down left. MARGARET stands by the door up left.*)

Ah – Dr Bahru – did you hear what I said?

BAHRU: (*Uneasily.*) Yes, Mr Dawlish. It is true, of course. There are such times – such words.

STEPHEN: (*Rather grimly.*) There are. But – you are still feeling uneasy.

BAHRU: (*Moving left of STEPHEN: hotly and excitedly.*)
Forgive me, Mr Dawlish – but this is not fair. It is hard
for one man, no matter how good his training may have
been, to conquer at once three thousand years of
superstition based on ignorance. (*He breaks down right.*)
And Mrs Dawlish knows this.

MARGARET: (*Interrupting; coolly.*) I have never been to
India. The only superstition based on ignorance
I understand, in this argument between us, is the
superstition based on ignorance that Dr Bahru's training
has given him.

BAHRU: (*Sharply.*) That is not true. I am sorry – but...

STEPHEN: (*Rising; interrupting, weightily.*) All right, Dr
Bahru. Let us say it isn't true. Let's assume – though
nothing could be more dangerous, in my experience –
that my daughter-in-law doesn't know what she is
talking about, (*He moves up the steps and stands right of
MARGARET.*) being only a dreamy, fanciful, half-
educated woman...

BAHRU: (*Hastily interrupting.*) I never said that.

STEPHEN: (*Moving down the steps; sternly.*) Please, Dr Bahru.
I am trying to give you the largest possible benefit of the
doubt.
(*ROSALIE enters up left and stands on the steps, leaning
against the wall left.*)
(*He addresses himself to all three visitors, carefully and
forcefully.*) Let it apply to all of us here. Rosalie is another
fanciful creature, young and ignorant, who doesn't know
what the world is like. And Christopher there is only a
musical farmer in an obscure corner of a forgotten
island. And I am an old man in his broken-down
mansion that is now only an impoverished farmhouse.
There – will that do? We are all, as Mr Heimer has told
us, small-time people...

HEIMER: (*Coming out of his reverie to protest.*) Now – look –
Mr Dawlish...

STEPHEN: (*Turning to HEIMER.*) No, sir, you will have
your opportunity soon, but this is mine. All right, we are
all small-time people – survivors from a wreck, from the

war of split atoms and split minds – who crawled out of the darkness into the daylight. A dark clutter of rubbish was cleared away for us. Now you come to dump the rubbish back on us again. For what? There is not one of you three who knows. We don't ask you to live as we do. Live as you please – and take the consequences. But who are *you* to come here and tell *us* how to live? Look at you now...

CHRIS: (*Rising; protesting.*) Grandfather, they are still our guests...

STEPHEN: (*Interrupting; sternly.*) I am not talking to them now as guests. They came here in another capacity, and now propose to act in that capacity. (*To the visitors.*) I say – look at you now. The rulers of the world, ready to shape our lives to your pattern. (*He pauses and moves to right of IRINA.*) One of you trembling before the endless tears begin to flow –

(*IRINA turns and faces front.*)

– one of you shouting the nonsense of his student days, to try to quieten a warning voice that is his and not ours. (*BAHRU sits on the plinth right centre.*)

(*He looks at HEIMER.*) The other frustrated, angry and helpless...

HEIMER: (*Excitedly protesting.*) If you mean me...

STEPHEN: (*Interrupting; gently.*) Yes, I mean you, Mr Heimer. And I'm not trying to be offensive. I like you. (*He turns and moves up the steps.*) But let's have no further argument. I'm too old for it. Too old for any more changes. I can only hope that the first excavator of yours that bites into these Downs will take my bones between its teeth. (*He turns abruptly and exits up left.*)

(*There is a long pause.*)

ROSALIE: (*Quietly.*) There isn't any more to say. There's your machine. Tell it to set all the other machines into motion. Hurry up, Mr Heimer – you must be wasting valuable time.

HEIMER: (*After a pause.*) Nobody knows but us whether that T-V-Com's working or not. We can stall on that. And we don't know yet when we can get away from here.

MARGARET: (*Calmly.*) You will know quite soon.

HEIMER: Why – have you heard something?

MARGARET: Yes – in my own way. Though Dr Bahru would say that is quite impossible – mere ignorance and superstition.

BAHRU: No, please – this is something quite different.

HEIMER: All the same, I doubt it.

(*FRED enters down right.*)

CHRIS: I wouldn't if I were you. (*He turns to FRED.*) What is it, Fred?

FRED: (*Crossing to HEIMER.*) It's a message for Mr Heimer. (*He takes a note from his pocket.*) Came to the post office – and Margery Briggs asked me to bring it up. (*He hands the note to HEIMER.*)

(*HEIMER rises and reads the note. FRED moves to the door up left and exits.*)

HEIMER: Transport. We move off tonight – to make the airport in the morning.

(*IRINA rises and stands facing up stage.*)

They're sending an atomicar from Shrewsbury, and it ought to be here between eleven and twelve tonight. (*He resumes his seat on the bench left.*) So – that's that.

CHRIS: (*Moving to IRINA; eagerly.*) Irina...

IRINA: (*Turning to CHRIS; firmly.*) No, please, Christopher. Afterwards – soon – we can talk, but now I must talk with Mr Heimer and Dr Bahru.

MARGARET: Come on, Christopher – Rosalie.

ROSALIE: (*Moving to the door up left: warningly.*) Mr Heimer.

HEIMER: (*Almost groaning.*) I know, I know.

(*MARGARET, ROSALIE and CHRIS exit up left. IRINA turns to HEIMER. HEIMER rises and moves in left of IRINA. BAHRU rises and moves in right of IRINA. The atmosphere is weighty, and there is a pause.*)

(*Uneasily.*) Well – here it is.

IRINA: (*Gravely.*) I should like to speak first, if you please.

HEIMER: Go ahead.

IRINA: You will soon see why I wish to speak first. For you two this affair of the chalk here is simply a matter of business. For me it is something different, more serious. Not because the chalk is really important to us Russians – I think it is not – but because I am a Russian official here on an official duty. And if it should be discovered that I have not carried out my duty properly – the result would be very serious for me. Even if it should not be discovered, I would wish to resign from the Commission...

HEIMER: (*Interrupting.*) Now wait. Let's put a few cards on the table. You and this boy Christopher are crazy about each other – aren't you?

IRINA: (*Very quietly.*) Yes. We are in love.

HEIMER: Okay. Then why go back to Russia at all? Why don't you stay here?

IRINA: That is not possible. There is a very strict rule against it. I would be sent back. There might be trouble too for my family.

BAHRU: That is true.

HEIMER: Too bad.

IRINA: (*Proudly.*) Besides, that is not how I wish to behave. I am not afraid to ask permission to retire, but I will not hide and tell lies. I am a woman, yes – with all a woman's feelings, but I am also a good citizen of my state – proud of being a Russian.

HEIMER: (*Easing down left.*) Well, that's up to you. Now you've made the point that this business of ours is all very serious for you, because you're a Soviet official on duty. So what, Madame Shestova?

BAHRU: (*Gloomily.*) She is reminding me that we must not weaken now, whatever we may be feeling.

HEIMER: (*Irritably.*) All right – who wants to weaken? I know my duty as well as you folks do.

BAHRU: Yes, yes, Mr Heimer. I was not suggesting you didn't. We are all agreed upon what we must do.

HEIMER: (*Gloomily irritable.*) Okay – okay – we're all agreed – so you two needn't go on and on about it.

IRINA: (*Urgently.*) No, no, you do not understand.
(*BAHRU and HEIMER stare at her.*)

(*Quietly.*) That is why I wished to speak first – to show you what I feel, although I take so much the greater risk. (*She pauses, then looks gravely from one to the other.*) Mr Heimer – Dr Bahru – we cannot bring unhappiness to these people. Let us leave them as we found them. The decision rests with us. You have not yet made your report, Dr Bahru?

BAHRU: No, not yet.

IRINA: And you, Mr Heimer. You spoke to America – to your Corporation?

HEIMER: Yep. But I wasn't allowed to say anything. Too busy taking orders – get to Sweden – then get back home.

IRINA: (*Brightly.*) Then let us say we cannot make our synthetic substances here.

BAHRU: (*Moving right and turning.*) My early report was favourable, but that doesn't matter. The final decision rests with Mr Heimer.

(*There is a pause. HEIMER turns and moves thoughtfully on to the steps. BAHRU and IRINA both look anxiously at him. After a few moments he turns with a completely blank face, then a slow grin lights up his features.*)

HEIMER: Okay – let's leave 'em as we found 'em.

(*IRINA moves to the balustrade, sits on it and starts to cry softly to herself.*)

(*He crosses to BAHRU. Decisively.*) We'll get through to the Corporation again – and I'll pass the word along to old G.J. and the boys that I'm moving out tonight and flying in the morning – and that there's nothing doing here. The stuff's not too promising – the conditions aren't right – and the natives are hostile. Let's get going with the T-V-Com.

(*BAHRU crosses to the T-V-Com. HEIMER moves to right of IRINA and pats her shoulder.*)

Don't cry. Don't cry. Everything's going to be fine. (*He moves to BAHRU at the T-V-Com.*)

IRINA: (*Through her tears.*) Yes. Everything's *going* to be fine. (*She is still crying quietly as the curtain falls.*)

Scene 2

Scene – the same, Night. The same day.

When the house lights are lowered and a few moments before the curtain rises, soft music is heard coming from backstage. It is an oboe and violin duet, has an English pastoral feeling and great tenderness. It can be heard clearly but rather distantly, and it should be so presented to the audience that they feel it is an essential part of the scene before them, but not itself a performance. Sufficient time should be allowed for the audience to be quiet, and the music continues during the opening speeches of the scene.

When the curtain rises, the scene is lit by soft but fairly bright moonlight, coming from the front. There is a dim light coming from behind the open door up left. MARGARET is leaning against the pillar right of the steps, listening to the music. After a few moments, FRED enters up left. He carries three suitcases, moves quietly down left and places them on the ground against the bench. He then turns and speaks quietly with MARGARET. Their voices must however cut clearly through the music.

MARGARET: (*In a slow easy tone.*) Is everything there, Fred?

FRED: Everything that was left at the top of the stairs, as you said.

MARGARET: They'll be ready to go, then, as soon as the car comes for them?

FRED: (*Moving to the steps and sitting on them left of MARGARET.*) Yes. Back to where they came from, And not going to do us any harm after all. D'ye hear me give a cheer when they told us?
(*There is a pause, during which the music, very softly now, can be heard. They listen to it and stare out at the night.*)
Beautiful night, Mrs Dawlish.

MARGARET: (*Dreamily.*) It has a bloom on it like a ripe plum. A lovely summer night with the moon at full, and everything made of blue silk, dark green velvet, and silver – and all so gentle and calm.

FRED: That's it. Rests a man just to look at it.

MARGARET: In the daytime when you're so busy and the light's so sharp, and the clocks are ticking in your ears, only the living are real and alive, and the dead are dead-and-gone and more than half-forgotten. But while I was standing here, listening to the music, I remembered them all, and then they weren't dead-and-gone, but all here, very close, listening as I was.

FRED: (*After a pause.*) We don't know very much – for certain, do we?

MARGARET: (*Slowly.*) No, Fred, we don't know very much. And the best knowledge we have is in our hearts and not in our heads. I think that's something we're beginning to understand again. Our hearts are older and wiser than our heads.

(*The music fades slowly out and ceases.*)

FRED: When I was young we were a cocky lot – thought we knew everything – and sat about in air raid shelters proving it. But we had a lesson or two coming to us.

(*There is a faint flash of white light off right.*)

MARGARET: (*Looking off right.*) What's that?

FRED: (*Looking off right.*) Did you see something?

MARGARET: Yes, a great white light flashing in the valley.

FRED: (*Rising.*) Where?

MARGARET: (*Pointing off right.*) It's lost among the trees.

(*The light flashes faintly again.*)

There you are.

FRED: (*Crossing to right.*) That'll be the car that's been sent for 'em. It's about time for it. They'll be twisting and turning down by Five Lanes – trying to find this house. I'd better go down. Everybody in the village'll be in bed and asleep now.

MARGARET: Go on then, Fred.

(*FRED exits down right. The light flashes again and MARGARET stands for a few moments staring off right. ROSALIE and HEIMER enter up left.*)

ROSALIE: You should have listened to the music.

MARGARET: I heard it out here. It came out into the wide night for me. Look at the light down there – turning and flashing among the lanes.

(*The light flashes faintly again off right.*)

ROSALIE: (*Moving down the steps to right centre and gazing off right.*) It's the rolling eyeball of a great beast, angry and blind.

HEIMER: Maybe. But I'll bet it's our transportation – looking for us.

MARGARET: That's what Fred thinks. He's just gone down to direct them here.

ROSALIE: Glaring and lost – that's what it is. And that's what you'll be soon, Mr Heimer.

HEIMER: Now I'll tell you something. For all my big talk about camps an' finishing an' a boy's long afternoons, about taking it easy an' relaxing with you folks, I want to be on the move again, to go places, to tear right into the job, to get some action, and maybe find a tough fight or two on my hands. And I say – that's a man's life.

MARGARET: (*Moving down the steps to centre.*) It's one kind of man's life. And I like a fighter myself.

ROSALIE: (*Rather shocked.*) Aunt Margaret!

HEIMER: (*Moving down the steps to right of MARGARET; delighted.*) Why – say – Mrs Dawlish – I could kiss you for that.

MARGARET: (*Demurely.*) Well, Mr Heimer, seeing that you're leaving us... (*She lifts her face to him.*)

HEIMER: (*Delighted.*) No fooling?

(*ROSALIE watches them with amusement. HEIMER gives MARGARET a hearty kiss, which she accepts demurely.*)
(*He turns triumphantly to ROSALIE.*) What do you know about that?

ROSALIE: You're getting out of hand now that your famous transportation has nearly arrived. All right – go places and get some Action. But don't try and make other people run away from themselves. Don't choke them with your dust.

HEIMER: (*Turning to ROSALIE; wonderingly and half-humorously.*) Beats me why I have to take all this from you. You're only a kid. You've been nowhere. You've done nothing. But I let you bawl me out as if you were my grandmother and they'd just given you the Nobel Prize. Will anybody tell my why?

MARGARET: (*Turning and moving up the steps.*) I must see if anything's wanted in the house. (*She turns.*) But I'll tell you why, Mr Heimer. Any girl is old enough to talk to you like a grandmother, because the way you like to behave, tearing about and plotting and being important about things that don't really matter – puts you at about ten or eleven years old.

HEIMER: (*Humorously indignant.*) Whoa – steady.

MARGARET: (*Smiling.*) Little boys of that age are delightful – in their place. (*She turns and exits up left.*) (*ROSALIE and HEIMER are silent a moment, looking out at the night.*)

HEIMER: (*Sitting on the steps; sighing.*) Certainly is a swell night.

ROSALIE: It certainly is.

HEIMER: Shall I tell you something – the real truth about myself?

ROSALIE: (*Easing to the balustrade.*) I wish you would.

HEIMER: Don't get me wrong, Rosalie. When I've talked about duty and responsibility and doing a big job for the hell of it, I've meant what I said.

ROSALIE: (*Sitting on the balustrade.*) Yes, I know you have.

HEIMER: (*Slowly and confidentially.*) But there's something else – that's kept me on the run, brought me a couple of million dollars, made me one of the chief executives of one of the biggest businesses in the world. It's the hollow place in the middle.

ROSALIE: (*Puzzled.*) The hollow place?

HEIMER: Right bang in the middle of things – a hollow place – just where there ought to be something lasting and good. You get through to it, and there's nothing but a tray full of cigarette butts, empty bottles, stale sandwiches, fellows yawning over the last story, some woman giving you one of their queer looks, cold daylight coming round the curtains, a hangover, and just a dead hollow place where there ought to have been something. You give it one look – and – hell! You're on the run again.

ROSALIE: Because you think that next time it will be better.

HEIMER: Check. So next time you come back with a bigger deal all tied up, with everything bigger and brighter and better, and you think that there you'll be – the happy boy, leading the life of Reilly. But no. Sooner or later the party won't stay alive, the liquor gives out or turns to acid in your guts, all the women look fat and sleepy or thin and angry, and – hell's bells – there it is again, the dead cold hollow place in the middle. You think it's New York that's doing it, so you try California. Then you think it's the coast that's wrong, so you try the desert or the mountains. Then you go back to the old hometown, and the real folks, but it's there waiting for you just the same – the big dead spot, the ashcan a thousand miles deep where nothing moves, nothing grows, nothing lives. (*He pauses. Almost angrily.*) You don't know what I'm talking about, but wait till you're older.

ROSALIE: I am older.

HEIMER: (*Almost angrily.*) And that's another thing – the way the women take it. They look at you as if it's all your fault, as if it had nothing to do with them, as if you'd promised them something different and had fallen down on it. What's the matter with 'em, anyway?

ROSALIE: I can't tell you. Or perhaps they're feeling what one of our English poets felt when he wrote: 'I, a stranger and afraid, in a world I never made.'

HEIMER: That poet should have stopped bellyaching and gone out and started making the world. That's what we've done, haven't we?

ROSALIE: Have you?

HEIMER: Now you're giving me just the same kind of look. Oh, I get you. If we think we've made our world, then what are we beefing about? Well, I never pretended to know all the answers. (*He pauses, then looks at her.*) What are *you* thinking about, young Rosalie?

ROSALIE: There was a moment tonight, when Christopher was playing, when it was as if we had all broken through into a larger and different sort of time, like that of a clear happy dream. Everybody there was so completely and wonderfully themselves – and everything, from the light on a hand to the shadows on the wall, was so inevitable and satisfying and right – that my heart nearly burst with joy.

HEIMER: (*Wonderingly.*) I was in that...?

ROSALIE: Yes, of course. We were all in it.

HEIMER: And all right and happy?

ROSALIE: We were more than that. We were like demi-gods. We sat by the fountains of wonder and glory. (*She pauses for a moment, looking at the night.*) Now of course it's different. A curtain has come down. Soon we shall be dwarfs shouting good-bye – midgets waving under the cold moon.

(*They sit in silence for a few moments, then MARGARET, BAHRU and STEPHEN enter up left. ROSALIE and HEIMER rise.*)

BAHRU: (*As he enters.*) Here, it is small and almost empty of people, and there is room for your charming and poetical fancies. (*He moves down the steps and crosses to right.*) But my country is vast and contains hundreds and hundreds of millions of people not very different from myself, and without science, I should go mad.

(*STEPHEN leans against the wall left at the top of the steps. MARGARET eases centre. ROSALIE moves up the steps and stands right of them at the top. HEIMER eases right of the balustrade.*)

Or else I would persuade myself, as our religious men used to do, that none of it is real, all an illusion, a dream.

MARGARET: (*Smiling.*) Then you return to your science and leave me to my fancies, as you call them. And one of them is that we men and women are part of a great procession of beings, many of them infinitely stronger and wiser and more beautiful than we are.

BAHRU: But where are they – these beings? I cannot touch them. I cannot hear them. I cannot see them.

MARGARET: (*Sitting on the plinth right centre.*) How many insects are there in your jungles that know anything about the Chemical Research Department of the South Asia Federation?

BAHRU: It is not the same thing. Mr Dawlish – I appeal to you...

STEPHEN: Don't appeal to me. I ought to be in bed, and if I'm to be kept up talking, then I'll choose my own topics.

HEIMER: (*Chuckling.*) You're a character.

STEPHEN: (*Sitting at the top of the steps, at the left end of them.*) Of course I'm a character. And when I was your age and as busy as you are, I was a pretty bad character. It's only since I've become an old man of the ruins I'm turning into a good character. But I'll say this, Dr Bahru, I'm not in favour of taking away your test-tubes and retorts, and I'm equally not in favour of bullying Margaret out of her angels and goddesses. Help yourself, I say – the world of ideas and images is rich enough, so take what you need out of it. (*He pauses.*) Where's this car that's coming for you important persons?

HEIMER: (*Pointing off right.*) Down there somewhere, I guess.

ROSALIE: If you look, you'll see a great glaring light. (*She sits on the steps, right of STEPHEN.*)

STEPHEN: I don't want to see a great glaring light. I've seen too many already. What I'd like to see is the small and quiet illumination of wisdom.

MARGARET: You are too impatient to see it.

STEPHEN: Don't lecture me, woman, but instruct the visitors, who are about to go.

BAHRU: (*Crossing HEIMER and sitting on the downstage end of the balustrade.*) And go – as friends.

MARGARET: But of course, Dr Bahru.

HEIMER: I'm not going to forget this in a hurry. And Mrs Heimer and the girls are going to hear about you folks.

STEPHEN: Well, come back here when you can. You too, Dr Bahru. Come in Spring when the primroses are out. Come in Autumn when the apples are ripe. We'll have a bit of magic ready for you whenever you come.

HEIMER: (*Sitting on the upstage end of the balustrade.*) I'll bet.

STEPHEN: And in the meantime, gentlemen, accept our thanks. And God be with you.

MARGARET: You don't know anything about God.

STEPHEN: I've never pretended to, my dear. But man is a god-worshipping creature, and if he doesn't choose to worship a mysterious universal power of goodness and love, then he'll find something else – and something much worse – to adore. The State, which is about as sensible as making a god out of the local gasworks. Business, which asks you to adore dividends and bank balances. Science, which means that a man's mind worships one bit of itself – idiotic. Or the Devil himself, who can easily masquerade as God.

BAHRU: But there is no devil.

STEPHEN: (*Rising; in a sharp ringing tone.*) Stupidity and Pride, booted and spurred in power, are the Devil – and for sixty years I watched his temples and instruments multiply, until a thousand cities vanished in flame and dust, and a hundred million bodies were consumed in agony upon his altar.

(*From off right there is a rushing Sound, suggesting a very fast, powerful vehicle, and there is a great white glare, like a searchlight. They all rise and turn towards the light. ROSALIE gives a sharp little scream. Then a harsh voice, much amplified, is heard speaking off.*)

VOICE: (*Off right.*) All right, folks. Ready when you are. Let's go.

STEPHEN: (*Quietly.*) Don't be alarmed. It's only civilisation catching up with us again.

(*FRED enters down right.*)

Is that you, Fred?

FRED: (*As he enters.*) Yes, Mr Dawlish, I came up with the car.

STEPHEN: All right, Fred, Tell Madame Shestova and Christopher that the car is here.

(*FRED crosses to the door up left and exits.*)

HEIMER: (*Moving down left; heartily.*) Well, this is it. We've got all the baggage out here, I guess.

BAHRU: (*Picking up two suitcases.*) Yes, the baggage is here.

HEIMER: (*Picking up the third suitcase.*) It's tough luck on those two. We ought to leave 'em alone a minute. Whichever way they work it – might be quite a time before they can meet again.

MARGARET: (*Calmly but impressively.*) They will not meet again for thousands of years.

ROSALIE: (*Shocked.*) Oh – Margaret.

STEPHEN: (*Dryly.*) Well – it'll seem like thousands of years – so we'll leave it at that. Come along. Have you got everything, Mr Heimer?

HEIMER: Yes, *sir.* Every little thing.

(*MARGARET, followed by BAHRU and HEIMER, moves down right.*)

ROSALIE: What about this T-V-Com thing?

HEIMER: We're leaving the T-V-Com for you to play with.

(*ROSALIE moves down right. MARGARET, followed by ROSALIE, exits down right.*)

STEPHEN: (*Moving down right.*) Well, that's an idea, I might call up your friend Copplestone from time to time – and give him our local news – hay looking good – corn harvest promising. One or two nice girls getting married – nobody down with ulcers or delirium tremens.

(*BAHRU, followed by HEIMER, exits down right. STEPHEN follows them off, chuckling. As he goes CHRIS and IRINA enter slowly up left. IRINA has changed into her uniform. They stand on the steps for a moment, looking off right, then they turn to each other.*)

VOICE: (*Off right.*) Ready when you are. All set. Let's go.

(*The bright light right swings away and goes out.*)

IRINA: (*Quietly.*) It is only the driver of the car.

CHRIS: (*Quietly.*) No, it isn't. It's hell-on-earth, and in a moment it will swallow you, my darling, my love, and then it will have swallowed the best of me, too. Lost. Gone.

IRINA: (*Very quietly and carefully.*) Everything that has happened between us – the smallest thing – every look you have given – every word you have spoken, my darling – the bird singing in the moonlight – the sun among the leaves – everything – I have safely here in my heart. (*She turns away with a heartbroken little laugh.*) They are my rations, I must live on them a long time.

CHRIS: (*Urgently.*) No, we shall meet again soon – somehow.

IRINA: (*Moving down the steps to centre.*) Please, my darling, we have said all these things. It is too late to begin again now. (*She turns to him.*) I love you.

VOICE: (*Off right.*) Madame Shestova. Let's get going. We're behind time.

(*CHRIS moves down the steps to left of IRINA.*)

IRINA: (*Through her tears.*) It is you and I who have been behind time. And I shall always be there with you – for ever and ever. (*She turns and runs to the exit down right.*) Good-bye. (*She turns and exits hurriedly.*)

(*CHRIS starts to follow her.*)

CHRIS: (*With a cry of despairing appeal.*) Irina.

IRINA: (*Off; calling.*) Good-bye.

CHRIS: (*Moving to the exit down right.*) Irina. (*He suddenly checks himself and stands staring, lost.*)

(*FRED enters up left and moves down the steps to centre. The rushing sound off right re-commences. The bright light swings on to the stage, then begins to move slowly off as if the car were moving. A confused and rather distant sound of good-byes is heard off. The rushing sound increases for a moment, then diminishes and fades out with the light.*)

FRED: (*Sympathetically.*) Christopher – lad…

CHRIS: (*Turning slowly.*) Yes, Fred?

FRED: Wouldn't you like a drink – or a bite to eat?

CHRIS: No, thanks, Fred. Not now. Later perhaps.

FRED: It's quite late now.

CHRIS: I'd like to be alone, Fred. If the others are coming in at once, then I'll clear out. If they're not, then I'll go in.

FRED: You ought to play something.

CHRIS: (*Moving to the door up left rather dazed.*) Yes, Fred, perhaps I ought to play something.

(*He exits up left. As he does so, STEPHEN and ROSALIE enter down right.*)

189

STEPHEN: Where's Christopher?

FRED: He's just gone in. He wants to be by himself – poor lad.

STEPHEN: (*Moving and sitting on the balustrade.*) I'll wait a minute, though I ought to have been in bed hours ago. (*ROSALIE crosses and sits on the steps. FRED eases up right of the balustrade. MARGARET enters down right, crosses, moves up the steps and leans against the pillar at the right end of them.*)

FRED: (*After a pause.*) I never said good-bye properly to them three – and I got to like 'em in the end – and now I don't suppose I'll ever see 'em again.
(*The music of CHRIS's violin, played very softly, is heard off up left, and blends with the speeches. There is a feeling of wide night, tranquillity and tenderness, with the voices floating out easily.*)

MARGARET: (*Slowly and dreamily.*) I think you will see two of them again. They will come back just as friends, drawn by some sense of loss.

ROSALIE: (*Sadly.*) But not Irina, you said… I saw her face in the car and already it was frozen white, lost in a long winter.

FRED: What is it politicians have got that's more important than a young fellow and his girl loving each other like that?

STEPHEN: (*Grimly.*) Nothing – nothing. And I wish the wreck of war had been wider still, so that every seat of power had been torn down. (*He pauses.*) There is an old tried pattern, a faded map, offering some chance of happiness, and still they pay men to rule thick lines across it.

ROSALIE: After that horrible dazzling light everything seemed dark at first, but now I can see again. The night has closed behind them without a scar, and every tree is like a candle burning in a quiet room.
(*The music fades out.*)

STEPHEN: I see the hawthorn that the Roman stared at – and soon I shall have gone with the Roman – leaving the green old tavern of the world.

MARGARET: We are nourished by this planet's clay and the flame that comes from beyond the stars.

STEPHEN: And I have lived long enough to understand at last that what is neither clay nor flame, neither Earth nor Spirit, can only leave us famished and frustrated. (*He pauses.*) Send down your roots and lift your faces to the sun and stars.

(*MARGARET moves down the steps and stares intently out, as if at the audience, The lights start to fade.*)

What is it, Margaret? What do you see?

MARGARET: (*Clearly and slowly, with her voice fading as the light fades.*)

A thousand eyes narrowing to watch us here,

Eyes that may never reach this time we show,

But see us as so many shadows on the *wall*...

(*The music re-commences softly, and as the last glimmer of light hesitates a moment – the curtain slowly falls.*)

The End.

THE GLASS CAGE

Characters

JOHN HARVEY

MILDRED McBANE
his aunt

MALCOLM McBANE
Mildred's brother-in-law

ELSPIE McBANE
David's daughter

BRIDGET
the housekeeper

DR EDWARD GRATTON

DAVID McBANE
Malcolm's brother

JEAN McBANE
David's niece

DOUGLAS McBANE
Jean's brother

ANGUS McBANE
Jean's brother

The Glass Cage was first produced at the Piccadilly Theatre, London, on the 26 April 1957, with the following cast:

JOHN HARVEY, William Job

MILDRED McBANE, Margot Christie

MALCOLM McBANE, William Needles

ELSPIE McBANE, Janet Reid

BRIDGET, Edna Pozer

DR EDWARD GRATTON, James Edmond

DAVID McBANE, Frank Peddie

JEAN McBANE, Barbara Chilcott

DOUGLAS McBANE, Murray Davis

ANGUS McBANE, Donald Davis

Director, Henry Kaplan

Setting, Hutchinson Scott

SYNOPSIS OF SCENES

The action of the play passes in the parlour of the McBane house in Toronto.

Act I	Scene 1: An evening in the year 1906.
	Scene 2: Evening, four days later.
Act II	Scene 1: Evening, five days later.
	Scene 2: Later that night.

ACT ONE

Scene 1

Scene – the parlour of the McBane house in Toronto. An evening in the year 1906.

It is a solidly-built, solidly and comfortably furnished parlour, obviously belonging to solid, comfortable people. There are double doors up left leading to the entrance hall and other parts of the house. There are ground-glass panelled folding doors right leading to a conservatory and thence to a newly-added big room. The room is amply and fussily furnished in the style of the period, but is not over-decorated. There is a couch right centre with a small circular table above it; a love-seat left; a settee up centre and a pouffe left centre. In the corner down right is a bookcase. Upright chairs stand down right and right and left of the hall doors. A potted palm stands on a pedestal down left. In the conservatory there is a table, an armchair and potted palms on stands. In the hall there is a settee. Heavy curtains drape the hall and conservatory doors. At night the room is lit by oil lamps, one on a pedestal down left, one on a pedestal up centre, one on the table centre, one on the bookcase down right and one on the table in the conservatory. A bell-cord hangs in the corner up centre.

When the curtain rises, it is not yet dark. The lamps are lit but turned low. MILDRED McBANE, ELSPIE McBANE and MALCOLM McBANE are seated cosily listening to JOHN HARVEY reading aloud. MILDRED is seated on the couch at the left end, working at some embroidery. She is a woman in her fifties, very English in type, rather grander socially than the others, a rather hard but brittle nervous woman. MALCOLM is seated on the downstage side of the love-seat, looking through a hand stereoscope. He is about fifty, a Scots-Canadian business man of the period, quietly well-dressed, apparently a sedate and rather finicky bachelor. ELSPIE is seated on the pouffe, darning. She is in her early twenties, a rather petite, fluffy blonde, very feminine. JOHN is seated below Mildred on the couch. He is in his middle twenties, well-built and good-looking, with a fine rich voice that he already likes the sound of, a theological student who will soon be a popular minister.

JOHN: (*Reading.*) 'The old Minister's secret was out at last, his heart hunger and unshed tears could now be understood. The village helper laid the sketches carefully back in the portfolio and tied a piece of white ribbon about the cover to prevent prying eyes from seeing the contents. And when the old minister, looking noble and majestic, lay in his coffin, she very gently placed the portfolio beside his pulseless heart. If you ever visit the village cemetery you cannot fail to see his grave.'
(*BRIDGET enters from the hall.*
DR EDWARD GRATTON follows her on. He is an Irish-Canadian, in his early sixties, a battered old G.P. He is carrying the familiar old black bag. He and BRIDGET stand by the door, listening.)
'It is the tallest white shaft there, and above the usual inscription, high up on the shaft, are the words – 'They shall hunger no more'.' (*He closes the book.*)
(*There is a moment's silence.*)

MILDRED: Thank you, John dear. It's a beautiful little story – and I'm sure you read it beautifully.
(*JOHN rises, moves to the bookcase down right, puts the book away, then stands behind the couch.*)

ELSPIE: (*Smiling at JOHN.*) Yes, you did, John.

BRIDGET: It's Dr Gratton – mum... (*She exits to the hall, closing the door.*)

MILDRED: (*Apologetically.*) Oh – Dr Gratton...

GRATTON: (*Moving to the table centre.*) I enjoyed the performance. (*He puts his bag on the table.*) And what would it be out of – this sad little tale?

ELSPIE: The book's called *Where the Maple Sugar Grows*. And you're not to be horrid about it.

GRATTON: I won't. I've a great respect for sugar of all kinds. (*To JOHN.*) Young man. You've a noble style of reading...

MILDRED: You know my nephew – John Harvey, don't you, Dr Gratton?

JOHN: (*Smiling.*) You attended to me once, sir, after a
football game...

GRATTON: Of course I did. And a great game you played,
too, that day. Where are you now?

JOHN: I'm a theological student – in my last year.

GRATTON: You'll have a grand manner in the pulpit. But
take care, later on, not to enjoy the sound of your voice
too much. Not like old Evan Williams, who always
sounded as if he was doing God a great favour.
(*GRATTON laughs with no response from MILDRED.*)
(*He moves down centre.*) Malcolm – what are you staring
at there – when you can't even say 'Hello' to an old
friend?

MALCOLM: (*Looking up from the stereoscope.*) A new set of
stereographs. Yosemite National Park. That was the
Bridal Veil Falls – wonderful.

GRATTON: (*Returning to the table and opening his bag.*) I'll
take a look sometime – when we've found a cure for
influenza. Well, to business. (*He takes two bottles of
medicine and a box of pills from the bag.*) Thought I'd bring
these myself as I was passing. (*He hands a bottle of
medicine to ELSPIE.*) This is yours, Elspie – three times a
day after food. (*He hands the box of pills to MILDRED.*)
I've had these pills made up for you, Mrs McBane – try
'em for two or three days, but if you begin to feel your
heart or any pressure round the temple, stop taking 'em
and let me know. (*He holds up the second bottle of medicine.
To ELSPIE.*) This is for your father, Is he in? (*He puts the
bottle on the table.*)

MILDRED: No. David's gone down to the station – to meet
some people who are staying with us. (*She says this as if
she did not want to say it, and puts the pills on the table.*)

ELSPIE: (*Brightly.*) Some people! Really, Aunt Mildred!
(*She rises and moves to GRATTON.*) They're my three
cousins – whom I've never seen. I think it's exciting,
though nobody else seems to.

JOHN: (*Smiling.*) I do.

MALCOLM: (*Dryly.*) We don't get excited as easily as you
do, Elspie.

ELSPIE: (*Sitting on the pouffe.*) Oh, Uncle Malcolm!

GRATTON: You'd rather see 'em in your stereoscope, eh, Malcolm?

MALCOLM: (*With a short laugh.*) You're dead right – I would.

MILDRED: (*Sharply and with a warning glance.*) Malcolm!
(*There is an awkward silence. GRATTON, obviously curious, looks round at them.*)

GRATTON: (*Moving down centre; rather maliciously determined to know.*) I seem to remember your brother Charlie left three children – didn't he, Malcolm? Married a wild girl somewhere up in the Thunder Bay country – part Indian, wasn't she?
(*MALCOLM puts a slide in his stereoscope.*)
Must be well into their twenties now, those three. Don't tell me it's them you're having to stay with you?

ELSPIE: (*Impulsively.*) Yes, it is. My father…

MILDRED: (*Cutting in; coldly.*) All right, Elspie.
(*MILDRED is clearly not going to say anything else. GRATTON looks quizzically at MILDRED, then looks at MALCOLM.*)

GRATTON: It's queer that in this matter of children, poor Charlie should have done better than the rest of you put together. Look at you. David a widower, with only little Elspie here. And Robert McBane left you a childless widow, Mildred. And Malcolm there is not even married at all. (*He crosses and stands above the love-seat.*) Are you taking Charlie's three into the business, Malcolm?

MALCOLM: No, we're not.

GRATTON: (*Dryly.*) You don't surprise me. But what – then?

MALCOLM: (*Elaborately casual.*) A deed of transfer has turned up. It must have been overlooked when Charles left the business. And as his wife died a year or two ago, the three children will have to sign whatever has to be signed. Not that they need have been brought here. The whole caboodle is only worth a few hundred dollars.

MILDRED: But David thought it best to have them here so that he could explain everything to them himself. You know how conscientious and thorough he is.

GRATTON: (*Crossing to MILDRED.*) And obstinate. Mulish. (*He turns to ELSPIE.*) Ah – Elspie – I'd forgotten you were here – mustn't talk about your father like that.

ELSPIE: (*Smiling.*) But it's true.

MILDRED: (*Rising and moving to the lamp down right.*) So he insisted on their coming – (*She turns up the lamp.*) after taking a great deal of trouble to find them – they'd gone roaming all over the place. And now, feeling responsible, he's gone to meet their train. That's all. (*She crosses to the lamp down left and turns it up.*)

GRATTON: I see. (*He holds up the box of pills.*) Take one of these directly after supper. Start 'em tonight. And remind David to take this medicine of his tonight, too. And don't forget your nice pink mixture, Elspie. Coloured specially for you. Well... (*He picks up his bag and moves to the hall door.*)

JOHN: (*Crossing to the hall door.*) I'll see you out, sir.

ELSPIE: (*Rising and moving to the hall door.*) So will I.

GRATTON: Come on, then. Though I was finding my own way in and out of this house the night you were born. Good night, Mildred – Malcolm.

(*MILDRED and MALCOLM murmur 'good night'. GRATTON, ELSPIE and JOHN exit to the hall. JOHN closes the door. MILDRED and MALCOLM are silent for a moment.*)

MILDRED: (*Moving to the lamp centre and turning it up.*) Why did you have to tell Edward Gratton all about this deed of transfer? And telling him, too, that it's only a matter of a few hundred dollars. (*She moves to the lamp up centre and turns it up.*)

MALCOLM: Because it's true. And also I didn't want him to imagine something tremendous has come up. He likes to talk. I've heard him at the club.

MILDRED: (*Shocked.*) Not about his patients?

MALCOLM: No, of course not. But general unprofessional gossip. So I didn't want to give him a lead.

MILDRED: (*Moving down centre.*) That's probably just what you have done, Malcolm. He'll be asking himself now why David should have gone to all that trouble for the sake of a few hundred dollars.

MALCOLM: (*Dryly.*) It's a good question. I remember that you and I asked it several times.

MILDRED: (*Moving to MALCOLM; sharply.*) That's quite different – and you know very well it is. Don't pretend to be stupid, Malcolm, just to annoy me. I know it's one of your favourite pastimes – but tonight's the wrong night. I've been furious all along with David about this whole idiotic business – it's so senseless bringing those three here.

MALCOLM: What are you afraid of?

MILDRED: (*Sharply.*) I didn't say I was afraid. I'm not. But while they're in this house, I'll have them on my hands. (*She turns away.*)

MALCOLM: (*Contemptuously.*) Two boys and a girl from the back of beyond. You're forgetting who they are and where they come from. Charlie never had any brains, and that woman he married probably couldn't count beyond ten. So what can these three be? Loggers. Farm hands. Or if they've gone urban – two bellhops and a chambermaid. They've never been in a house like this before. (*He rises, crosses and puts the stereoscope and slides on the bookcase down right.*) They won't have known people like us. I don't suppose they'll want to stay more than a day or two.

MILDRED: (*Hastily.*) I know, I know. I've thought of all that. I don't say it's reasonable to be worried, to feel on edge as I do. I just want you to remember that's how I'm feeling. And don't pretend you're outside all this, Malcolm.

MALCOLM: It isn't pretence. *I* haven't a conscience...

MILDRED: (*Cutting in; sharply.*) We're not talking about consciences...

MALCOLM: (*Cutting in; calmly.*) I am. And not having one... (*He breaks off.*)
(*They look at each other for a moment. MILDRED cannot reply to this and keep calm, so she does not try. She turns up*

*centre. After the pause, it is clear MALCOLM is deliberately
changing the subject.)*
(He moves below the couch.) What do you think young
Elspie and your nephew are doing – spooning?

MILDRED: *(Crossing above the couch to the conservatory door.)*
Certainly not. And I wish you wouldn't use that vulgar
expression.
They're probably playing ping-pong in the big room.
(She listens.) Yes, there they are. *(She moves to the couch and
sits.)* You might remember, Malcolm, that all men haven't
the same tastes. And John has a very serious nature.

MALCOLM: *(Moving up centre.)* I know. It weighs a ton.

MILDRED: *(Angrily.)* Please don't talk like that – you know
how I dislike it.

MALCOLM: And you ought to know by this time, Mildred
dear, that I've had as much as I can take of all these
serious natures round here. It's like living in a Methodist
mission. *(He moves below the couch.)* I mustn't offend
Brother David, the lay preacher. I mustn't shock sly
little Elspie or that milksop nephew of yours. But surely
I don't have to pretend with you all the time? It might
be good for you if I didn't.

MILDRED: *(Angrily.)* Oh – be quiet!
(BRIDGET enters from the hall.)

BRIDGET: *(Pleased and excited.)* They're here – all three of
'em with the master – but big and black and not a smile
between 'em.

MILDRED: *(Rising and crossing to BRIDGET.)* Tell Miss
Elspie – and ask her to show them their rooms – hurry.

BRIDGET: I will.
(BRIDGET exits, closing the door.)

MALCOLM: I'd better go out and be civil to them.

MILDRED: *(Crossing to MALCOLM; urgently.)* No, don't,
please, Malcolm. You heard what I said to Bridget. I want
to meet them here – and not start by showing them their
rooms. But if you go and meet them it'll look as if I'm
deliberately avoiding them – whereas if we're both here
– it'll seem quite natural – and give us a certain
advantage right from the beginning... *(She breaks off.*

With an exasperated tone.) Oh – don't look at me like that.
You know very well what I mean. Stop pretending you
don't care.

MALCOLM: Well, I don't, not as much as you do. And I've
told you why.

MILDRED: Yes – and for goodness' sake don't let's have
any more of *that* sort of talk – now they're in the house.
(*She moves to the pouffe and sits.*)

(*MALCOLM sits on the couch. DAVID McBANE enters from
the hall. He is rather older than these two, about sixty, and a
thicker, more commanding personality than MALCOLM, very
much the head of the business and the family. He has the loud
voice and the over-confident manner that often go with
enormous self-deception, for he is not a hypocrite but an
enthusiastic self-deceiver. There is something vaguely parsonical
about his dress, general appearance and manner. He crosses
to the table, picks up some letters and opens them.*)

(*She addresses DAVID at once, to explain herself.*) David,
I thought it would be much better if I received them in
here.

DAVID: Just as you please, Mildred. Elspie's looking after
them now.

MALCOLM: What are they like?

DAVID: You'll see for yourself, shortly. Quiet, decent
young folks, I'd say. Shy, of course. What you'd expect –
I've done all the talking so far. I've made it plain that
this is a God-fearing household. And I think we'll have
short family prayers when they're all down and before
we have supper.

MILDRED: Quite right, David. I'm glad.

DAVID: They understand why they're here – but I haven't
made too much of that. I wanted them to feel they were
welcome.

MALCOLM: (*Dryly.*) Didn't they ask why they haven't been
welcome earlier?

DAVID: They didn't. And I don't see them asking that sort
of question, Malcolm. But I told them frankly it would
have been difficult while their mother was alive.

MILDRED: And how did they take that?

DAVID: Quietly and decently enough. They've been travelling for some time – the girl, Jean, and the younger lad, Angus, all the way from Chicago...

MALCOLM: Chicago, eh? Not straight out of the wilds, then. What were they doing in Chicago?

DAVID: I don't know.

MILDRED: (*Hastily.*) And the less we say about it the better. Please do remember that, Malcolm.

(*MALCOLM does not reply.*)

DAVID: Well, Malcolm? You heard what Mildred said?

MALCOLM: Yes. And I think she's making too heavy weather of this visit. But I'll try to remember not to ask them embarrassing questions.

(*JOHN enters from the hall.*)

DAVID: See that you do. Ah – good evening, John.

JOHN: Good evening, Mr McBane. (*He crosses above DAVID and stands behind the couch.*) Now it's finished, that makes a fine big room along there.

DAVID: (*Pleased.*) Glad you think so, John. It'll hold a hundred and fifty people – maybe more. We're having our first prayer meeting and concert there, next Tuesday night. I hope you'll be able to be with us, lad.

JOHN: Thank you, sir. I hope so, too.

(*MILDRED rises and moves above the love-seat.*)

DAVID: Have you met Elspie's three cousins yet?

JOHN: Not properly, sir. She took them away, and I went back to the big room to take down the ping-pong table.

DAVID: That's a foolish game for an upstanding serious young fellow like yourself, John. But no doubt Elspie made you play. Like she made me buy the game – table an' all. We're spoiling her between us.

(*ELSPIE enters from the hall. She looks troubled but DAVID does not notice it. She leaves the door open and moves to the pouffe.*)

MILDRED: Elspie!

DAVID: I'm just telling John here we spoil you between us. But why didn't you wait to bring your cousins down?

ELSPIE: (*Sitting on the pouffe.*) Bridget'll show them where to come.

(*MILDRED moves down left.*)

DAVID: No doubt. But I wish you'd stayed. They're not used to this kind of house. They're shy. Especially the girl – Jean.

(*MILDRED moves to left of ELSPIE.*)

ELSPIE. I don't think she's shy, Father.

MILDRED: (*Touching ELSPIE.*) What is it, then, dear? And what's the matter?

ELSPIE: It's nothing. I'm being silly.

MILDRED: No, you're not. Tell me.

ELSPIE: (*With a touch of distress.*) There's nothing to tell.

MILDRED: (*Persisting.*) You don't like them, do you?

ELSPIE: (*As if at bay.*) I wish you wouldn't, Aunt Mildred. I think – I'll go up to my room – I have a headache. (*She rises.*)

DAVID: (*Sternly.*) You've no headache, girl. And you'll stay down here for prayers and for supper.

(*ELSPIE sits on the pouffe.*)

And if your aunt asks you a question, you'll give her a civil sensible answer.

ELSPIE: (*Distressed.*) Father – please! I can't give her a sensible answer. I haven't got one to give. I can't say I dislike them. I can't say I like them.

DAVID: Well, that's sensible enough. You don't know them yet. You haven't made up your mind.

MILDRED: That's not what she means, though, David. I saw at once something was wrong.

ELSPIE: (*Rising and moving to the hall door; vehemently.*) Nothing was wrong – nothing was wrong…

(*MILDRED crosses to right of ELSPIE.*)

DAVID: (*Sharply.*) Stop that – or there'll be something wrong now.

(*ELSPIE, suddenly quiet, smiles with an effort, then looks gravely at the others. She obviously tries very hard to put her thoughts into words.*)

ELSPIE: (*Moving below the love-seat.*) It's no use asking me if they're shy or not shy, if I like them or dislike them. What I felt – and it upset me, gave me the queerest shaky sort of feeling – was that they were so strange.

Really strange, not just people I didn't know. There weren't any thoughts or feelings I could understand behind their eyes. (*She sits on the downstage side of the love-seat.*) All three have the same sort of eyes – they just look at you.

(*DAVID breaks in urgently. He looks around to command their attention, then drops his voice.*)

DAVID: (*Moving above the love-seat.*) I'll tell you what's strange about their eyes. Quite simple. No need to get worked up about 'em. They're Indian eyes. Their mother was part Indian, remember.

JOHN: (*Almost cutting in; heartily.*) Of course – that's it, Mr McBane. There was a fellow in the team with me...

DAVID: (*Really cutting in.*) So you see, Elspie, you're just making a fuss about nothing. Don't start making up all kinds of nonsensical stuff about them. Or treat them as if they were wild heathens. They're just decent, simple, shy young folk, who don't happen to have had the advantages you've had. And it's up to you to make them feel they're welcome here. We'll do what we can, we older ones, but they'll lose their shyness much sooner with you and John. So all you must do...

BRIDGET: (*Off.*) They'll all be here. They've been waiting for some time. This way now.

(*DAVID moves and stands above the hall door. MILDRED moves to left of the couch. ELSPIE rises and stands left of the pouffe MALCOLM rises and moves down right.*

DOUGLAS, JEAN and ANGUS McBANE enter from the hall, rather slowly, not at all hesitantly but with great deliberation. They look neither shy nor cheerfully brash. All that can be said is they look watchful and patiently purposeful. Their clothes are rather less conventional and respectable than those we have already seen, but they are not loudly dressed. There is some colour link between their clothes so that, without being dressed alike, there is a strong likeness in their appearance. There is a pause, then their quietness and negativeness make the others louder than usual. JEAN stands centre of the rostrum, with DOUGLAS above her, and ANGUS below her.)

DAVID: (*Very bluff and hearty.*) Well – well – well, here you are, then. All I have to do is to make you all known to each other. Now then – this is Jean – that's Douglas – that's Angus. (*To the three arrivals.*) This is your Aunt Mildred, who was married, as I told you, to my older brother Robert. She's the big boss of the house.

MILDRED: (*Smiling at them; graciously.*) You're not even *intended* to believe *that*. You must have seen already it can't be true. But your rooms are my responsibility – and I hope you like them.

(*They nod affirmatively, with a little smile. DAVID hurries on with his introductions.*)

DAVID: This is your Uncle Malcolm. I told you about him.

MALCOLM: Glad to know you at last. Knew I'd one pretty niece – Elspie here. Didn't know I'd two. It's great.

(*The three behave as before.*)

DAVID: And this is John Harvey, the only one here who isn't a McBane. He's your Aunt Mildred's nephew on her side.

JOHN: (*To the three.*) I hope you'll be as happy under this roof as I have always been. And I'm sure you will be, once it's not so strange, for you'll find them all the kindest people.

DAVID: (*Bluffly.*) My daughter Elspie you already know. (*He moves to the three and breaks up the group.*) Well, now, there's a few minutes before prayers and supper – so let's break this up – and get acquainted. Elspie – take charge of Angus.

(*ANGUS and ELSPIE move to the love-seat and sit, ANGUS on the downstage side.*)

Jean – you go over there with Malcolm –

(*JEAN and JOHN move to the settee up centre and sit. MALCOLM closes the door and sits on the settee, with JEAN and JOHN.*)

– and, Douglas, you come with your Aunt Mildred and me. (*DOUGLAS, MILDRED and DAVID move to the couch. During the ensuing dialogue, MALCOLM and JOHN talk in animated dumb show to JEAN. ELSPIE and ANGUS pretend to talk, but it is slower and with more sense of strain.*)

MILDRED: Shall we sit over here on the couch, David?
(*MILDRED, DAVID and DOUGLAS sit on the couch.*)
I suppose you are the eldest – are you, Douglas?

DOUGLAS: Yes. By a year and a half.

DAVID: Then you're the one I'll have to do business with, my boy.

MILDRED: (*Hastily.*) Never mind about business tonight, David. (*To DOUGLAS.*) Besides, you must be tired after your journey.

DOUGLAS: No. I'm used to moving around. We all are.

DAVID: Not much harm in it while you're young. But don't forget the old saying about rolling stones not gathering any moss.

DOUGLAS: No, I won't.

MILDRED: Soon you'll want to marry and settle down and make friends, with nice people...

DAVID: (*Heartily.*) And for that – and sometimes for business, too – there's nothing like regular attendance at a place of worship – and not just being a member of a congregation – but doing all you can to serve your church or meeting place – it's made all the difference to me, I can assure you, lad.

DOUGLAS: (*Without any tone.*) It must have done.

MILDRED: Your uncle never spares himself...

DAVID: (*Cutting in; bluffly.*) Oh – I do what I can. We all do here, as you'll see, lad. Are you a member of any congregation?

DOUGLAS: (*Smoothly.*) I'm afraid not.

DAVID: What about your brother and sister?

DOUGLAS: (*Smoothly.*) We haven't seen much of each other just lately. So I'll have to ask them. (*He raises his voice and calls.*) Jean.

JEAN: (*Looking across at DOUGLAS.*) Yes?

DOUGLAS: (*Smoothly and without any colour.*) Uncle David wants to know if you're a member of any church or meeting.

JEAN: (*In the same tone as DOUGLAS.*) No, I'm not, Uncle David.

DOUGLAS: What about *you*, Angus?

ANGUS: (*Shaking his head.*) Not yet, Uncle David. Never been in one place long enough to get round to it.

DAVID: (*Bluffly.*) Well, I don't suppose that's your fault, lad. But you will – you will – or if you don't, you'll regret it. I know I...

ELSPIE: (*Cutting in; with some urgency.*) Oh – Father – no...

ANGUS: (*Cutting in; with faint mockery.*) Cousin Elspie, don't interrupt your father. What were you saying, Uncle David?

DAVID: I was just about to say...

MILDRED: (*Hastily and anxiously.*) No, David. If we're going to have prayers, you'll have to begin now. It's nearly supper time.

DAVID: (*Taking charge; solemnly.*) You're quite right. (*He rises and moves right centre.*) Now then – (*He looks round at them all, but is really addressing the visitors.*) we can't do this every night – I wish we could – but this is certainly an occasion when we ought to submit ourselves to the will of the Lord. So I'll lead you in prayer, to ask a blessing on this house and the souls of all within it. (*Rather ostentatiously he kneels in a prominent position down centre, bending his head and covering his eyes with his hands.*)
(*The others do not kneel but lean forward, elbows on knees, hands covering eyes. There is an unctuous quality in DAVID's praying that is carefully revealed without being burlesqued. During pauses, which are marked, there are murmurs of 'Amen' from MILDRED, MALCOLM and especially JOHN.*)
We beg Thee, O Lord, to accept our humble petition for Thy blessing on this house – Amen.
(*ANGUS sits up.*)
We come to Thee with contrite hearts, knowing full well that in Thy sight we are all miserable sinners – Amen.
(*DOUGLAS sits up.*)
We have done those things we ought not to have done, and have left undone those things we ought to have done – Amen.
(*JEAN sits up. DOUGLAS, ANGUS and JEAN abandon all pretence of joining in the prayers. They sit upright, as tall*

and straight as they can make themselves, exchanging glances about the bowed figures, ANGUS with mocking derision, DOUGLAS with cold contempt and JEAN with angry scorn. And as they thus reveal themselves, DAVID goes droning on and the curtain slowly starts to fall.)
Our ways have not been Thy ways – accept our repentance, O Lord – Amen. Accept our thanks that Thou has seen fit to grant us health and strength and the fruits of Thy bounty…

Scene 2

Scene – the same. Evening, four days later.

When the curtain rises, the room is empty and the lamps are turned low. The centre section only of the conservatory doors is open. The lamp in the conservatory is fully lit. A piano solo, 'Jesus the Joy of Living Hearts', is being played in the room off beyond the conservatory, and we can just hear it coming along the corridor. After a moment or two, ANGUS, dressed as before, enters from the hall. He crosses to the conservatory door, listens for a few moments, then takes a cigarette from his pocket, and lights it. He goes to the lamp up centre and turns it up, then takes a flat half-bottle of whisky from his pocket and takes a drink. He turns up the lamp on the table centre and closes the hall door. JEAN and DOUGLAS enter from the conservatory. JEAN wears a different blouse. DOUGLAS, who is dressed as before, closes the conservatory doors and the music is no longer heard. The opening to the scene is very relaxed and rather slow, nobody making hurried movements.

JEAN: (*Giving ANGUS a warm smile.*) Angus – I was hoping you'd be here.
ANGUS: (*Returning her smile.*) Just made it, Jeannie. (*He crosses to the palm pot down left and deposits the spent match in it.*) Want a drink? (*He indicates the bottle.*)
JEAN: (*Moving to the couch and sitting.*) Yes, please. *And* a cigarette.
(*ANGUS crosses to JEAN, gives her a cigarette, lights it for her, then sits on the floor in front of the couch. DOUGLAS*

sits right of JEAN on the couch. They settle down, sprawling comfortably in an easy huddle.)

ANGUS: How's the prayer meeting and concert along there?

DOUGLAS: What you'd expect.

JEAN: (*Taking the bottle from ANGUS.*) No talent. (*She takes a drink and returns the bottle.*)

DOUGLAS: It was no use staying. Nothing we could do in there.

JEAN: Except suffer. And that's not what we're here for.

ANGUS: I'm glad you mentioned that, Jeannie.

JEAN: Think I needed reminding? I'm not delaying anything.

DOUGLAS: Don't start rushing it, Angus. We're about where we ought to be. And I need time for what I'm trying to do.

JEAN: So do I. Besides, don't forget I've been switched. John didn't exist in our original plan. And of course it would be much easier if he lived here.

ANGUS: Or if he lived at all.

JEAN: No; Angus, you're wrong there – he's alive all right. And when he has a few emotions of his own, instead of those he's been told to have, he might go off with a bang. Anyhow, he's a better prospect than little Cousin Elspie, who seems to be just afraid of you.

ANGUS: She has intuition. I'm afraid of myself sometimes. But I've been busy following up something else.

DOUGLAS: What would that something else be, apart from sampling all the saloons?

ANGUS: Tell you later. The saloons come into it. Did our good kind Uncle David say anything to you tonight about signing his nice document?

DOUGLAS: No, he hadn't time. Later he will.

JEAN: (*With mock gravity.*) I'm afraid dear Aunt Mildred is beginning to feel the strain. But then she's had trouble with her nerves for years and years. Dr Gratton, who's been looking after the family for such a long time...

ANGUS: Except us, of course.

JEAN: We're not including the riff-raff. Anyhow, clever Dr
    Gratton hardly knows what to do for the best – her
    nerves give her so much trouble.

ANGUS: (*Bitter behind his easy mockery.*) She ought to try
    cooking for thirty lumberjacks. That's good for the
    nerves – you haven't time to remember them.

JEAN: I need a little drink. (*She takes the bottle from
    ANGUS.*)

ANGUS: (*Taking the bottle from JEAN.*) Just let Douglas and
    me finish this one, girl. There's only room for one
    enthusiastic drinker in a family. And I'm it – not you.
    I don't want little sister beating me to the bottle every
    time.

DOUGLAS: Also, you could easily have one too many and
    then blow up too soon.

JEAN: I don't say it couldn't happen.

DOUGLAS: You never liked hard liquor before, Jean.

JEAN: No, but before *what?* Before quite a lot of travel
    and experience. In a way, I don't like hard liquor now. If
    I really felt gay, I wouldn't call for it. But it keeps the
    light burning. And the floor isn't too cold when you take
    your shoes off. Moreover, gentlemen, if I hadn't taken to
    short stiff drinks, I don't think we'd be here.

ANGUS: This is news.

DOUGLAS: You'd better tell us how you did it.

JEAN: Many and many a time – oh, after the last show, too
    tired at first to do anything but take a quick drink – or
    on the railroad with nothing to look at but dust or snow
    – or undressing in flea traps on one night stands – I've
    imagined this so clearly that I think I must have made
    it happen. Just as I wanted it. The three of us here,
    camping in the middle of them, just as we are now. All
    of them open a mile wide... (*She breaks off.*)

DOUGLAS: Well?

JEAN: (*Sitting up.*) Well, it's happened, hasn't it? Just as
    I imagined it.

ANGUS: And now you don't like it.

JEAN: (*Hastily.*) I didn't say that. I love it.

213

DOUGLAS: Why did you suddenly break off like that, then? (*JEAN rises, crosses to the palm pot down left, and puts her cigarette in it.*)

JEAN: (*Rather confusedly.*) Oh – I'd said what I wanted to say – and my voice was trying to run on when my thoughts had stopped. (*She turns up the lamp down left. With more confidence.*) But I've thought of something since – something important. Perhaps we ought to have some sort of signal. (*She turns to the others.*)

DOUGLAS: To do what?

JEAN: Look – one of us is with one of them – and it's a good chance. But not if the other two of us are still around. So some sort of signal to clear off... (*She moves centre.*)

ANGUS: (*Rising and semaphoring to JEAN.*) Oh – we'll just wave large green and red flags.

JEAN: (*Entering into this.*) Wouldn't that be wonderful? Would you keep them in your pocket?

(*DOUGLAS rises and moves to the conservatory door.*)

ANGUS: (*Moving behind JEAN.*) I shouldn't – no. (*He picks JEAN up and spins round with her in his arms, to the love-seat.*) I'd begin to carry a mast around...

JEAN: (*Laughing.*) And run them up.

ANGUS: (*Laughing.*) And red and green lights for evening work. (*He sits on the downstage side of the love-seat, with JEAN on his knee.*)

DOUGLAS: (*Crossing to right of the pouffe; with authority.*) That's enough of that. We're wasting time. And we don't need any kind of signals. We know what's happening. And we're not dense. Now, let's see how far we've got. Angus, you and I know where we are...

JEAN: (*Rising and moving to the pouffe.*) And I know where I am.

DOUGLAS: Tell us then.

JEAN: (*Sitting on the pouffe.*) There are things you can bring yourself to do so long as you don't tell anybody – not even yourself – what exactly you *are* doing.

DOUGLAS: My mind doesn't work like that.

ANGUS: Mine doesn't. But I know what she means. Just as I always knew what mother was trying to say – whatever mess she made of saying it.

JEAN: Yes, you did, Angus. Better than I did, I think.

ANGUS: But everything she said about *this* was plain enough. She hammered it in.

JEAN: And perhaps knocked us out of shape. I've sometimes wondered...

DOUGLAS: (*Kneeling right of the pouffe; cutting in.*) No, Jean, let me do the talking now.
(*MALCOLM enters from the conservatory and stands in the doorway.*)
So – let's look at it. So far – what have we got?

JEAN: (*Indicating MALCOLM.*) I think we've got a visitor.
(*They all look at MALCOLM, who stands in the open doorway, staring at them sprawling at ease, drinking, smoking, with JEAN showing a certain amount of leg. None of them attempts to change position.*)
(*She mutters.*) What happens to us now, boys?

ANGUS: (*Not in as low a tone as her question.*) Nothing. Leave this to me.
(*MALCOLM comes deliberately into the room, closes the door and stands behind the downstage end of the couch.*)

MALCOLM: I've good ears. What does she leave to you, Angus?

ANGUS: (*Cheerfully.*) Anything that worries her. I like to look after my little sister.

JEAN: Give me another drink then, Angus dear.
(*ANGUS rises and hands the bottle to JEAN, who takes a drink.*)

MALCOLM: (*Coolly.*) There aren't going to be any pretences then. I'm glad of that. You notice I'm not surprised.
(*ANGUS puts out his cigarette in the palm pot down left, and sits on the back of the love-seat.*)

ANGUS: (*Mockingly.*) And you can notice that we don't care whether you're surprised or not, Uncle Malcolm. It just isn't worrying us at all.

JEAN: I'm so bad I don't even mind your staring so hard at my legs. Of course, I know they're all right. I've had to display them for a living. Still, there's no performance tonight. So...

(*She sits up, adjusts her skirt and looks quite demure.*)

MALCOLM: (*Waiting, until she is ready to listen.*) I'm not surprised because I knew from the first moment you walked in here that you were too good to be true. You didn't take me in for a second. I'm not so naive as the others here.

ANGUS: Of course you aren't. We knew that.

MALCOLM: So far I've kept my suspicions to myself.

DOUGLAS: Good!

MALCOLM: I wanted first to discover what you were up to. (*He crosses to centre.*) But you realize, of course, that if my brother David had walked in and found you like this, he'd have had you out of this house tonight. He'd have given you just time to pack.

DOUGLAS: (*Rising.*) Without our having signed anything for him? (*He takes the bottle from JEAN, puts it in his pocket and moves up centre.*)

MALCOLM: He'd have risked that. You'd have had to go.

ANGUS: (*Mockingly.*) Too bad! But you're not like Uncle David, are you, Uncle Malcolm?

MALCOLM: (*With sudden loss of temper.*) And serve you right for your damned impudence.

(*The result of this is startling. ANGUS springs up like a cat, bristling, blazing with fury, ready to fling himself at MALCOLM.*)

ANGUS: (*Crossing to left of MALCOLM.*) You hypocritical bastard!

JEAN: (*Rising; in alarm.*) No, Angus – no!

DOUGLAS: (*Pulling ANGUS back.*) Don't be a fool – or you'll bitch up everything.

(*ANGUS controls himself and sits on the couch.*)

MALCOLM: (*To DOUGLAS.*) I wasn't at the office yesterday. But I understand you spent some time there. (*JEAN sits on the love-seat.*)

DOUGLAS: Yes. Fascinating! Just as Jean likes theatres and Angus likes saloons, I like offices. Your old chief clerk was quite impressed.

MALCOLM: (*Still angry.*) So I gathered this morning. In fact, old Cutler spoke to my brother David, who now has some notion of offering you a job with us. Some sort of clerkship. Not here but at our branch office in Kingston.

DOUGLAS: (*Moving up left centre; with marked irony.*) I'm flattered.

ANGUS: (*Mockingly.*) Isn't Uncle David *good* to us?

MALCOLM: (*Angrily making his point.*) And now when I tell him what I'm certainly going to tell him, he'll feel all the more that he's been made a fool of – and out you go.

ANGUS: (*Rising.*) We're all going to run and tell tales to the big boss, are we?

MALCOLM: Some of us are.

DOUGLAS: I don't think if I were you...

ANGUS: (*Cutting in.*) No, Doug, this is all mine – I told you I had something... (*He moves down right.*) Jeannie, you wanted a signal. This is one.

JEAN: (*Rising and crossing to ANGUS.*) What to do?

ANGUS: Go listen to the music – and make eyes at Good Boy John.

JEAN: Because something unfit for my ears...?

ANGUS: It could be, too.

JEAN: Then you've forgotten where my ears have been lately. I've heard things that would keep you boys awake at night.

ANGUS: Stop it, sis, you're frightening me to death.

JEAN: No, but seriously, Angus... (*She crosses below ANGUS to the conservatory door.*)

ANGUS: (*Following JEAN.*) Seriously, Jeannie – I'll do it better if you're not listening. And it might make it easier – and safer – if you don't know.

JEAN: (*Resigning herself.*) Oh – well – if that's how you feel...

MALCOLM: I'll go with you, Jean. (*He moves towards the door.*)

(*JEAN exits to the conservatory. As she opens the door, the sound is heard of a violin playing 'Traumerei'.*)

ANGUS: (*Standing between MALCOLM and the door.*) Oh – no – you won't. You've said your piece. Now I'll say mine.

(*MALCOLM and ANGUS stand looking at each other, a contest of wills. ANGUS wins. MALCOLM gives a shrug, turns away from the door and crosses to the pouffe. ANGUS quickly closes the conservatory door and the sound of the music ceases. DOUGLAS moves down left.*)

(*He moves above the couch. Relaxed.*) You know, Uncle Malcolm, I like to visit a few bars and saloons...

MALCOLM: (*Dryly.*) You're not telling me anything I didn't know.

ANGUS: (*Moving above the table centre and leaning on it.*) Oh – there won't be much you don't know already. One little thing, though. I've a kind of professional interest in bars and saloons. Among other things I've been a bartender. Just imagine that. A McBane serving behind a bar – wearing a clean white jacket – 'Good evening, Mr Smith – the usual is it, sir?' – 'Damn you, Joe, you call this stuff whisky?' – 'Sorry, sir!' They call you Joe, most of 'em, fat slobs that like to find fault and keep you apologetic and busy – until they've had three too many and tell you you're a pal, ask you where they can find a red-headed girl who'll be nice to them or start crying because it's such a cruel world. Most of 'em are what I called you a few minutes ago – hypocritical bastards.

MALCOLM: (*Angrily.*) I don't have to listen to this. (*He turns and moves towards the hall door.*)

ANGUS: (*Crossing to centre.*) You'll either listen now – or hear it given out at the supper table.

MALCOLM: (*Stopping and turning.*) Hear what given out?

ANGUS: The private life of Malcolm McBane, Esquire. (*He moves below the table centre and sits on it.*) Now, Uncle Malcolm, once you've been a bartender yourself, you're not just a customer but one of the fraternity. When business is quiet, the other fellow will lean on the mahogany and have a nice professional gossip. He'll answer questions he wouldn't even take from a customer. And that's how I came to know about Mrs O'Dwyer.

MALCOLM: (*Moving centre; doing his best.*) And who's she? Am I supposed to know?

ANGUS: (*Rising and moving to right of MALCOLM.*) You've been keeping her for the last three or four years. Molly O'Dwyer. Good-looking plump brunette.

(*MALCOLM turns away.*)

I've seen her so we needn't argue about that. Lives at forty-one Peel Street. Her husband used to be foreman up at Blackwater until you had him fired. He went out to Vancouver. Molly stayed here. And you know why. At least you think you do.

MALCOLM: (*Turning to ANGUS.*) What do you mean – I *think I do?*

(*DOUGLAS, before ANGUS can reply, interrupts and moves to the hall door.*)

DOUGLAS: Let's leave that, Angus?

ANGUS: All right, Doug. He might be in love with her, though I doubt it. This sort use 'em, they don't love 'em.

(*MALCOLM crosses and stands down right.*)

Now, Uncle Malcolm, we were talking about Uncle David, the big boss, being made a fool of – telling us to clear out...

DOUGLAS: Yes. And remember, not even any hints, winks, nudges...

MALCOLM: Of course, that's understood. (*He stares at them for a moment.*) I thought I hadn't any family pride. Now I find I have – and it's puking at the thought of you insufferable young blackguards.

DOUGLAS: (*Bitterly.*) That's what's wrong with us. We haven't any family pride at all. You saw to that.

MALCOLM: Charlie might have been a wild drunken fool – but he'd be turning in his grave if...

ANGUS: (*Moving to MALCOLM and facing him.*) I've heard him turning in his grave all my life. Now go and sing a few hymns.

(*ANGUS and MALCOLM stare at each other a moment, then MALCOLM turns and exits to the conservatory, closing the door behind him.*)

(*With a short, rather unhappy laugh.*) So much for Uncle Malcolm. (*He sits on the couch.*)

DOUGLAS: (*Moving down centre.*) Was that the whole story?

ANGUS: I don't know very much more – and none of it's to his credit. The gossip is that he deliberately worked O'Dwyer's dismissal and that Molly O'Dwyer thought he was going to marry her. Now that she knows he isn't, she's deceiving him with a mate off one of the lake boats.

DOUGLAS: You nearly told him so.

ANGUS: Glad you stopped me.

(*DOUGLAS turns away left.*)

(*He leans forward.*) Why should poor Molly O'Dwyer lose her rent just because we don't like our uncle? But look – Doug – what about Jean?

DOUGLAS: (*Rather coldly.*) What about her?

ANGUS: I never wanted her in this. Now I like it still less.

DOUGLAS: We're not amusing ourselves.

ANGUS: I am – part of the time. (*He rises.*) But Jean's different, for all her tough backstage talk. And she's the only sister we've got. This can turn very ugly, don't forget, and she might become too involved. (*He crosses to DOUGLAS.*) I think she ought to go.

DOUGLAS: (*Bitterly.*) Go where? She hasn't anywhere to go – and whose fault is that?

ANGUS: (*Turning away.*) I still don't like it.

DOUGLAS: And if I started to tell you what I don't like, I could go on all night. I want to build things up, not knock 'em down, however rotten they are. You won't understand this – but you'll have to believe me. Yesterday, down at the office, I ached to take hold of the whole goddam organization and clean the muck out of it, sweat the fat off it, make it all run easy and sweet like a fine engine. I tell you, Angus…

(*JEAN enters from the conservatory, leaving the door open behind her. A number of voices off are heard singing 'Tell me the Old Old Story', accompanied by a harmonium or American organ.*)

JEAN: (*Crossing hurriedly below the couch to ANGUS.*) Urgent signal, boys. I think I'm being followed. Don't stay or you'll spoil it.

ANGUS: Perhaps it ought to be spoilt.

JEAN: (*Rather annoyed; sharply.*) I know what I'm doing. Go on – quick. That way. (*She pushes ANGUS and DOUGLAS towards the hall door.*)

(*DOUGLAS and ANGUS exit to the hall. DOUGLAS closes the door behind them. JEAN moves to the pouffe and sits, looking pensive and sedate.*

JOHN enters rather hesitantly from the conservatory, closing the door behind him and shutting out the sound of the singing.)

(*As if surprised.*) John! Don't you like that hymn?

JOHN: (*Standing by the door; rather confused.*) Yes – it's one of my favourites – but... (*He hesitates.*)

JEAN: (*Encouragingly.*) But what, John?

JOHN: (*After hesitating; apologetically.*) You're a strange girl, Jean – if you don't mind me saying so.

JEAN: (*Rising and moving up centre; belligerently.*) Oh – you think I'm strange – do you?

JOHN: (*Moving down right centre.*) Well – yes – I do. I'm sorry.

JEAN: (*Moving to JOHN; laughing.*) You don't know much about girls or you wouldn't apologize. Girls love being told by men that they're strange. They lap it up, even if they're about as strange as a helping of mashed potatoes. But did you risk sneaking out of there just to tell me I'm strange?

JOHN: No. It was something else.

JEAN: What then?

JOHN: (*Hesitating; embarrassed.*) I hope you won't think me conceited...

JEAN: I think most men are – but there have to be exceptions. Go on.

JOHN: (*Hesitantly.*) Several times I've – er – caught you looking at me...

JEAN: (*Moving down centre.*) Wait a minute. You've *caught* me looking at you? I don't like the sound of that. It really *is* rather conceited...

JOHN: (*Moving just above JEAN; embarrassed.*) Oh – no – I didn't mean...

JEAN: (*Ignoring his interruption.*) It suggests I've been staring at you all the time – and now and then you've given me a glance and *caught* me at it.

JOHN: (*Moving level with her.*) No, I didn't mean that.

(*JEAN turns away.*)

Of course I've been looking at you – and then I've seen you looking at me – that's all.

JEAN: All right, then. You looked. I looked. We both looked. (*She turns to him.*) So...?

JOHN: I'm trying to explain what happened just now, why I followed you out. You see – just before you left, I thought you looked at me as if –

(*JEAN reacts.*)

– even if you didn't know it – you wanted to talk to me. So – as this seemed a good chance, I took the risk of following you out. Was I wrong?

JEAN: No. I think it was very sweet of you, John. Thank you.

(*As JOHN is standing before her, JEAN puts out her hand as if to thank him with it. He takes JEAN's hand, not knowing what to do with it. JEAN watches him smilingly. For a moment it looks as if JOHN is about to kiss it, but then in an awkward way he quickly presses it with his other hand, that is, between both his hands, then lets it go and moves away as if embarrassed and disturbed. JEAN looks at him, without his noticing, with a gleam of triumph in her eyes. JOHN crosses to the couch and sits on it at the right end.*)

(*After a considerable pause.*) Well, John?

JOHN: (*Looking at her.*) I can't help feeling – that – you're unhappy.

(*JEAN looks gravely at JOHN but does not reply.*)

I've felt it right from the first – when you came in here with your brothers to meet everybody.

JEAN: (*Moving above the table.*) Did you feel my brothers were unhappy, too?

JOHN: No. Only you.

JEAN: Have you had a lot of practice at this, John?

JOHN: (*Bewildered.*) At what?

JEAN: (*Moving behind the couch.*) At telling girls what they like to hear. First, you tell me I'm strange. Good! Then you tell me I'm unhappy. *Very* good. Now all you have to tell me is that I'm strange and unhappy because I'm not like other girls – I'm more sensitive than they are – and people don't understand me as you do. Now, John, be honest, *were* you going to say that? (*She puts her hands on his shoulders.*)

JOHN: (*Miserably.*) Something like that.
(*JEAN laughs, but not maliciously, and crosses below the couch to centre.*)

JEAN: If you have a congregation with plenty of women in it – and you don't neglect your visiting – you'll soon be a wonderfully popular minister, John. I can see you...

JOHN: (*Rising and cutting in sharply.*) No, Jean. Say what you like about me – but don't sneer at my calling. I'm not preparing for the ministry just for something to do. I shall go out and preach the Living Word, to offer men and women the hope of salvation – and *not* to flatter foolish women. (*He looks defiantly at her.*)

JEAN: (*Mildly.*) I never said they were foolish. Of course we all are, to some extent. (*She moves to left of him.*) But I'll tell you a secret about women, John. Most of their foolishness is on the surface – they wear it like scarves and ribbons – fluttering it in the world's eye – but deeper down, just where solemn pompous men become idiots, women are far from being foolish. What is it you men preach, as if you'd made a great discovery?
(*JOHN turns to her.*)
The gospel of love. But even the silliest woman has never believed in anything else.

JOHN: But it's not the same kind of love...

JEAN: (*Cutting in.*) Oh – you mean there are nasty sinful bodies mixed up in our kind of love? You're quite right.

(*JOHN looks down.*)
We women can't help thinking we have bodies – we're reminded about them all the time – and if we completely forget about them, soon there wouldn't be any men to look longingly at them or to reproach us for having so much flesh and blood...

JOHN: (*Rising; urgently cutting in.*) Stop – please! (*He crosses below JEAN and stands below the pouffe.*)

JEAN: (*Moving to right of JOHN.*) Oh – I'm sorry, John.
I may not look it but I'm rather an argumentative sort of girl. And this is the first chance I've ever had to talk to a theological student. I once argued with a de-frocked priest in a boarding-house in Buffalo – he was drunk at the time and a bit difficult to understand...

JOHN: (*Turning away.*) I'd rather not hear about him, if you don't mind.

JEAN: (*Crossing slowly below JOHN and turning to face him.*) No, I don't mind, John. But after daring to leave the hymn-singing, because you thought I looked unhappy and ought to be talked to, you shouldn't be sulky and silent.
(*JEAN looks at JOHN. He does not look at her. She goes to him, standing close and putting a hand on his arm to turn him gently round, smiling at him. As JOHN faces her, it is clear he is tremendously aware of her physical nearness. JEAN, of course, knows exactly what she is doing. JOHN does not speak but looks as if he wants to say something.*)
Yes, John?

JOHN: (*Gripping her upper arms; urgently.*) Why do you laugh at me when all I wanted to do was to help you? I thought you were unhappy and might like to talk to me. I still think you're unhappy. I don't believe you want to argue. I think you'd like to confide in me – to tell me what's making you so unhappy – but that now you daren't. Isn't that true?

JEAN: You're hurting me.

JOHN: (*Releasing her.*) I'm sorry. I wasn't noticing what I was doing.

JEAN: And you're very strong, aren't you?

JOHN: Yes, I am – but I believe you're laughing at me again.

(*JEAN crosses below JOHN and leads him to the couch.*)

JEAN: Come on – we'll never be sensible standing here like this. (*She sits on the couch.*)

(*JOHN sits above JEAN on the couch.*)

What is it you'd like to know, John?

JOHN: I want to know why you're unhappy – and if I can help you, Jean.

JEAN: Very well. I'm one of those people who always look rather unhappy unless they're actually and blazingly happy. And as I'm not blazingly happy here – and I doubt if anybody ever was in this house – then I probably look miserable And you can help me by talking and listening – so long as you don't get sulky or squeeze my arms black and blue...

JOHN: (*Rising and moving centre.*) I said I was sorry.

JEAN: Let's forget it. Now – Aunt Mildred. Remember she's my aunt as well as yours. Aunt Mildred, then.

JOHN: What about her?

JEAN: Are you as devoted to her as she is to you?

JOHN: I try to be. She's been wonderfully kind and good to me, Jean. She's a good person – exceptionally good – you know. She's not been very well lately – she's very highly strung – so you haven't seen her at her best.

JEAN: (*Blandly.*) No, I thought I hadn't. In fact, I was saying to Douglas and Angus just now that I didn't think Aunt Mildred was at her best. And they agreed.

JOHN: (*After a small but significant pause.*) You think I'm a fool, don't you?

JEAN: Certainly not.

JOHN: (*Indignantly.*) Then why do you talk to me like that? I'd have to be a fool to believe you were sincere. I could hear the mockery. You think Aunt Mildred doesn't like you.

JEAN: She hates the sight of me. And you know it.

JOHN: No, I don't. You're exaggerating. (*He moves and sits above JEAN on the couch.*) Don't you think if you took

225

Aunt Mildred into your confidence, you wouldn't feel so unhappy – and I *know* you're unhappy – and you'd also find she didn't really dislike you – or you her. She's too good...

JEAN: (*Rising and moving down right; cutting in sharply.*) Don't say any more. You've said it. She's too good.

JOHN: (*Rising and moving down right centre.*) I didn't mean it in that way.

JEAN: But it's true.

JOHN: (*Trying to interrupt.*) Jean, I was...

JEAN: (*Moving to right of him.*) No, listen to me, John. I haven't been much among the good for some time. When you're a girl who has a living to earn, all in a big rough world, you don't see much of the good. You don't find yourself in places where they are. They're at home, being good, and you're not. So you have to get along with the wicked. And now I seem to like the wicked much better than I like the good.

JOHN: (*Annoyed.*) This is just silly flippant talk.

JEAN: (*Flaring.*) No, it isn't – and shut up! I don't say I like the *wicked* wicked – the horrors – the monsters – oh, yes – I've met a few of them. And don't think they'll go to Hell one day. The point about them is that they're in Hell now – you can smell it all around them. But those are the really *wicked* wicked. The people the good call wicked are the people I like best. My father and mother were wicked – my brothers are wicked – I'm wicked...

JOHN: (*Shouting angrily.*) I don't want to listen to such stupid childish talk...

JEAN: (*Cutting in.*) Childish! I knew more about life when I was ten than you know now – (*She moves left centre.*) or probably ever will know. Where have you been? What have you seen? What thoughts have you ever had that were your own?

JOHN: (*Annoyed.*) Oh – rot! You're no older than I am.

JEAN: (*Moving to him; smiling seductively.*) I'm a thousand years older than you are, John dear. (*She strokes his cheek, then, holding one cheek with her hand, she lightly kisses the other.*) There!

(*JOHN is obviously physically attracted to JEAN and is controlling himself, the effort making him scowl at her.*) Oh – dear! Have I gone wrong again? (*She steps back from him.*)

JOHN: (*Troubled.*) That depends.

JEAN: On what?

JOHN: On your motive – for doing what you did.

JEAN: (*Crossing to the chair down right and sitting.*) Oh! We wicked ones aren't very strong on motive. We're apt just to do things without bothering too much why we're doing them.

JOHN: (*Moving below the downstage end of the couch.*) So then you play with fire.

JEAN: Often we do – yes. Isn't it queer that should be bad? It sounds such a lovely thing to be doing – *playing with fire*. I can imagine glorious beings who live in the sun just to play fire – blue, green, crimson, golden fire – lakes and peaks and fountains of white flame…
(*ANGUS enters from the hall. He leaves the door open and stands right of it. He is a little drunk.*)

ANGUS: (*Magnificently.*)
'O, who can hold a fire in his hand
By thinking on the frosty Caucasus?'

JOHN: (*Surprised.*) Shakespeare?

ANGUS: (*Moving left centre.*) The Bard himself, Mr Harvey, sir. And don't look surprised. We bartenders, bellhops, and wandering riff-raff often have a fancy for noble language, Mr Harvey, sir. We roll it on our tongues, tasting its spice and honey, as we perform our humble and ill-rewarding tasks. (*He moves centre.*) One old soak I waited on got all his drink, after the first, by offering to fit any mood or occasion with a Shakespeare quotation. There are worse careers, my friends. Are you two sparring or billing?

JEAN: Sparring mostly. And I know what you've been doing.

ANGUS: You're quite right, Jeannie. (*He moves up centre.*) She's often right, y'know. Don't think she's always wrong. But what's happening at the musical meeting, among the decent folks?

(*ANGUS exits to the conservatory, leaving the door open. DAVID's voice is heard off, preaching.*)

JOHN: (*Moving towards JEAN; quickly and quietly.*) Will he leave us now?

JEAN: Probably not.

JOHN: (*Urgently.*) If they're not coming out at once, couldn't we go outside and finish our talk? I haven't said what I wanted to say – you wouldn't be serious – if we could be alone just for a few minutes, I could explain what I meant.

JEAN: (*Rising and smiling at him.*) All right, John – (*She leads JOHN left centre.*) it's a nice night, let's take a little walk. (*ANGUS enters from the conservatory and stands up right of the table.*)

ANGUS: (*With mock gravity.*) Our Uncle David is giving them an *address*. On the subject, I think, of sincerity. (*With an obvious burlesque of DAVID's manner.*) 'We must ask ourselves what it means to be sincere. We must not pretend to ourselves that we have it. God will not be deceived. And He demands sincerity.'

JOHN: (*Moving up centre; rather sharply.*) Don't expect me to laugh. I respect your uncle – and happen to share his beliefs about God and sincerity.

JEAN: (*Moving to JOHN.*) Come on, John.

ANGUS: (*Sharply.*) Where are you going?

JEAN: To finish our talk outside.

JOHN: Have we your permission?

JEAN: (*Hastily.*) John – shut up!

ANGUS: (*Crossing to JOHN and facing him; with one of his lightning tempers.*) Yes, you have my permission. And if you were being funny, then don't expect *me* to laugh. Because while we're here Jean and Douglas and I are giving one another permissions – we're a kind of team...

JEAN: (*Warningly.*) Angus!

ANGUS: (*To JOHN; angrily.*) And don't give me any sermons about God and sincerity. Not in this house. I don't know how much sincerity God demands. I'm not in His confidence the way some of you seem to be. But

I know how much a man needs – to be a man and not a talking rat.

JOHN: (*Cutting in; braving ANGUS's anger.*) There are no talking rats here.

ANGUS: (*Moving close to JOHN; sinister rather than angry.*) You don't know what there is here, Harvey. You run in and out of this house all the time – to be patted on the head like a good little boy – and anybody might be here, anything might be happening – and you'd be too damn stupid to know.

JOHN: I know you smell of liquor – and if Mr McBane notices it…

ANGUS: (*Cutting in; mockingly.*) Oh, yes, Uncle David mustn't smell it. Let's not be too sincere about that. Take him away, Jeannie – and scream if you need any help. (*He turns away.*)

(*JOHN, angry, is about to say something, but JEAN hastily checks him and hurries him out to the hall. ANGUS waits a moment, then crosses to the conservatory door which he opens to reveal ELSPIE standing on the threshold. She wears a different dress, more a party frock. The sound is heard of a violin playing 'Meditation' from 'Thais'.*)

(*He steps back. With a mock flourish.*) Well – well – well – little Cousin Elspie. What were you doing – spying on us?

(*ELSPIE comes into the room, crosses above the couch and moves down centre. ANGUS closes the door. The music ceases.*)

ELSPIE: No, I wasn't. I was coming in here – and then I heard you and John quarrelling – and I hate it when people sound so angry.

ANGUS: That comes of living a sheltered life, Cousin Elspie. Out there – (*He waves a hand at the wide world.*) some people are angry all the time.

ELSPIE: What people?

ANGUS: (*Moving to the couch and sitting.*) Cops – foremen – nigger-drivers – old men in saloons whose livers are turning into leather – disappointed women who run boarding houses for the overworked and underpaid – angry, angry all the time – just vats of smoking acid.

ELSPIE: You enjoy talking in that exaggerated way, don't you?

ANGUS: Sometimes, it's been the only amusement I could afford.

ELSPIE: Where have John and your sister gone to?

ANGUS: I don't know. Down the road – into the garden – on the porch – anywhere. Just to finish a talk they were having without you and me listening. Are you jealous?

ELSPIE: (*Protesting.*) John and I aren't engaged, or anything.

ANGUS: Are you jealous?

ELSPIE: I'm very fond of him because we've been friends for such a long time – but he's not in love with me and I'm certainly not in love with him.

ANGUS: Are you jealous?

ELSPIE: (*Stamping her foot; crossly.*) Oh – stop it, Angus! (*She suddenly laughs a little.*) But I suppose I am, a little. And you know what I think? I think she's deliberately trying to make him fall in love with her.

ANGUS: Why should she do that?

ELSPIE: Some girls can't help it. They're born flirts and men-stealers.

ANGUS: Bitches, you mean. (*He sits up.*) But if you're suggesting that Jean's one...

ELSPIE: (*Cutting in.*) No, nothing as bad as that. But John's very attractive, you know.

ANGUS: No, I didn't know.

ELSPIE: All my friends think he is. And some of them are jealous of me.

ANGUS: (*Rising and moving to right of ELSPIE.*) Lots of jealousy round here, isn't there? The sheltered life again, I suppose. Too many regular meals and nothing else to do. You ought to import some of those angry people into your circle, and then have to take 'em on an empty stomach...

ELSPIE: (*Crossing to the love-seat.*) I don't know what you're talking about.

ANGUS: (*Looking at ELSPIE; wonderingly.*) So dense. Yet so sensitive. Like something from another species.

ELSPIE: (*Sitting on the downstage side of the love-seat.*)
I thought for a moment you and John were going to
fight – I mean, really fight.

ANGUS: (*Crossing to the pouffe.*) Sorry to disappoint you.

ELSPIE: Don't be silly. I'd have been terrified.

ANGUS: (*Kneeling on the pouffe.*) You'd have had a
wonderful time.

ELSPIE: What a horrible thing to say.

ANGUS: I've been where dainty refined little darlings like
you have screamed with delight to see men bleeding.
You retreat from Nature but you do it in a circle, and
meet it again when it's panting, sweating and bleeding. If
ever we have a big war, you'll be tripping about, fresh as
roses, your eyes brighter, your lips redder than ever –
giving yourselves to the prize butcher boys. (*He moves to
the table.*) No – don't say it – you don't know what I'm
talking about.

ELSPIE: If there had been a fight, you wouldn't have liked
it. John's terrible when he loses his temper – and he's
very strong – as strong as you are, perhaps stronger.

ANGUS: He might be, but I'm a dirty fighter. Not from
choice, but from necessity. Where I've been, all the
fighting's been dirty. (*He moves to right of the love-seat.*)
Nasty rough men, Elspie dear, in a nasty rough world.

ELSPIE: I don't understand you, Angus. You're always
boasting about the horrible work you've had to do in
horrible places – as if you were just a lumberman or a
sailor or something like that – yet all the time you talk
in this clever way I don't understand and you can quote
poetry...

ANGUS: (*Sitting on the upstage side of the love-seat.*) I know.
Isn't it fascinating?

ELSPIE: (*Keeping still and looking at him.*) Yes, in a way – it is.

ANGUS: (*Leaning close to her.*) What way?

ELSPIE: (*Almost in a whisper.*) I'm not sure. (*She pauses.*)
I suppose – you've met – all kinds of girls.

ANGUS: (*Almost in a whisper.*) No. Mostly big heavy dark
girls. And I don't like big heavy dark girls. I like

delicious small fair girls. (*He takes her face in his hands, obviously preparing to kiss her.*)

ELSPIE: No, you mustn't – somebody'll come in – no, please don't. (*But she makes no attempt to break away.*)

(*ANGUS kisses ELSPIE with notable skill and some appearance of passion. It is a fairly long kiss and the movement of ELSPIE's arms suggests that after the first moment she is eagerly responding to it. At the end she releases her arms but leans back a little in his and looks solemnly into his face.*)

Why did you do that?

ANGUS: You mean, why did *we* do that?

ELSPIE: I don't know. I never thought I would. I didn't seem like me – but somebody else who made me do it. You've been drinking, haven't you?

ANGUS: A few nips. Nasty?

ELSPIE: It would have been to me – but it wasn't to – the somebody else. *She* rather liked it.

ANGUS: Then, she's the one I'd better talk to.

ELSPIE: *She* doesn't want to talk.

(*ELSPIE puts her face up again and they go into a mutually passionate embrace and kiss.*

DOUGLAS enters from the hall. ELSPIE gives a little scream when she sees DOUGLAS, breaks away, rises, crosses and exits hurriedly to the conservatory, closing the door behind her. ANGUS and DOUGLAS watch her go, then look at each other.)

DOUGLAS: (*Moving down coldly; centre and rather slowly.*) Why this canoodling?

ANGUS: Why not?

DOUGLAS: You answer me first.

ANGUS: Well, she's a pretty little thing – and like most of 'em she enjoys being kissed. Of course, I enjoy it, too. But I thought you might be asking on her behalf.

DOUGLAS: Now, I'll answer your question – *why not?* Either you're just idly amusing yourself or you're not. If you're idly amusing yourself, it isn't fair to the girl.

ANGUS: (*Rising and moving to left of DOUGLAS.*) We didn't come here to be fair to people, did we?

DOUGLAS: No, but she doesn't count. She doesn't belong to their generation.

ANGUS: We're told that the sins of the fathers shall be visited upon the children...

DOUGLAS: That may be good enough for the Ancient Hebrews, but it isn't good enough for us. Then, if you're not idly amusing yourself, if you're beginning to take the girl seriously, then that isn't fair to Jean and me. By the way, where is Jean?

ANGUS: She went out with young Harvey.

(*DOUGLAS is about to protest.*)

No, I don't think you'll have to talk severely to Jean, too. She nearly has the good boy on a string, but she'll pull it to upset dear Aunt Mildred. But I wasn't working for the cause. I felt it was after hours and I needed a little innocent amusement. Not that it would be innocent long with sweet little Elspie, who has a convenient secondary self, clinging, hot, almost ready for anything.

(*DOUGLAS does not reply but stares at ANGUS with cold disgust.*)

Don't look at me like that, Doug.

DOUGLAS: (*Distastefully.*) Did you hear yourself then?

ANGUS: Yes – I was talking like a load of manure. And when I've heard other fellows talking like that, I've wanted to put my boot to their backsides.

DOUGLAS: (*Moving up centre.*) I'm glad to hear it.

ANGUS: (*Following DOUGLAS; fiercely.*) Don't give me that stuff, Doug. I'm not taking any of it from you. You persuaded me I ought to come here. All right, I'm here. But I'm not like you. I can't be cool and calm and work to a plan. I can't be detached. If I go wrong, it's because I feel wrong. If it upsets your plan, I'm sorry. But – by God – you're not going to stand there, turning your nose up at me, as if I were a bad smell, just because I do and say a few things you don't approve of. I have to work this out as best I can. If I don't risk overdoing it, I can't do anything at all. And if you ask me, Jean's the same.

DOUGLAS: (*Moving to right of ANGUS.*) No, she isn't. And at least she keeps sober.

ANGUS: I'm not drunk – far from it.

DOUGLAS: You're not sober. If you had been, you'd have left that girl alone.

ANGUS: (*Urgently.*) All right, all right, I need a few drinks. There are some jobs – you know them as well as I do – that have to be done on a few drinks. And to me this is one of them. (*He turns to DOUGLAS.*) If it isn't to you, then count yourself lucky. But for God's sake don't pull a sour face on me – just because you've sent me up the chimney and I've come down black.

DOUGLAS: (*Angrily.*) And don't you pretend now, when you're beginning to lose your head, that all this is something I've just cooked up. You know damned well we're all three in it together, we've always been in it together, we made the same promises...

ANGUS: (*Cutting in.*) In short, we're all three equally in it.

DOUGLAS: Yes, of course.

ANGUS: Then who the hell made you the boss man?

DOUGLAS: (*Looking steadily at ANGUS; quietly.*) Do you want me to tell you?

ANGUS: (*Moving down left; not meeting the challenge.*) No, I'd rather talk about something else. (*He suddenly grins disarmingly.*) But you can give me a cigarette.

DOUGLAS: (*Moving to ANGUS and offering him a cigarette.*) They'll be out of that meeting very soon.

(*ANGUS takes a cigarette and lights it.*)

ANGUS: And catch me smoking? All right, then. I'm the one who smokes – the really bad one – Hellfire Angus...
(*MILDRED enters from the conservatory, leaving the door open. She moves up right of the couch and sniffs in disgust.*)
I'm just saying, Aunt Mildred – I'm the one you must blame – I smoke – I drink – I...

MILDRED: (*Cutting in; coldly.*) This room reeks of tobacco and liquor. Your Uncle David will be here soon – they're about to sing the closing hymn – and don't be surprised if he's extremely angry.

ANGUS: You're not, of course.

MILDRED: No, merely sorry. I hoped that somewhere you might have picked up a few manners. But you're behaving like an ill-bred lout. This is our house – you are our guests – we are entitled to some consideration. Whatever faults your father had, at least he had the instincts of a gentleman. He wouldn't have allowed you to turn your hostess's drawing-room into a saloon.

ANGUS: (*With a rueful laugh.*) *Touché!* (*He disposes of the cigarette rather elaborately into the palm pot down left.*) (*MILDRED looks accusingly from one brother to the other. Voices are heard off singing 'Now the Day is Over'. It is clearly heard at first but the sound is cut down, though not faded out altogether, when the dialogue starts.*)

DOUGLAS: (*Moving centre; dangerously quiet.*) Is there anything else you want to tell me about my father?

MILDRED: (*Moving to right of DOUGLAS; firmly.*) No. But I want *you* to tell *me* what happened to Elspie, who came out here and then returned to the meeting, distressed about something. And also what has become of my nephew John. (*She looks from one to the other.*) (*DOUGLAS and ANGUS do not reply.*) (*She loses her temper.*) Oh, don't be stupid! There isn't much time. What happened?

DOUGLAS: (*Crossing below MILDRED and standing above the couch.*) I'm not stupid. And to me there seems to be plenty of time. (*He sits on the back of the couch.*) As for what happened, I don't know.

ANGUS: (*Moving to left of MILDRED.*) I do. I don't know why Elspie left your meeting, though I could easily guess. But she talked to me, chiefly about fighting, of all things – you'll have to watch her there – and she went back, I imagine, because Douglas interrupted us. As for your nephew John, I believe he followed my sister out...

MILDRED: (*Indignantly.*) I saw her making great eyes at him. Well, where are they?

ANGUS: Out somewhere, still talking.

MILDRED: (*Incredulously.*) Talking!

DOUGLAS: Why not? What did you think they were doing?

ANGUS: I don't know about John, but I'll bet Jean's still talking. Most singing waitresses and chorus girls will

235

argue about *something*. Jean's the only one who'll argue about *anything*. They're probably up to the neck now in the doctrine of infant baptism.

MILDRED: Nonsense!

ANGUS: (*Moving above the love-seat.*) All right – nonsense, then.

MILDRED: (*Moving above the table; to Douglas.*) Was your sister a chorus girl – and a – what is it – singing waitress?

DOUGLAS: (*Smooth and deadly.*) I think so – yes. Angus knows more about it than I do. But if you like, Aunt Mildred, we can give you a list of the things we've done to earn a living, You might find it quite amusing.

MILDRED: Indeed! And what exactly is a singing waitress?

ANGUS: (*Listening.*) You'd better ask Jean. She's here.

(*JEAN and JOHN enter from the hall.*)

MILDRED: John!

JOHN: (*Hastily.*) Oh – Aunt Mildred – I...

MILDRED: (*Cutting in; with authority.*) Time for excuses later. They're still singing the final hymn and if you hurry you can help Uncle David with his 'good nights'. But hurry.

(*JOHN crosses to the conservatory door.*)

ANGUS: (*Calling to JOHN.*) Don't forget – his address was about sincerity. (*He sits on the arm of the love-seat.*)

(*JOHN exits hastily to the conservatory, closing the door behind him. The sound of the singing ceases.*)

MILDRED: (*To JEAN; severely.*) Where did you take him?

JEAN: (*Sitting on the pouffe.*) To a house near the waterfront – furnished in the Oriental style – its air thick with the fumes of Chinese incense and opium...

ANGUS: (*Laughing.*) Good old Jeannie!

MILDRED: (*Moving to right of the pouffe; angrily.*) But you can't evade my question by talking impudent nonsense. Where have you been?

JEAN: We've been walking round the block – arguing. You know, I always feel my mind's in a muddle about everything, but poor John's is even worse...

MILDRED: John is doing exceptionally well at the theological training college. Who are you to criticize him? And tell me – what is a singing waitress?

JEAN: (*Cheerfully.*) Oh – did Angus tell you I'd been one? Well, it's slow murder. You have to be a work horse and pet kitten at one and the same time. You have to wait on the customers, lugging round a dozen steins of beer, while you dazzle and torment them with short skirts and low necks. You're giving the boys a good time, one of the girly-girls – with flat feet, cramp and laryngitis. Don't suggest it to Elspie – she wouldn't last a week.

MILDRED: (*Outraged.*) Elspie! David McBane's daughter!

JEAN: (*Rising; flashing out.*) And I'm Charles McBane's daughter.

(*ANGUS and DOUGLAS rise.*)

MILDRED: I suppose you are. (*She looks at them and realizes she has gone too far. Hastily.*) No – no – of course you are. Now, listen to me.

(*JEAN sits on the pouffe.*)

I'm not a wealthy woman. But if you will leave this house at once I'll give you a thousand dollars, to divide as you please.

(*The others exchange surprised glances, then stare at MILDRED.*)

Well?

DOUGLAS: (*Moving above the couch.*) We haven't signed that deed yet, you know.

MILDRED: (*Moving towards DOUGLAS.*) You can still sign the deed. In fact, you must. But I'm only asking you to leave this house and to promise never to return to it. You'll have a thousand dollars to divide between you. And I warn you that if you refuse, I shall do all I can to persuade my brother-in-law to tell you to go – and of course in that case I shan't give you a cent.

DOUGLAS: (*Sitting on the back of the couch.*) Why waste a thousand dollars, then?

MILDRED: Because I prefer not to have to explain to him why I want you to go. There are some things I understand

that he doesn't understand, and I'd rather he didn't
understand. (*She turns up centre. Suddenly letting go.*) Oh –
what on earth induced him to ask you to stay here?

DOUGLAS: I can tell you that. I did. No visit, no signature.

MILDRED: (*With passionate emphasis.*) And I knew at once
you'd make mischief. You've only been here – what –
three days – four days – yet everything's going wrong.
We were a peaceful, contented, happy household...

JEAN: (*Very sharply.*) Never!

MILDRED: (*Moving down centre.*) What did you say?

JEAN: (*With great emphasis.*) I said – *Never!* You weren't
peaceful, you weren't contented, you weren't happy –
never – never – never – never! And now I wouldn't
leave at once if you offered me ten thousand dollars.

ANGUS: (*Moving to left of the entre pouffe.*) That's the stuff
Jeannie! And I'll tell you a secret, Aunt Mildred dear.
Not half an hour ago I was wanting to leave – without
anybody paying me anything – but now I've changed my
mind. Or you've changed it for me. Y'know, you're one
of those unlucky people who always manage to talk
themselves out of their own argument, who add a final
clincher or two and blow their whole case to
smithereens.

MILDRED: (*Moving below the table and turning to
DOUGLAS.*) You seem to have more sense than these
two, Douglas...

DOUGLAS: (*Calmly.*) I'm glad you think I've more sense
than Jean and Angus. I've always felt I had. In fact, I've
always believed that with half a chance I could do very
well in business...

MILDRED: (*Cutting in: impatiently.*) Yes – yes – but what do
you say to my offer?

DOUGLAS: (*Smiling; calmly.*) I say – 'No'.

MILDRED: (*Angrily.*) Then you're a fool, too.

DOUGLAS: (*Smiling.*) We'll see.

(*DAVID enters from the conservatory. He wears a frock coat
and appropriate trousers, etc.
MALCOLM, ELSPIE and JOHN follow him on. DAVID is
very expansive following his meeting, not happy so much as*

238

full of himself. He is laying down the law as he enters. JEAN
rises, moves and sits on the upstage side of the love-seat.
ANGUS moves to the hall door and leans against the upstage
doorjamb. ELSPIE moves to the chair down right and sits.
JOHN stands above ELSPIE. MALCOLM stands up right
centre. MILDRED moves to right of the pouffe. DAVID crosses
to centre.)

DAVID: (*As he enters.*) ...and I say, it's not a lot to ask. I'm
not asking for it as any return for anything I may have
done for all of you. It's not my work but the Lord's work
I'm bringing to your notice.

MILDRED: (*With forced enthusiasm.*) A splendid meeting,
David. And what a fine address you gave us.

DAVID: Glad you thought so, Mildred. It *was* a good
meeting – but as I've just been saying, it would have
been a better one for me if I hadn't seen members of my
own family, who ought to set an example, sneaking out
and sneaking back again...

MILDRED: Have they told you what was wrong?

DAVID: Haven't given 'em a chance to, yet. (*He looks at*
JOHN and ELSPIE.) Well, what *was* wrong?

MILDRED: (*Before they can reply; hastily.*) No, David. I can
tell you, better than they can. The complete truth, too.

DAVID: Now – now – Mildred – you're getting worked up
about something – what *is* this? And who's been using
tobacco here?

ANGUS: I have. I'm a great user of tobacco, Uncle David.

DAVID: Not in this house you're not, lad. And if you
haven't the strength of mind to keep off tobacco, you'd
better take yourself somewhere else.

MILDRED: (*With force.*) Yes – and take his brother and
sister with him. David, I have to tell you that you're
entirely mistaken in these three young people. They are
their father all over again – and a good deal worse.
They've no decent respect for anybody or anything.
What happened at the meeting tonight was entirely due
to their influence – and to nothing else. I mistrusted
them the moment I first set eyes on them the other night.

But out of the goodness of your heart you were so determined we should make them welcome, I couldn't tell you what I felt. I'm convinced now they only came here to make mischief. (*She sits on the pouffe.*)

(*MALCOLM moves down a little.*)

DAVID: But, Mildred...

MILDRED: (*Rather faintly but still urgently.*) No, David, please – let me say what I have to say. I came out early – to try and persuade them to leave us, before worse happened. They refused, laughed at me. I beg you – to order them out of this house. You don't understand yet – you haven't seen as much of them as the rest of us have – I tell you they're *wicked*. Ask the others – if they'll only tell you the truth.

DAVID: (*Moving to MALCOLM.*) Anything in this, Malcolm?

MALCOLM: (*Hesitating.*) Well – er – I wouldn't say...

ANGUS: (*Moving above the love-seat; cutting in, pointedly.*) I'm sure Uncle Malcolm wouldn't like to see us turned out, having to take rooms downtown – *you* know the kind of place, Uncle Malcolm – or should I explain...

MALCOLM: (*Giving in; hastily.*) That'll do. No, David, I can't agree with Mildred – she's not well – so she's exaggerating. (*He moves up centre.*)

DOUGLAS: (*Smoothly but pointedly.*) I'm sure Cousin Elspie wouldn't like us to go – would you, Cousin Elspie? (*ANGUS moves down left.*)

ELSPIE: (*Flashing a look at ANGUS.*) No. I want them to stay, Father.

JEAN: And so does John – (*To JOHN.*) don't you?

JOHN: (*Eagerly.*) Yes, I do. I really do, Mr McBane.

MILDRED: (*Deflated.*) Help me upstairs, John, before you make a bigger fool of yourself.

(*JOHN crosses to MILDRED.*)

I won't stay down for supper, David. (*She rises.*) Bridget can bring me a tray.

DAVID: I'll tell her. You have some rest, Mildred – and don't go fancying things are worse than they are.

(*MILDRED and JOHN exit to the hall.*)

I've still a bit of business to transact with these young
people. (*He moves centre.*) And that's something we can do
this very night, Douglas lad. You have the document and
the three of you can sign it.

DOUGLAS: (*Smiling calmly.*) No, not tonight, Uncle David.
I left the deed today with a friend of mine downtown.

DAVID: (*Disturbed at this.*) That was a foolish thing to do.
What friend?

DOUGLAS: (*Calmly.*) He knows you – but you wouldn't
know him.

DAVID: I don't know about you folk, but I'm sharp set. The
Lord's work puts a fine edge on a man's appetite. (*He
exits to the hall.*)
(*MALCOLM follows him out. ELSPIE rises, crosses and exits
to the hall. JEAN, ANGUS and DOUGLAS linger behind,
as DAVID's voice can be heard booming outside the room.
ANGUS and DOUGLAS are jubilant, JEAN troubled.
ANGUS hastily takes the bottle of whisky from his pocket.
DOUGLAS rises. ANGUS crosses and stands above the table.
JEAN rises and moves towards the hall door.*)

ANGUS: (*Jubilantly.*) We did it. We did it. And every shot
rang a bell.

DOUGLAS: I rang the old man's with the last cartridge.
Now we go when we're ready to go, not before.

ANGUS: (*Holding out the bottle.*) Here, Jean, one for victory.
(*JEAN shakes her head.*)
Well, we did win, didn't we?

JEAN: (*Sombrely.*) Yes, we won. (*She turns to go.*)
(*ANGUS and DOUGLAS, puzzled, watch JEAN as she goes
and follow her towards the hall door as – the curtain falls.*)

End of Act One.

ACT TWO

Scene 1

Scene – the same. Evening, five days later.

When the curtain rises, the room is empty but the lights are full on. The hall door is closed and the conservatory door is fully open. For a few moments the audience must be able to take in the empty, silent, lighted, expectant room, then the voices of GRATTON and BRIDGET are heard off in the hall. GRATTON enters from the hall, peers into the room to see if anyone is there, then speaks over his shoulder. He carries his bag.

GRATTON: We'll talk in here, Bridget. (*He comes into the room and puts his bag on the table.*)
    (*BRIDGET enters from the hall, closes the door, looks at GRATTON with keen expectancy and moves to left of him.*)
    (*His manner is easy but confidential.*) Now, Bridget, I'm taking you into my confidence. I want to impress upon you, Bridget, that your mistress – Mrs McBane – is really a sick woman this time. There have been occasions when she'd little the matter with her. But not this time. She needs all the care and rest we can give her. I don't want her to feel worried and anxious. So whatever happens down here, keep her out of it.

BRIDGET: Yes, Doctor.

GRATTON: Now – tell me what's happening in this house.

BRIDGET: Well, now, the three of 'em's still here – and wouldn't be, I'm thinking, but himself, Mr David McBane, was called away three or four days ago, and only came back late last night an' has been out all day today.
    (*JEAN, DOUGLAS and ANGUS enter from the hall. The two men are dressed as before, but JEAN's costume is chosen with an eye to what follows in this scene. ANGUS moves down left. JEAN stands just above ANGUS and DOUGLAS just above JEAN. GRATTON looks curiously for a few moments at the three.*)

GRATTON: (*Clearly dismissing her.*) Now, Bridget, remember what I said about Mrs McBane.

BRIDGET: I will that, Doctor.

(*BRIDGET hurries out to the hall. The three face GRATTON as a group.*)

GRATTON: (*Taking a prescription from his bag.*) I'm Dr Gratton – and I'd like a word with you.

JEAN: I'm Jean McBane. These are my brothers – Douglas – Angus. You've seen Aunt Mildred?

GRATTON: Yes. I'm the family doctor here.

JEAN: How is she?

GRATTON: Far from well. A heart condition. And I'll tell you what I've just told Bridget – don't do or say anything to excite her. I've ordered her to stay in bed – so all you have to do is to keep away. I don't suppose she'll ask to see you, because from what I can gather – she doesn't like you.

ANGUS: We don't like her.

JEAN: (*Warningly.*) Angus!

GRATTON: No, young woman. He's right and you're wrong. Don't cover anything up for my sake. (*He crosses above the sofa and puts the prescription on the bookcase.*) I've been looking after this family for over thirty years. I knew your father very well...

JEAN: (*Crossing to right centre; eagerly.*) Of course – you must have done. How stupid I've been. Why didn't I think of that before?

DOUGLAS: (*Moving down centre.*) Because we didn't come to this house to hear about our father.

GRATTON: (*Looking curiously at DOUGLAS.*) You didn't, eh?

DOUGLAS: (*Curtly.*) No.

(*GRATTON regards DOUGLAS speculatively a moment longer, then moves to the couch, sits and looks at JEAN.*)

GRATTON: Can you remember your father, Jean?

JEAN: (*Kneeling at GRATTON's feet.*) Not really. Just somebody very big – a smell of cigars and whisky – and a story about a bear – and he was telling that to Douglas, not to me.

GRATTON: I liked Charlie McBane. A lot of people didn't.

DOUGLAS: (*Sitting on the pouffe and facing up stage; bitterly.*) We know that.

GRATTON: (*Dryly.*) So I imagine. But it's all old history – over and done with.

ANGUS: (*Moving above the love-seat.*) Is it, Doctor? How do *you* know? Suppose now and then I get fighting mad just because once – let's say – I wanted a pair of skates and couldn't have them – and I couldn't have them because some people didn't like my father. Is that old history, over and done with?

GRATTON: Are you asking me something or telling me something?

ANGUS: I'm asking you. What's the answer?

GRATTON: You won't like it.

ANGUS: Go on.

GRATTON: (*Rising.*) You're a grown man, not a child. If you can't get over once wanting a pair of skates and not having them, you'd better start blaming yourself, not other people.

ANGUS: (*Moving down left; stung.*) That's too simple...
(*GRATTON looks at ANGUS, then turns to move to the table.*)

JEAN: (*Breaking it up.*) Tell me about my father, Dr Gratton – please.

GRATTON: (*Stopping and turning.*) Your grandfather – Donald McBane – who built up the business – was a hard man, strict and severe with himself and with everybody else. There was wild blood in him somewhere but old Donald had it bottled in iron. But it had to come out – and it came out in Charlie. He was wild all right. But he only behaved like a lot of the men he preferred to work with – up in the logging camps. That's where Charlie belonged, where he always wanted to be. (*He moves to the table and closes his bag.*)
(*ANGUS sits on the back of the love-seat.*)
He was as out of place here in Toronto, in the offices and parlours and churches, as a bull moose. He couldn't be

fitted into a tame pattern, like his three brothers. I went
up into the rough country with him once, and there
seemed nothing wrong with him there – indeed, there
wasn't – you had to have men like him to break that
country. And the old man, though he gave poor Charlie
hell, understood this in his way…

DOUGLAS: (*Cutting in; bitterly.*) But nobody else did. Or if
they did, they didn't care.

GRATTON: How old are you?

DOUGLAS: Twenty-seven. Why?

GRATTON: Take an old doctor's advice – and get rid of
that bitterness. Another ten years of it and you won't
have any digestion left – then you'll have to start eating
yourself – the ulcers you'll have will do that.

ANGUS: (*Rising.*) Now look here…

GRATTON: No, let's leave it at that. I don't want to know
why you're here or what you think you're doing. Family
business isn't my concern. (*He moves above the couch to
right of it.*) But some things are – I'm the doctor round
here – and some of the mess I'll have to clear up. I liked
your father. I'm prepared to like you. But only if you
make up your minds either to go away or to behave
yourselves.

ANGUS: And not make any trouble for our nice, quiet,
respectable, rich Toronto relations – your patients and
good friends.

GRATTON: (*Crossing below the couch to centre; losing his
temper.*) Don't talk like a jackass. Who do you think lives
here? The Governor-General? Andrew Carnegie?
(*ANGUS sits on the love-seat.*)
All you're dealing with are an elderly disappointed
woman with a weak heart, an elderly worried man with a
high blood pressure, a rather unstable inexperienced girl
– and here you are, the three of you, young and strong as
horses, able to earn a living…

JEAN: (*Rising; breaking in hotly.*) Yes – and you ought to see
the looks on their faces when we tell them what jobs
we've had…

GRATTON: (*Cutting in.*) They're shocked. Of course they're shocked. I've heard about that. (*He moves to the table.*) And don't tell me you haven't done your damnedest to give them a shock. All right, try shocking *me* now.

ANGUS: Why should we? You don't come into this.

GRATTON: Into *what?* Just tell me that.

DOUGLAS: (*Rising; smoothly but with force.*) Into the family business that you've told us isn't your concern, Doctor.

GRATTON: (*Trying to interrupt.*) Listen here...

DOUGLAS: No, Doctor. You listen to me. You've told me that feelings of bitterness can produce ulcers. On the same interesting theory, perhaps some other sort of feeling, if it goes on long enough, can produce bad hearts and high blood pressures – perhaps some sort of guilty feeling. (*He moves up centre.*)
(*DAVID enters from the hall and stands a moment glaring at DOUGLAS, who stares back at him defiantly.*)

GRATTON: (*Picking up his bag and crossing to the hall door; hastily.*) David, I'd like a quick word with you about Mildred – and I can't wait.

DAVID: (*Motioning GRATTON out of the door.*) I'll see you out, Edward.
(*GRATTON exits to the hall.*)
You three stay here. I've something important to say to you. (*DAVID exits to the hall, leaving the door open.*)

DOUGLAS: (*Crossing to the couch and sitting; rather grimly.*) This is it, I think. The big blow up.

ANGUS: (*Rising and moving up left.*) I'm in the mood. (*He moves down left.*)

DOUGLAS: Well, stay in the mood, but keep quiet. This is where I do the talking.

JEAN: I hated that rather nice old doctor. Then I hated myself for hating him. That's too much hate. (*She moves up centre.*) Now I can't decide whether I want to go away and have a quiet cry or stay down here and do the cakewalk.

ANGUS: (*Crossing to centre and imitating a Negro.*) Wal, Miss Jean, Ah'd jus' soon do that o' cakewalk. (*He bows to JEAN.*)

(*JEAN moves to left of the pouffe, enters into the spirit of it and adopts the same style as ANGUS.*)

JEAN: Massa Angus, Ah wanna tell you it might do me a whole heap o' good to do the cakewalk.

ANGUS: (*Moving below the pouffe; louder.*) If dat's so, Miss Jean – (*He moves up centre.*) den we's all set to do de cakewalk an' den de ol' buck an' wing.

JEAN: (*Moving down left; laughing.*) De buck an' wing, Massa Angus…

ANGUS: Yas indeedy, ma'am.

DOUGLAS: (*Angrily.*) Oh – for God's sake – I'm trying to think.

ANGUS: (*In his ordinary voice.*) And we're trying not to think. Right, Jeannie?

JEAN: Right, Angus. And he'll never understand the way it takes us.

ANGUS: I keep telling him so. He doesn't see that you and I have to have a safety-valve – to blow off steam.

DOUGLAS: (*Rising.*) You think *I* don't need one? If so, it's you two who don't understand. (*He moves down right.*) And if you don't, then I'm alone.

JEAN: (*Wonderingly.*) So you feel that, too, Douglas. I wonder. (*She sits on the upstage side of the love-seat.*)

ANGUS: (*Sitting on the pouffe.*) No wondering – not yet. Not until we know what our good Uncle David has to say. (*There is a moment's pause. DAVID enters from the hall, carefully closes the door, then stares at the others for a moment.*)

DAVID: (*Crossing to centre; in curt authoritative style.*) You three young people have a lot of wrong ideas. One of them is about me. I like to sing hymns, bow my head in prayer, worship my maker. By your way of thinking that means I'm a fool. That's one of your mistakes, among a lot of others. I've been the head of a successful commercial house, engaged in very competitive business for over twenty years. If you'd made a few enquiries about me…

DOUGLAS: (*Moving right centre; cutting in curtly.*) I've made a lot of enquiries about you.

DAVID: (*Curtly.*) Then you haven't the sense to understand what you've been told. I brought you here to sign something. Now you'll sign it – and leave in the morning. Or tonight, if you prefer it.

DOUGLAS: I told you the other night, before you went away, I hadn't got the deed. I still haven't got it.

DAVID: No, but I have. (*He produces a folded document from his inside pocket.*) Now, let's stop playing boys' games and attend to business. Once you've signed this I give each of you a cheque on the firm for seven hundred and fifty dollars. Do what you like with the money – (*He moves to right of ANGUS.*) smoke it, drink it – throw it in the gutter – and as far away from this house as you can go. (*He is in a rage now.*) I brought you here to give you a chance – dead against what I know now was good advice – you'd bad blood in you and had been dragged up like ragamuffins…

ANGUS: (*Rising and fiercely cutting in.*) Drop it, you damned old hypocrite.

DOUGLAS: (*Fiercely.*) Shut up, Angus. Leave him to me. (*To DAVID. With cold precision.*) Go on. You were giving us a chance.

DAVID: (*To DOUGLAS; still angry.*) Don't think I'm blind and deaf. I know what goes on under my own roof. Every filthy monkey trick. Now sign – and you'll get your cheques. Then clear out. (*He holds out the document to DOUGLAS.*)

DOUGLAS: (*Taking the document; coolly.*) Anything more to say?

DAVID: (*Crossing below DOUGLAS and standing down right, still angry.*) No – no – no. Go on – get on with it.

DOUGLAS: (*With a step towards DAVID; smiling at him.*) All right. I will. (*He tears up the document and flings down the pieces.*)

(*DAVID aghast, turns to DOUGLAS but is unable to speak for a moment.*)

DAVID: (*Shouting with rage.*) Why – you – you young idiot – you won't get a cent now.

DOUGLAS: My grandfather left his four sons equal shares in the firm. My father was tricked out of his share. The rest of you have had it. For twenty-five years. Two hundred thousand dollars is a modest estimate of what his share is worth during all that time. You've taken more than two hundred thousand from us. But we'll call it that – a nice round figure.

DAVID: (*Cooler now.*) So that's it. Just childish – childish. We don't owe you a cent. Nobody tricked your father out of anything. He made a bad choice. He was unlucky. But then he never had a good head for business.

ANGUS: (*Grimly.*) We know that.

DAVID: (*Crossing below DOUGLAS to right of ANGUS.*) It's time you knew a bit more. Your father never liked office work, never wanted to stay here in Toronto. We had a subsidiary company called Northern Timber Territories. Your father took over all our shares in that company in exchange for his holding in McBane and Sons. That suited him, it suited us. It was a straightforward business transaction. Unfortunately, Northern Timber Territories went to pieces in his hands.

DOUGLAS: (*Moving down right; promptly and grimly.*) And left him without a cent. He had to take a foreman's job. It killed him.

DAVID: Drink killed him, not work.

JEAN: (*Bitterly.*) You're a great Christian, you are. When they're stoning sinners you're right out in front with a rock in your hands.

DAVID: A man pays himself the wages of sin.

(*JEAN rises and moves down left.*)

But if you think we're hard-hearted here, let me tell you this. After your father died, we offered your mother an allowance, enough to bring up you three decently and respectably.

(*JEAN sits on the arm of the love-seat.*)

She refused it. She insulted us.

DOUGLAS: (*Moving right centre.*) Shall I tell you why?

DAVID: No, *I'll* tell *you.* Because she was an ignorant, foolish woman...

ANGUS: (*Very sharply cutting in.*) That's enough.

DAVID: (*Moving to left of DOUGLAS.*) Like you, she imagined she had a big claim on us. She wanted your father's original share – or nothing. Childish nonsense! (*JEAN sits on the downstage side of the love-seat.*) Like your two hundred thousand dollars. Now, don't waste any more of my time and patience. (*He turns and moves up centre.*)

DOUGLAS: (*Following DAVID.*) Just a minute, if you don't mind – *Uncle David.* It's true my mother knew nothing about business. But my father had told her something she couldn't forget. He'd told her – not once but a thousand times – that he never remembered signing himself out of McBane and Sons into Northern Timber Territories.

DAVID: Charles never remembered doing anything he was sorry for afterwards. One reason why he was useless in business. But of course he signed all the necessary transfers.

DOUGLAS: In what condition?

DAVID: He was never sober very long when he came to Toronto. We couldn't help that.

DOUGLAS: You could that time. You made sure he was drunk – very drunk.

DAVID: (*Sharply.*) That's not true. He was the only one of us who took liquor. And he must have known what he was doing. He signed the transfers. There was a witness, of course.

DOUGLAS: (*Staring hard at DAVID; rather slowly.*) Yes, an assistant cashier called Fricker who left Toronto just afterwards – *oddly enough.*

DAVID: He went out west somewhere.

DOUGLAS: (*Moving below the couch and standing down right of it.*) He went to Winnipeg.

DAVID: Yes, Winnipeg, I believe it was. He died out there a few years ago.

DOUGLAS: He wasn't dead when I talked to him yesterday.

DAVID: (*Turning to DOUGLAS; staggered.*) You're sure it was the same man?

DOUGLAS: (*Leaning on the back of the couch.*) I made sure of a lot of things before I told you that you owed us two hundred thousand dollars.

DAVID: What did Fricker tell you?

DOUGLAS: Plenty. There's a fuse waiting for a match. And I can supply the match.

DAVID: What did Fricker tell you?

DOUGLAS: Enough to confirm what my mother had always told us. My father signed away his inheritance – ours, too – when he was too drunk to know what he was doing.

(*JEAN rises. ANGUS moves above the love-seat.*)

JEAN: (*Together with ANGUS. She gasps.*) It's true then!

ANGUS: (*Together with JEAN.*) The psalm-singing cheats.

DOUGLAS: (*Moving in front of the couch.*) The pen had to be put into his hand and guided to the paper. When Fricker knew who I was, he discovered he had a conscience. He admitted he'd been bribed to act as witness...

DAVID: (*Bursting in.*) I don't believe it. Either he's lying – or you are. Where is he?

DOUGLAS: (*Sitting on the couch.*) Find him. I had to.

DAVID: Don't think I can't. I remember he has a brother here. (*He moves towards the hall door.*) I'll find him tonight.

DOUGLAS: No doubt. But don't offer him too much to change his mind.

DAVID: (*Passionately.*) I never bribed him. And I wouldn't bribe him now.

DOUGLAS: It's here in black and white. (*He takes a document from his pocket.*) Want to see his signature?

DAVID: No, I want the truth. And I'll find him and get it out of him if it takes all night. (*He exits hurriedly to the hall, slamming the door behind him.*)

(*DOUGLAS puts the document in his pocket and relaxes, rather exhausted.*)

JEAN: (*Crossing to DOUGLAS.*) Is it really true, Douglas? (*ANGUS moves slowly up left, then down centre and crosses to left.*)

DOUGLAS: Every word. Though I must admit this fellow Fricker is now a boozy, muddle-headed old man, whose memory isn't too reliable. But there's no doubt he was there – and that he knew very well father was in no fit state to sign anything.

ANGUS: 'We beg Thee, O Lord, to give us a blessing on this house.' Why – the canting old son of a... (*He moves up centre.*)

JEAN: (*Cutting in sharply.*) No, Angus.

ANGUS: Don't cramp me, Jeannie. I have to expand, to blow off steam.

DOUGLAS: And I'm feeling like that – for once. Got a bottle upstairs, Angus?

ANGUS: (*Jubilantly.*) Yes – a bottle of whisky. (*He exits to the hall.*)

JEAN: (*Sitting beside DOUGLAS on the couch.*) You're very like mother in some ways, aren't you, Doug? You're very hard, aren't you?

DOUGLAS: I don't think so. Look – Jean. They were his brothers – and they deliberately cheated him. The company they persuaded him to take never had a chance – and they knew it. They could have bought him out between them. But no, they were too greedy for that. They had to cheat him. And to make certain, these Toronto Teetotallers filled him with drink...

JEAN: That's the most horrible part of the story. (*She rises and moves centre.*) But – (*Rather slowly and hesitantly.*) suppose Uncle David didn't know what really happened...

DOUGLAS: Why suppose anything of the sort?

JEAN: Because, right at the end – when you were talking about bribery, I couldn't help feeling he was really sincere – as if he hadn't known...

DOUGLAS: (*Cutting in; impatiently.*) Of course he knew. Everybody says David's always been the boss, ever since the old man died. They couldn't have worked a scheme like that without him. He was up to the neck in the rotten business. (*He rises and moves behind the couch.*) This house stinks of it. Piety, swindling, and nobody very well.

JEAN: (*Moving up centre; impulsively.*) Oh, let's stop thinking about them. All this hate and plotting and accusing is beginning to make me feel a thousand years old.
(*ANGUS enters from the hall. He carries a full bottle of whisky, three glasses and a concertina. He puts the bottle and glasses on the table and tosses the concertina to DOUGLAS.*)
(*She moves to left of ANGUS. Delighted.*) Oh – this is wonderful, Angus. We'll have a party. You've still got that thing – can you play it?

ANGUS: After a fashion. So can Douglas. (*He pours three drinks.*) But, before we have music and mirth, children, we must drink a toast.

JEAN: (*Clapping.*) A toast – a toast!

ANGUS: (*With mock pomposity.*) It will be proposed by the Right Honourable Angus McBane, Chairman of the Board of Governors, Minister of Forests, Fisheries and Feathers, and Canadian Gold Stick-in-Waiting to His Majesty King Edward the Seventh. (*He hands drinks to DOUGLAS and JEAN.*)
(*JEAN sits on the pouffe. DOUGLAS sits on the couch.*)
(*He now becomes the proposer of the toast, as if ending a long speech.*) And so – Mr Chairman, my Lords, Ladies and Gentlemen – I gratefully accept the privilege – for indeed a great privilege I feel it is – of asking you to rise – and to drink with me – a toast in memory – the glorious memory – of that enterprise typical of so many enterprises of this rich, fair land of ours – the Northern Timber Territories. (*He raises his glass.*)
(*JEAN rises, moves to left of ANGUS and raises her glass. DOUGLAS rises, moves to right of ANGUS and raises his glass.*)

DOUGLAS/JEAN: (*Together; with mock solemnity.*) The Northern Timber Territories.
(*They all drink. ANGUS sings softly in French, the first verse of 'Youpe! Youpe!'.*)

DOUGLAS: (*Over the singing.*) Come on, pass it round. (*He sits on the couch.*)
(*ANGUS, still singing, refills the glasses.*)

JEAN: (*Moving below the pouffe; over the singing.*) Do you remember when Louis and old Paddy Riley used to come down the Black River singing that? And that Indian – what was his name?

DOUGLAS: Henry Newblanket. They took me with them, once.

ANGUS: Chorus – me boys!

(*They all sing the refrain. After the refrain ANGUS turns to JEAN for her to sing the second verse.*)

Sing, girl – I'm behind with my drinking. (*He drinks.*)

JEAN: I've forgotten the words – something about lighting a pipe...

(*DOUGLAS drinks, then sings the second verse, followed by the other two. At the end of the second verse, they all sing the refrain. JEAN starts to sing 'Ma Pere'.*)

DOUGLAS: (*Putting his glass on the table.*) Oh, yes, let's try that one. (*He rises.*) I'll play – you two dance. (*He moves behind the downstage end of the couch and plays the concertina.*)

(*JEAN and ANGUS put their glasses on the table. JEAN jumps on to the love-seat and dances. ANGUS dances on the pouffe removing his jacket and waving it.*)

JEAN: (*Crying out.*) Oh – damn this skirt – I can't move in it.

ANGUS: Take it off then, girl – take it off –

(*JEAN removes her skirt.*)

– get back into the chorus line.

(*JOHN and ELSPIE enter from the conservatory. The music and dancing continue through the following dialogue.*)

ELSPIE: (*Half shocked, half excited.*) Jean, what are you doing! Look at you! Honestly, you must be crazy. John – look at her.

(*JEAN does some high kicks.*)

No, don't look at her.

JOHN: (*Shocked but fascinated.*) Jean – really – I don't think I ought to stay.

JEAN: (*Laughing at him.*) Don't be silly.

JOHN: (*Bewildered.*) What is it? Are you all drunk?

ANGUS: Not yet. Want to join us? Help yourself.

JOHN: (*Moving to the table.*) You think I daren't. You think I'm a prig, don't you? (*He picks up one of the glasses from the table and hastily swallows some whisky, choking a bit.*)

ELSPIE: (*Crossing to ANGUS.*) Angus – Angus – dance with me. John can't take his eyes off Jean, now.

(*ANGUS jumps from the pouffe and dances up and down left centre with ELSPIE. JEAN jumps from the love-seat and moves provocatively to JOHN.*)

JEAN: (*Teasingly.*) Little Johnny Harvey's afraid of dancing. Little Johnny Harvey's frightened of girls. (*She picks up a glass.*)

JOHN: No, I'm not. But they shouldn't drink whisky. (*He takes the glass from JEAN.*)

JEAN: Drink it yourself, then.

JOHN: I'm not afraid of it. (*He drinks and chokes.*)

(*From now on until MALCOLM speaks, the two girls, aided by ANGUS, tease and bait JOHN, who is timid and clumsy, anyhow, at first and then angry and rather drunk. JEAN provokes him and when he makes a clumsy grab for her, she eludes him and dances with ANGUS, who releases ELSPIE, who in turn provokes JOHN and eludes him, though not as thoroughly as JEAN does. When ELSPIE joins ANGUS again, he releases JEAN who once more goes to work on JOHN. No dialogue is necessary for the music is too loud, and the dancing and miming carry the simple story. During this, JOHN hastily swallows two or more drinks.*

MALCOLM enters from the conservatory when the JOHN-baiting is at its height. The others are so excited and making so much noise, they do not notice MALCOLM, who stands by the door, watching for a few moments.)

MALCOLM: (*Moving up right of the couch; to JOHN.*) Well, now we *are* seeing something – aren't we?

(*The music ceases and the others notice MALCOLM and he can be heard. The music stops naturally because they are exhausted and have had enough of it. JEAN sits on the couch. DOUGLAS moves down right. ELSPIE sits on the pouffe. ANGUS moves and stands above the love-seat. JOHN is at the table.*)

And I'm afraid you're risking your soul for nothing, my pious young friend. The girls are busy making a monkey out of you – which is what they'll always do if you don't show them plainly you're a man with all they want a man to have...

(*ANGUS moves up centre.*)

JOHN: (*Cutting in; shouting angrily.*) I won't listen to any of your horrible, filthy talk, Malcolm McBane. I always felt you were like that – sly and lascivious.

DOUGLAS: Drop it.

(*ANGUS moves down to JOHN. ELSPIE rises and moves up centre.*)

MALCOLM: Then tell him if he can't treat 'em rough when they take their skirts off, he'd better get back to his milksop college...

JOHN: (*Moving close to MALCOLM; shouting, ready to go for him.*) I'll knock you senseless for that – you...

(*ELSPIE screams. JEAN rises and gives a cry of warning. ANGUS and DOUGLAS restrain JOHN who shouts and struggles.*

MILDRED enters from the hall. The struggle stops abruptly and there is a moment's quiet.)

MILDRED: (*Very sharply.*) John! What does this mean?

JOHN: (*Loudly.*) I don't want to talk to you. I don't want to talk to anybody. I'm going. I'll get drunk. To hell with it all.

(*JOHN pushes MALCOLM aside and exits hurriedly to the conservatory. ELSPIE gives a cry of alarm.*)

JEAN: (*Urgently.*) Angus – follow him – it's all our fault – go after him – hurry.

(*ANGUS exits to the conservatory.*)

ELSPIE: (*Moving to MILDRED.*) Aunt Mildred – please – don't tell father – please. (*She weeps.*)

JEAN: It was my fault.

MILDRED: (*To ELSPIE.*) Very well. Now stop crying. (*She sits on the settee up centre.*)

(*ELSPIE exits to the hall.*)

DOUGLAS: (*Sitting on the arm of the couch; to MILDRED.*) I'm very sorry if we disturbed you – brought you downstairs.

MILDRED: You didn't.
(*MALCOLM moves towards the hall door.*)
Going, Malcolm?

MALCOLM: For some air. That young idiot rather shook me up.

MILDRED: Well, I've no doubt you know where to go to recover from the shock.

MALCOLM: (*Blandly.*) Does that mean anything, Mildred?
(*MILDRED looks at MALCOLM without replying.*)

DOUGLAS: If it means what I think it means, you're not keeping your secrets very well, Uncle.

MALCOLM: There are times when I don't care. This is one of them. (*He exits to the hall.*)

MILDRED: (*To DOUGLAS.*) So you know about that woman of his. I might have guessed.

JEAN: (*Moving to left of MILDRED; not aggressively.*) Well, Aunt Mildred, why don't you say it? – you'll feel better.

MILDRED: (*Staring at JEAN; rather absently.*) Say what?

JEAN: (*Rather defiantly.*) What you're thinking, of course. That we've been drinking and dancing and playing the fool – half dressed – that we've deliberately encouraged poor Elspie to misbehave – and John to shout and swear and fight and go off threatening to get drunk. That's what you were thinking, wasn't it?

MILDRED: No. I was thinking how like your father you looked. (*She rises.*) I'd never noticed it before. (*She exits to the hall.*)

DOUGLAS: Well, it was fun while it lasted – but it didn't last long.
(*JEAN picks up her skirt, moves to the table and puts the glasses together.*)

JEAN: (*Looking at DOUGLAS.*) Except for the first few minutes, when we forgot who we were and where we were, it wasn't fun even while it lasted.
(*DOUGLAS looks at JEAN and shrugs. There is a tinkle as JEAN puts the glasses one in the other.*
Curtain.)

Scene 2

Scene – the same. Later that night.

When the curtain rises, the room has been cleared and tidied up a little. The doors are closed and the lamps are lit, but the lamp down right is turned low. JEAN is sitting on the pouffe. DOUGLAS is standing by the conservatory door. For a few moments they do not speak. They are restless and uneasy, obviously waiting.

JEAN: What time is it?

DOUGLAS: (*Pulling out his watch.*) Nearly half past eleven.

JEAN: Go on about what you've been doing.

> (*DOUGLAS moves down right and crosses below the couch to centre, picking up the scraps of the document from the floor as he moves.*)

DOUGLAS: Why? It's not worth talking about.

JEAN: It passes the time.

DOUGLAS: And I've told you before. Don't you read my letters? (*He puts the pieces of paper on the table.*)

JEAN: Yes, but I've forgotten what jobs you had. Now I want to know.

DOUGLAS: (*Sitting on the couch.*) Well, I was with those implement people nearly a year, then I wanted a change – so I got a job with a firm of millers – doing the same thing – book-keeping. I'm good at figures.

JEAN: I know. But is that all you wanted to do? Book-keeping isn't much, is it?

DOUGLAS: It's less than that. Usually done by ghosts – fellows who are dead but don't know it.

JEAN: But you used to be ambitious. Remember how we used to talk?

DOUGLAS: I'm still ambitious.

JEAN: Then your heart's not been in it. You're clever enough, Doug.

DOUGLAS: I suppose I was waiting.

JEAN: It's the same thing. Your heart wasn't in it. Like mine. Angus may be different.

DOUGLAS: I couldn't have drifted about as Angus has done – working in hotels, bartending, God knows what.

JEAN: It's the same as your book-keeping, really – just keeping alive. But Angus is different because he's not ambitious in your way. He could drift along for years – half dreaming, half laughing at everything – and then suddenly do something wonderful – write a book – a play...

DOUGLAS: He never even tries to write, now. I asked him.

JEAN: So did I – and he was furious – and told me to shut up. He knows he's wasting himself. Just as you are.

DOUGLAS: (*Rising, cutting in with protest.*) Wait a minute...

JEAN: (*Ignoring this; with more force.*) Just as I am. (*She rises and moves centre.*) We've all been wasting ourselves – throwing our years away as if they were garbage. We've spent all our time here looking at these people – as if they were specimens in a zoo – but now we're all three together again, why don't we look at ourselves?

DOUGLAS: (*Sharply.*) Because that's not what we came here to do.

JEAN: Never mind about that. We've heard enough about it. *Us* now. Where are we? Who are we? (*She moves up centre. Gathering force and urgency.*) It's worse for me than for you two. A young man can just do a job. A girl doesn't just do a job. She lives a kind of life, and it soon begins to mould her and colour her – she begins to smell of it. I've been where girls – young and lively girls, sometimes beautiful girls – are herded into jobs and their kinds of life as pigs are fed into the Chicago packing plants – and in a few years they come out coarse, brutalized, hopeless women – for ever. I've worked with them, lived with them, Douglas. (*She moves to left of DOUGLAS.*) Whether it's called industry or entertainment, it's all the same – they're crammed into the machines as if they were planks or scrap iron. They're spent and wasted, like dirty pennies. Yes – and right up in front –

(*ELSPIE enters from the hall, leaving the door open. She looks wan and still rather tearful. She wears a dressing-gown.*)

– spending and wasting herself is Jean McBane.

ELSPIE: I heard some of that. I don't think it makes much sense.

JEAN: (*Sitting on the pouffe.*) It's not meant to make any for you.

ELSPIE: (*Moving to left of the pouffe.*) Sometimes I think you three are just crazy.

DOUGLAS: We might be. Is that what you came down to tell us?

ELSPIE: No. But it was hopeless trying to go to sleep. You're waiting for John and Angus, aren't you?

DOUGLAS: And your father.

ELSPIE: I'm not worried about him. He often stays out late – usually talking business with somebody. But I'm terribly worried about John – going off like that – blazing wild. (*She crosses below the pouffe to DOUGLAS.*) Do you think Angus has found him?

DOUGLAS: It depends. (*He sits on the downstage end of the couch.*) If John dashed into the nearest den of vice, then Angus will have found him – and ought to be looking after him. But if he went back to the training college, Angus will *not* be there.

ELSPIE: You're making fun of me. Well, I'll tell you something, Douglas McBane. You may be the quietest of you three, but sometimes you seem to me the craziest.

DOUGLAS: Perhaps I am.

JEAN: Perhaps you are. And perhaps she's right about us.

ELSPIE: I wish you wouldn't talk about me as if I wasn't here.

JEAN: We're thinking about ourselves – that's why.

ELSPIE: (*Crossing to JEAN; brightening up.*) Perhaps we ought to have some coffee. I could make some.

JEAN: You do, then, Elspie. Black and strong.

ELSPIE: It's bad for the nerves. And we're all nervy already.

DOUGLAS: Let's risk it. (*He rises, turns up the lamp on the bookcase, then sits on the back of the couch.*)

ELSPIE: (*She moves towards the hall door, then stops and returns to JEAN.*) Jean, do you think I'm in love with John? Or do you think it's really Angus, now?

JEAN: (*Putting an arm around ELSPIE.*) If you can't decide which it is, then it isn't either. And Angus would be all wrong for you, Elspie. Like a dog walking out with a cat. Better make it John if you must be in love with somebody.

ELSPIE: (*Almost wailing.*) But poor John's in love with you. He's mad about you. Look what happened.

JEAN: (*Gently.*) It was all silliness and excitement. Tomorrow he'll be ashamed of himself and then he'll dislike me. I'll be all mixed up with his being ashamed of himself. Now go and make that coffee, please, Elspie.

ELSPIE: (*Moving to the hall door.*) All right. You know, it wasn't all silliness, though I agree about the excitement. I thought I was ashamed of myself and of everybody, but I don't believe I am really. Some of it was *wonderful*. I didn't care. I was *happy*. If it was wicked, then there's a lot of wickedness in me – deep, deep down – a *devil*. (*She nods, stares bright-eyed for a moment, then with a short laugh exits hurriedly to the hall, leaving the door open.*)

JEAN: (*Thoughtfully.*) If the lid really blew off, she *might* be a little devil, too. (*She rises and moves to left of the couch.*) You don't see that, do you, Douglas?

DOUGLAS: No. To me she's just a fool.

JEAN: Then be careful before you ask a girl to marry you. Better let me take a look at her first.

DOUGLAS: So long as I can take a similar look at your young man. Unless he's firmly fixed already. Is there one? I've never asked you.

JEAN: (*With some bitterness.*) No, you haven't, have you? But then, we didn't come here to discuss my lovers.

DOUGLAS: Have you any?

JEAN: (*With passionate bitterness.*) No, I haven't. I wouldn't take a man from the world I've been living in. No – no lovers. All I've got are two crazy brothers, two wicked uncles, a horrified aunt, a silly cousin, and a theological student who's just discovered sex.

DOUGLAS: (*Rather heatedly defensive.*) You're glaring at me as if it were all my fault.

JEAN: I don't say it's your fault. I don't say it's anybody's fault.

DOUGLAS: But you're complaining…

JEAN: (*Cutting in passionately.*) Of course I'm complaining. And you ought to be complaining. You want to – only you won't let yourself go, Doug. For God's sake – be honest. What do you like about your life as it is?

DOUGLAS: (*With careful emphasis.*) I'll tell you. *Only one thing.*

(*DAVID enters hurriedly from the hall. DOUGLAS takes him in, but JEAN, intent on DOUGLAS's answer, does not.*)

JEAN: (*Impatiently.*) Well – what is it?

DOUGLAS: (*Indicating DAVID.*) Your answer's here.

DAVID: (*Standing up left.*) What's all this?

JEAN: (*Moving centre.*) We've had a lot of excitement here – but the story'll keep – and I doubt if you'd understand it. But we're still recovering. So we're edgy.

DAVID: Why don't you go to bed, girl?

JEAN: Elspie tried that, but now she's in the kitchen – making coffee.

DAVID: (*Angrily.*) Then she oughtn't to be. It's too late to be making coffee.

JEAN: This is one night in this house when it's not too late for anything. The rules are suspended.

DAVID: (*Moving to JEAN.*) That's for me to decide. Where's the other lad – Angus?

JEAN: He's out somewhere – trying to pluck a brand from the burning.

DOUGLAS: It means that young John Harvey…

(*JEAN crosses below DAVID and stands up right of the love-seat.*)

JEAN: (*Cutting in sharply.*) Oh – why tell him? (*She turns away from them.*)

DOUGLAS: (*Rising and moving to DAVID.*) Well, did you find Fricker?

DAVID: Yes, I did.

DOUGLAS: So? Go on.

DAVID: He tells a certain story. What he told you, he says, might be true. Might not be. He admits to having taken a bribe.

DOUGLAS: If he was inventing it, he'd hardly accuse himself, would he?

DAVID: He might – if it was made worth his while. Men like Fricker don't improve with age. And he never could be trusted.

DOUGLAS: (*Bitterly.*) Not like his old employers – men of honour – men of integrity – *good men.*

DAVID: (*Sharply.*) Don't take that tone with me, lad. I'm entitled to some respect...

DOUGLAS: (*Moving down right; cutting in angrily.*) Respect? Well, I'll be damned!

DAVID: (*Angrily.*) And don't use bad language in this house. I won't have it.

DOUGLAS: (*Moving to DAVID; angrily.*) You won't have it! You're entitled to some respect. Go on. What's next? Why don't you ask me to apologize because you cheated my father out of his inheritance? Or have you forgotten what I told you before you went to find Fricker?

DAVID: No – and don't shout at me. We don't need to make this a shouting match.

DOUGLAS: (*Sitting on the couch; calmer.*) Quite right, we don't. I'll be quiet, I'll be cool. But don't try any more of those big bluffing tactics. It's obvious you couldn't shake Fricker's evidence. It's equally obvious you unloaded a dud company on my father, and made him so drunk that he didn't know what he was signing...

DAVID: (*Moving to DOUGLAS; cutting in urgently.*) Never in my life have I made any man drunk – let alone my own brother. If you were any judge of men, you'd know that without my telling you. I wouldn't do such a thing for all the money in Canada. Whatever else I am, I'm a God-fearing man, Douglas McBane. My brother – your father – was a weak, foolish, sinful man. And it's true I was glad and not sorry when he was no longer a partner in McBane and Sons, for he had no sense, no judgement. But I believe men have immortal souls, lad, and that if those souls are black with sin, they'll be condemned to endure eternal torment. D'you think I'd have risked that

263

just so that I wouldn't see Charlie's foolish face across the boardroom table? (*He moves below the pouffe.*) Better for me to cut off my right hand than trap my own brother in his own sinful folly. You don't understand because you and I don't live in the same world, lad. You live in a sort of farmyard, like talking beasts, but I live where God and Satan are battling for immortal souls. (*He sits on the pouffe and puts his head in his hands.*)

JEAN: (*Impulsively.*) And you weren't there, were you? (*She turns to DOUGLAS.*) Because I believe him, Douglas. He means what he says.

DOUGLAS: Then it doesn't make sense.

JEAN: It does if he wasn't there – when father signed those papers.

(*JEAN and DOUGLAS look enquiringly at DAVID, who says nothing.*)

DOUGLAS: (*Rising and moving centre; to DAVID.*) Well, *were* you there?

(*DAVID does not reply.*)

JEAN: (*Crossing to DOUGLAS.*) Don't you see? He won't reply because he doesn't know what to say. If it happened that way, then the others, whoever *was* there, did something terribly wrong – and he doesn't want to admit that.

DOUGLAS: (*To DAVID; impatiently.*) You prefer to accuse me of bribing Fricker – to accuse Fricker of lying – is that honest, is that good? (*He pauses.*) Come on, say something.

DAVID: (*Slowly; with an effort.*) Your sister's quite right, of course. She saw a bit deeper into it than you did – they often do. I wasn't there when the transfers were completed – I wasn't even in Toronto – I was down in Kingston. Robert and Malcolm handled it. All they told me was that he was eager and willing to sign. They brought him here to do it.

DOUGLAS: And now you know why – so that if he had any misgivings, which he must have had, they'd only to see he had enough to drink...

DAVID: (*Painfully.*) Yes – yes – if that's the way it was.

JEAN: (*Kneeling right of DAVID; eagerly.*) And Aunt Mildred *knew* – she was here – and that's what's wrong with her – why she tried so hard to get rid of us – why she hates us – we're on her conscience. Her husband was dead. Malcolm didn't care – he wouldn't. But she did – in the wrong way – blaming us – and father and mother. Oh – didn't you ever feel there was something wrong?

DAVID: (*Painfully.*) Yes, I did.

DOUGLAS: (*Moving to right of JEAN.*) Well, what did you think it was, then?

DAVID: (*Rather evasively.*) We're weak and sinful creatures, all of us. I thought... (*He breaks off.*)

DOUGLAS: Well, go on.

DAVID: No, what I thought has nothing to do with this business. It's another sort of thing altogether.

(*ELSPIE enters from the hall. She carries a tray with a pot of coffee and three cups. DOUGLAS moves down right.*)

ELSPIE: (*With false brightness.*) Father – do you want some coffee?

DAVID: (*Rising and moving to ELSPIE; severely.*) No, I don't, Elspie. All I want is to see you get off to bed, where you belong, at this time of night. Now, put that down, and off you go, child.

ELSPIE: (*Crossing and putting the tray on the table.*) I couldn't sleep before – and I certainly shan't sleep now – not knowing what's happened to John and Angus – and not knowing what's happening here, either.

DAVID: (*Hastily.*) There's nothing happening here.

ELSPIE: (*Bravely.*) Father – I know that's not true.

DAVID: (*Angrily.*) Don't talk to me like that.

(*ELSPIE sits on the couch at the upstage end.*)

JEAN: (*Rising and moving to DAVID; angrily.*) And don't talk to her like that. She'd be an idiot if she didn't feel something was happening between us here.

DAVID: But it's no concern of hers. I know how to bring up my own daughter.

JEAN: You don't. You haven't a notion. Why don't you stop worrying about that bad-tempered old Israelite you call God – and try to understand your own daughter?

DAVID: (*Angrily.*) Any more of that blasphemous talk – and you leave this house tonight.

(*JEAN moves up centre.*)

Even if *you* don't know what's sacred...

JEAN: (*Cutting in fiercely.*) I *do* know what's sacred. It's about the only thing I do know for certain. And what's sacred isn't somebody's idea about who made the universe – what do *we* know about the universe? (*She moves to right of DAVID.*) None of that guesswork stuff is sacred – only people – life. And the least we can do is to try and understand it – and love it – and not just shout at it and bully it.

DAVID: (*Glowering at JEAN.*) If you were my daughter...

JEAN: (*Cutting in.*) Never mind about that – I'm not. And let me tell you this. Every time I'm beginning to feel sorry for you, as I was just before Elspie came in, you say or do something that puts me right back – hating you again. And I don't want to hate you. I don't want to hate anybody. I'm tired of hating. Yes, Douglas – tired of hating. (*She moves to the settee up centre and sits.*)

DOUGLAS: Perhaps you're not the only one.

DAVID: (*Moving to left of JEAN.*) If you'd had a proper Christian upbringing, you'd know we're commanded to love one another.

JEAN: And if there were fewer commands and more encouragement, people might make a start.

ELSPIE: (*Suddenly.*) Listen!

(*They listen a moment. ELSPIE runs and exits by the hall door. ANGUS and JOHN are heard off, stumbling and talking, but not so that the words are distinguishable. DAVID moves to the hall door.*)

(*Off.*) John! Angus!

JOHN: (*Off; but clearly heard.*) Quiet, Elspie. Coming in this way not to disturb anybody. Steady now, Angus.

ANGUS: (*Off; gravely.*) Steady it is, John.

266

DAVID: (*Moving below the table; disgusted and angry.*) They're drunk, the pair of them. *Drunk!* I won't have them in the house. (*He turns angrily towards the hall door.*)

DOUGLAS: (*Moving behind the couch.*) Yes, you will.

DAVID: (*Angrily.*) I tell you I won't.

DOUGLAS: (*Urgently.*) Listen – you don't understand what's happened tonight. So keep quiet for once. If you don't, I'll tell them all I know about you people – the whole rotten story.

(*JOHN and ANGUS enter from the hall, ANGUS upstage of JOHN.*

ELSPIE frightened, follows them on, and moves down left. Great care must be taken to make this entrance dramatic but not comic, so all suggestion of the usual stage drunkenness must be avoided. JOHN and ANGUS look as if they have been fighting. Their hair is untidy, they have a bruise or two on their faces with some suggestion of blood. Their clothes are disordered. ANGUS, who is leaning on JOHN, is deathly pale, a frightening sight. Their manner of speaking is wild but must not suggest usual stage drunkenness, no hiccups, no sloppy sibilants, etc.)

JEAN: (*Rising and moving to ANGUS; alarmed at his appearance.*) Angus, what's happened?

ANGUS: I found him. Then we ran into trouble.

JOHN: He saved my life. There was a big tough, full of booze – and he picked a quarrel with me – and started fighting. Then he pulled out a knife – and somebody hit me from behind – and he'd have used the knife if Angus hadn't tackled him. And I thought he wounded Angus – but Angus says he didn't...

ANGUS: A scratch. A mere scratch. Nothing to McBane – the Iron Man from the North – the Terror of the Wild.

JOHN: (*With eager penitence.*) It was all my fault. I'm to blame for everything.

ANGUS: Certainly not. Before that it was my fault, Jean's fault, Douglas's fault – we're all in it – all to blame – oh, good Uncle Scowler.

DAVID: (*Angrily.*) I don't care who's to blame – but you've been fighting – you're drunk – you're not fit to enter this house.

ANGUS: (*Shouting.*) Stop! (*He moves to DAVID, slowly and carefully, holding a hand to his side.*) Tell you something, dear Uncle Householder. You don't care who's to blame, 'cos you could never imagine *you're* to blame. You and God just dish it out. 'Pass the blame, God,' you tell Him. 'No, David,' He says, 'Your turn this time. Give it to 'em while it's hot.' (*He staggers above the table.*)

DAVID: (*Moving in front of the couch; turning his anger on ELSPIE.*) Elspie, go to bed.

ELSPIE: (*Sitting on the love-seat; protesting.*) I want to give Angus and John some coffee.

JOHN: Yes, please, Elspie.

DAVID: (*Moving towards ELSPIE; in a fury.*) Do what I tell you.

JEAN: Oh – leave her alone.

JOHN: (*Cutting in; with drunken gravity.*) Excuse me. I protect Elspie.

(*DAVID crosses and sits on the couch.*)

ELSPIE: (*Delighted.*) Oh – John – do you?

JOHN: (*Moving to ELSPIE.*) From now on – I protect you. But not as a minister. Can't be a minister now. Can't preach against sin. I'm loaded with it.

JEAN: (*Moving to left of ANGUS.*) Angus, are you sure you're not hurt? You look awful.

ANGUS: I am awful. Angry uncle quite right – not fit to enter his beautiful home, pride of Toronto. I want to make a speech, Jeannie, then I go to bed. (*He leans on JOHN.*)

JEAN: I'd rather do without the speech and lead you straight upstairs. (*She sits on the settee up centre.*)

ANGUS: No, must make speech – short speech – truth but in spirit of compassion. Thank you, dear Sis. (*He moves and leans against the up stage jamb of the hall door.*) First – financial statement – for you, Uncle. You owe me – a third of two hundred thousand dollars – what's that? Six six six six six – a lot of dollars. Keep 'em. Don't want 'em. No dollars, no revenge. 'Vengeance is mine, saith the Lord.' Let Him have it. I don't want it. 'Cos I'm drunk? Possibly. But why drunk? Answer that – Nuncle?

DAVID: (*Harshly.*) I will, lad. Because you like making a beast of yourself.

ANGUS: (*Moving above the table.*) A beast? Never! Do cattle distil whisky, do sheep brew beer? (*He moves behind the couch.*) The beasts, my dear Nuncle, with long faces and never a laugh, quietly but deter – determinedly attend to their own affairs like Toronto business men and pillars of the church. (*He moves above the table.*) When I drink, I drink to stop being a beast – to enjoy not the corn but the gold light and the green shadows of the harvest field – not to chew the grass but to hear its whispering music. There is a man in me – more *me* than I am – who moans in his sleep, hungry for Paradise. I wake him with whisky – which he loves because it is useless and dangerous, like the beauty of women, because its heart is not earth, water, air, but fire – and when he is awake – just for a little time – half an hour or only two minutes – he believes we are all on the road to Paradise. Outside in the Street, where the cops are waiting for the deadbeats, he can already hear the angels saying – (*He moves to right of the settee up centre.*) 'He hath made every thing beautiful in his time and in their heart he hath set eternity.' And then he cries, 'Holy! Holy! Holy! All things are Holy.' (*He lifts up his hands, and on the side where one has been pressed, the blood is running.*)
(*ELSPIE, pointing, gives a scream.*)

ELSPIE: (*High-pitched and hysterical.*) Look – blood! (*She is rigid with fear.*)
(*ANGUS sways, about to fall in a faint. JEAN rises and, with DOUGLAS, rushes to catch ANGUS, with JOHN and DAVID just behind.*)

DOUGLAS: (*To DAVID and JOHN; urgently.*) The doctor – quick. Let's get him upstairs.
(*DAVID crosses and exits to the hall. JOHN and DOUGLAS, helped by JEAN, lead ANGUS out to the hall. ELSPIE, still rigid with fear and horror, rises and moves slowly as if in a trance, towards the hall door. She stares down at the stained floor up centre, then slowly puts a hand down and brings it*)

*up stained with blood. She moves in front of the couch, in the
same trancelike state, staring at the blood-stained hand which
she holds rigidly in front of her. She is beginning to shudder
and shake, on the point of collapse.
DAVID enters from the hall.)*

DAVID: (*Crossing to right centre.*) Doctor's on his way.
(*Sharply.*) Elspie!

ELSPIE: (*Showing DAVID her hand; tonelessly.*) Look – blood!

DAVID: (*Angrily.*) What do you think you're doing, girl?

ELSPIE: (*Piteous but very simply.*) Don't be angry with me,
Father. You're always so angry – and I do try to be good.
(*She is shaking.*)
(*DAVID is moved deeply at last, and uncertainly holds out
his arms; ELSPIE, with a cry, moves into DAVID's arms and
begins quietly sobbing.*)

DAVID: (*With great tenderness.*) Elspie! Little Elspie. Don't
cry lassie. I'm not angry with you. I'm your father –
you're all I have to love. There's so much I don't
understand – and you've no mother now to make me
understand. I'll do better – you won't have to tell me
again I'm always angry – never, never again. Look – let
me wipe your hand. (*He takes his handkerchief from his
pocket and wipes ELSPIE's hand.*)

ELSPIE: Everything's so difficult, so strange. You think
life's so easy it seems boring – then suddenly it's all
different – and terrible – like a tiger in the room.
(*DAVID leads ELSPIE to the couch and sits her on it.*)

DAVID: Yes, that's how it is, Elspie. You might have
laughed at me sometimes – because I get down on my
knees in this room – to pray for us all – to ask for
strength – but I may have seen that tiger looking
through the window. There – that's better. (*He moves to
the table.*) Would you like a drink of coffee?

ELSPIE: (*Sitting shakily.*) Yes, please, Father.

DAVID: (*Pouring a cup of coffee.*) It'll be half cold now – but
better than nothing – and you've had a nasty fright –
though I doubt if it's as bad as it looks.
(*JOHN enters from the hall, looking pale and rather shaky.*)

270

JOHN: (*Moving centre.*) Are you all right, Elspie?

ELSPIE: (*Half teasing, half serious.*) You promised to protect me but you didn't – father had to do it.

(*DAVID moves behind the couch and hands the cup of coffee to ELSPIE.*)

Thank you very much, Father. Perhaps John would like some.

JOHN: I'll get it. (*He moves to the table and pours a cup of coffee.*) If anything happens to Angus, I'll never forgive myself. It was all my fault.

DAVID: I doubt that. He's a wild lad – like his father.

ELSPIE: (*Simply.*) I love him. No, John, it won't stop me loving you, if you really want me to – it's different. And he doesn't care about me. And he's wild and crazy and I never know what he's talking about –

(*JOHN sits on the pouffe.*)

– but I'll always love him.

DAVID: There was somebody who felt like that about his father – Charles. But when he married – and somebody not good enough for him, she thought – she was so mad jealous – it all went sour on her.

ELSPIE: You mean Aunt Mildred.

DAVID: (*Putting his hand on ELSPIE's shoulder.*) You never heard me say so.

(*MALCOLM enters from the hall, obviously having just come in from the street.*)

MALCOLM: Gratton's just gone upstairs in a hurry. Is Mildred worse?

DAVID: (*Moving above the table.*) No. Angus got into a fight – a knife wound.

JOHN: He saved my life.

MALCOLM: (*Moving to left of JOHN.*) Well, you know how much that's worth. I don't.

JOHN: Do you know what anything's worth?

MALCOLM: (*Angrily.*) I know when an idiot of a student begins to…

DAVID: (*Moving centre; cutting in sharply.*) That'll do, whatever it is. Where have you been, Malcolm?

MALCOLM: That's my business, David. But I believe if Elspie wasn't here, I'd tell you. I'm in that sort of mood.

271

DAVID: So am I. Do you remember Fricker? Perhaps you thought he was dead – as I did. But he's here in Toronto. Douglas talked to him yesterday. I talked to him tonight. You can guess what he told us.

MALCOLM: Do we have to talk about it tonight?

DAVID: (*Grimly.*) Yes – if it takes till daylight.

MALCOLM: Well, we needn't do it here.

DAVID: (*Grimly.*) Come up to my room. (*He exits to the hall.*)

(*MALCOLM, after a moment's hesitation, shrugs and follows DAVID off. JOHN rises, moves to the table and puts down his cup.*)

ELSPIE: I don't know what that's about – but I wouldn't be Uncle Malcolm for anything. And it serves him right, whatever it is. You can't go back to college tonight, can you? (*She rises and puts her cup on the table.*) Well, then, I'll have to make you up a bed in the little end room. And you'll have to help me. We won't go until somebody comes in. Aren't you going to be a minister now?

JOHN: I'm not sure. What do *you* think, Elspie?

ELSPIE: Sometimes I like you as a minister – and sometimes I think it could be very boring.

JOHN: I wouldn't be that kind of minister.

ELSPIE: What other kind is there?

JOHN: (*Hesitantly.*) Perhaps a long way from any big town. In country that's just being settled...

ELSPIE: Honestly, John, I couldn't. I'd be no use at all. I'd die. Oh – how difficult everything is. The minute you start talking seriously about anything, it turns difficult.

(*JEAN and DOUGLAS enter from the hall.*)

JOHN: (*Eagerly.*) What does Dr Gratton say about Angus?

JEAN: It's better than we thought – a clean wound – though of course he's lost a lot of blood.

ELSPIE: (*Picking up the coffee tray.*) We're going now. We have to make up a bed for John. We're unofficially engaged now. Come on, John darling. (*ELSPIE crosses and exits to the hall.*)

(*JOHN hastily follows her off.*)

DOUGLAS: (*Crossing and sitting on the couch.*) And what will happen to 'John darling'?

JEAN: (*Crossing to right centre.*) They've a better chance now than they had before we came. She wanted Angus, John wanted me. They've lost us. And now, coming alive, they've met in their double loss – and could make something between them. Adam and Eve outside Eden.

DOUGLAS: I thought I heard David shouting at Malcolm as we came along the landing.

JEAN: You did. I heard him. He's very angry.

DOUGLAS: (*Reproachfully.*) Yet you didn't tell me.

JEAN: (*Looking at him; gravely.*) No, Douglas, I didn't tell you.

DOUGLAS: Why?

JEAN: You know why.

DOUGLAS: I don't.

> (*JEAN looks reproachfully at DOUGLAS.*)
> (*He is suddenly angry.*) Why didn't you tell me? Don't look at me like that. I'm asking a simple question. (*He rises.*) Why didn't you tell me?

JEAN: (*Stung.*) Because I didn't want you back in the scheme again – working the plan.

DOUGLAS: What? You can say that – after we've waited for years…

JEAN: (*Cutting in.*) Yes – and Angus said it, too, said it for us, in front of everybody.

DOUGLAS: Tomorrow morning he won't remember *what* he said.

JEAN: (*Angrily.*) He won't if he thinks you disagree.

DOUGLAS: I *do* disagree. I want to finish what we began, what we all planned and waited for.

JEAN: (*Distressed.*) No. No. Please, Douglas, don't pretend not to understand.

DOUGLAS: I'm not pretending anything. And I'm only asking you to let things take their natural course.

JEAN: They've never taken a natural course with us – and they never will – unless we do something enormous and final. When Angus was talking to us all, I knew then what we had to do – to be free of the trap – free to start moving the other way. Then for a moment I felt free. *Free!* It was wonderful. I could have cried out for joy. Dear Douglas, please! If we don't do something now, we'll never be free.

(*GRATTON enters from the hall. He carries his bag.*)

GRATTON: (*As he enters.*) Well, your brother's a lucky young man.

(*DOUGLAS moves down right.*)

There were half-a-dozen very nasty things that knife might have done – but it didn't. He'll be all right. Nothing to worry about.

JEAN: (*Sitting on the couch.*) Can we see him?

GRATTON: (*Moving to the table and putting his bag on it.*) I'd rather you didn't. I've been trying to settle him down quietly for the night. And that's not been easy, for this family business you mentioned seems to have set David off like a rocket. I've tried to persuade him to let it all rest until the morning. But no – he's been on at Malcolm – and – dead against my advice – he's pulled Mildred into it. That brings me into it now. All because David McBane's obstinate, impatient, and over-conscientious.

DOUGLAS: (*With marked irony.*) Did you say over-conscientious, Doctor?

GRATTON: That's what I said, young man, and that's what I meant.

(*DAVID, MILDRED and MALCOLM enter slowly from the hall, reminding us of the first entrance of DOUGLAS, JEAN and ANGUS. They stand up left centre, MILDRED between DAVID and MALCOLM.*)

(*He continues rather angrily.*) So you wouldn't take my advice, David.

DAVID: Your advice is good, Edward, but God's is better. (*He looks at the others.*) Douglas – Jean – we're here to ask your forgiveness. I want you to forgive me – not because I did you a deliberate wrong – but because I was blind and foolish – and for too long I'd put you, my own brother's children, out of my thoughts. Your Aunt Mildred and your Uncle Malcolm, between them, did you a terrible wrong, which they've confessed to me and now they'll confess to you. When they've done that, we'll decide what retribution we can make...

JEAN: (*Urgently cutting in.*) No – no!

DOUGLAS: (*Angrily.*) Drop it, Jean. Let them talk. (*To MALCOLM and MILDRED. With obvious hostility.*) Well, go on.

MALCOLM: This is what you've wanted all along, isn't it? The Toronto McBanes baring their backs – while you three hold the rods of chastisement.

DAVID: (*Angrily.*) That's not what you came down to say, Malcolm.

MALCOLM: It's what I *am* saying.

DAVID: You were to ask their forgiveness.

MALCOLM: And now that I'm here, I don't want it. What do *you* say, Mildred?

MILDRED: (*Urgently.*) No, David, it's no use. Now that I'm face to face with them, I can't do it. I'm remembering how they first came through this door, pretending to be shy, tongue-tied, when all the time they'd planned to destroy every bit of happiness they could find here.

DAVID: And whose fault was that, Mildred? You've already admitted...

MILDRED: (*Cutting in.*) I won't be a hypocrite. I may have behaved badly. But I don't want their forgiveness – and I won't ask for it. They're vindictive savages – and I hate them.

JEAN: (*Rising and moving centre.*) Yes – and now I'll tell you why. You were in love with my father – and hate us because we're not your children.

MILDRED: It's a lie – a lie. Malcolm – a lie.

GRATTON: (*Firmly.*) Yes, Malcolm, you see her upstairs. No, David, that's enough.

(*MALCOLM and MILDRED exit to the hall. JEAN moves to DOUGLAS.*)

(*He turns to DAVID.*) I'm staying because of you, David. Remember – I've warned you.

DAVID: (*Who seems bewildered.*) What do I do? Go to bed when the house seems in ruins? Why can't we all behave like decent God-fearing folk?

GRATTON: (*Moving centre.*) Perhaps because we aren't decent – and God ought to start helping us instead of frightening us. Now, sit down, man –

(*DAVID sits on the love-seat.*)

– and give your clogged arteries a chance. I'll do the talking. Now, you two – what do you want?

DOUGLAS: What we were brought up to want.

(*GRATTON sits on the couch.*)

JEAN: (*Crossing to right of the pouffe.*) Our mother believed you'd all got rid of my father – not because he drank and gambled and was wild – most of the men she knew were like that – but because he married *her*. And of course that seemed as wicked and terrible to us as it did to her. She loved us – she slaved to bring us up properly – but she let us grow up in a cage...

DOUGLAS: (*Crossing to right of JEAN.*) No, Jean.

JEAN: Yes, Douglas. A cage of resentment and envy and vindictiveness and hate and revenge.

DOUGLAS: (*Protesting.*) I've never seen it.

JEAN: No – we couldn't see it – because it was a glass cage – but a *cage*...

(*ANGUS enters from the hall. He is wearing an old dressing-gown and pyjamas, and looks pale and shaky.*)

ANGUS: (*Moving to the pouffe.*) Can't have cages. (*He sits.*)

JEAN: Angus!

GRATTON: Good God – you young jackass – I can't have *you* wandering about. Get back to bed at once.

ANGUS: Go on, Sis – who are you arguing with?

JEAN: With Douglas. But not any more

(*DOUGLAS moves up left centre and stands with his back to the audience.*)

Either he sees it or he doesn't. I'll tell you, Dr Gratton. Because we grew up like that, we could see the world stretching before us – through the glass bars – but we couldn't go out to accept it. We wasted ourselves. Douglas and Angus are really brilliant young men – but what have they done –

(*DOUGLAS turns.*)

– where have they been going? And what have I been doing? Where is my lover, my husband, my children? What have we made of ourselves?

ANGUS: (*Rising.*) Don't quite know where we've got to –
but it seems to be up to you, Doug – and remember
you're carrying me with it, too.

JEAN: We'll never be out of our cage, never, never be free,
until we've committed ourselves to one big decision.
And I'm not going to argue any more. Either you see it
– or you don't.

DOUGLAS: (*Stubbornly.*) Well, I don't. We made a plan. It's
worked. Now you want me to throw it all away. It's all
very well for you two – but I've always had most of the
responsibility. I've had to keep your minds fixed on it –
I know what to do with the pieces when we've broken
these people. (*He crosses and stands down right.*)

GRATTON: (*Rising and moving to right of JEAN; softly, but
cunningly pitching his voice.*) There's a disease we haven't a
name for, though it's the father of half the ailments we
know about, for once you have it, energy goes draining
and draining away – hurry to nowhere. What's
remarkable about you, young woman, is not that you've
lived in a glass cage, but that you've discovered it's
there. (*He moves above the table and picks up his bag.*) We've
millions of 'em. Wasting enough energy, will and ability
to change the face of the world. Well, if you're out – stay
out – and don't let this obstinate brother of yours push
you in again.
(*DOUGLAS makes an inarticulate sound.*)
(*He moves towards DOUGLAS.*) Did you speak, young
man? Want to tell us how soon you'll be a millionaire?

DOUGLAS: (*Crossing to right of JEAN.*) Not this time. (*He
turns to JEAN and ANGUS, smiling.*) All right – we're out.
(*JEAN, overjoyed, embraces DOUGLAS.*)
Uncle David, we're through. No confessions, no
retributions. No more accusations, no more claims. You
must settle it yourself, do what you think best.

DAVID: (*Rising.*) Thank you, lad. But we have to make
some amends. I'll make sure of that.

GRATTON: (*Moving above the table.*) And I'll make sure you
go to bed this very minute, David McBane!
(*DAVID exits to the hall.*)

277

DOUGLAS: And we'll go as soon as Angus is fit to travel.

ANGUS: (*Cheerfully.*) That's tomorrow.

GRATTON: (*Moving to the hall door; indignantly.*) It is *not*, young man. Otherwise it's out of a cage into a coffin. (*He exits to the hall.*)

JEAN: (*Happily.*) You know, *you* told us how to get out of it, Angus.

ANGUS: (*Surprised.*) I did? When?

DOUGLAS: Tonight.

ANGUS: I was drunk. Perhaps that's when I'm worth listening to. Well – what next?

DOUGLAS: (*A little ruefully perhaps.*) What next – and where?

JEAN: We needn't decide that now. (*She smiles at them.*) It's a big country – and we're free.
(*Curtain.*)

The End.